THE LUCAS EFFECT

The Lucas Effect

George Lucas and the New Hollywood

Patti J. McCarthy

\<teneo\> //press
AMHERST, NEW YORK

Copyright 2014 Teneo Press

All rights reserved
Printed in the United States of America

No part of this publication may be reproduced, stored in or introduced into a retrieval system, or transmitted, in any form, or by any means (electronic, mechanical, photocopying, recording, or otherwise), without the prior permission of the publisher.

Requests for permission should be directed to:
permissions@teneopress.com, or mailed to:
Teneo Press
PO Box 349
Youngstown, NY 14174

Library of Congress Control Number: 2013943898

McCarthy, Patti.
The Lucas Effect: George Lucas and the New Hollywood .
p. cm.
Includes bibliographical references and index.
ISBN 978-1-934844-67-0 (alk. paper).

*For Caitlin & Callie,
With love...*

*And in memory of Michael Christensen,
Who will live in our hearts forever.*

Table of Contents

Acknowledgements ix
Chapter 1: Rise of the New Hollywood 1
Chapter 2: New Hollywood Mavericks 39
Chapter 3: The "High Concept" Blockbuster 73
Chapter 4: Building the Empire 137
Chapter 5: Digital Beginnings 211
Chapter 6: The New Age of Film 261
Epilogue 277
Bibliography 291
Appendix 309
Index 311

Acknowledgements

Since this book has developed over a period of years, including dissertation research conducted while at the University of Southern California, I would like to thank those faculty members who directly helped to shape the project: Allan Casebier, Tara McPherson, Drew Caspar, Paul Wolanski, Larry Ulman, Anthony Kemp, Dana Polan, and in particular, my dissertation chair, Michael Renov, who was extremely supportive and helpful throughout—a tremendously talented scholar and theorist.

During my time at USC, I was also working in the film industry at Rastar Productions at Sony Pictures Entertainment with many people who helped further my understanding of the "biz." A special thank you to John Morrissey, Larry Turman, MaryKay Powell, and especially, the late Ray Stark, who was not only a mentor, but also a kind and cherished friend.

Prior to USC, several teachers and professors at the University of the Pacific encouraged my film scholarship: Diane Borden, Lou Leiter and Joseph Subbiondo. Without their interest in my work and their continued enthusiasm I never would have made this long journey. I would also like to acknowledge Robert Gustafson at California State University, Northridge who made insightful comments regarding my work-in-progress.

I also want to thank George Lucas for his brilliant and visionary work, his love of film and filmmaking, and for being a constant source of inspiration. Not only have I come to respect his work as an entrepreneur and his talent as a filmmaker, but also admire his deep sense of integrity and commitment to his family and friends and his ability to forge friendships that have lasted a lifetime. He is a kind and gentle man—a good father, employer, and brother, whom I have come to know better through my research, my work with Lucasfilm employees, and his sister —and friend, Wendy. Watching *Star Wars* for the first time was a pivotal moment in my life and began my life-long love and appreciation of film. Thank you, George for the memories!

Much thanks also to my publisher, Paul Richardson, who has watched this work evolve and has been supportive throughout. Thank you, Paul, for believing in both the work and me.

I also want to thank my Mom, Pat Bridge; Dad, Jack McDaniel; and sister, Gina Daniels; and last, but certainly not least, a special thank you goes to my husband, Edward McCarthy and my two beautiful daughters, Caitlin Elizabeth and Callista Marie—to them, I dedicate this work.

The Lucas Effect

Chapter 1

Rise of the New Hollywood

> Walking down the street in the deserted Hollywood streets in 1951 with David [Selznick], I listened to my favorite movie boss topple the town he had helped to build. The movies, said David, were over and done with. Hollywood was already a ghost town making foolish efforts to seem alive. But now that the tumult was gone, what had Hollywood been?
> — Ben Hecht, 1954 (Schatz, *Genius of the System*)

> When they tell you it's not about the money...it's about the money.
> — Old Hollywood Adage

The Fall of the Old Hollywood System

As in most endeavors, before anything "new" can be considered, it's important to take a look at what might be considered the "old." In this case, the "old" defines the classic Hollywood studio system which held sway from roughly the 1920s into the late 1940s, which, after experiencing radical changes to its operating structure, fell into decline. For a number of years the demise of the classic studio system has been attributed primarily to the *United States v. Paramount Pictures* anti-trust decree of 1948 which forced the monopolistic Big Five (MGM, Warner Bros., Paramount, RKO, and Twentieth Century-Fox) to divest themselves of their movie theatres. This divestiture effectively put an end to the distribution and exhibition guarantees that supported the classic studio business structure. Only recently has the full implication of this case been acknowledged in light of the New Hollywood system. The *Paramount* case and other important events during this time irrevocably set the stage for Hollywood business practices used today. For this reason, I will examine specific historical events in Hollywood at the end of World War II that shaped and helped to structure a New Hollywood system and sensibility.

The Golden Age was called "golden" for a reason. From the early 1920s through the 1940s, the "studio system" referred to a factory-based mode of production and a vertical system of integration of film production which allowed the Big Five collectively and collusively to control the film marketplace (they produced the film, they distributed the film, they screened the film in their theatres). Even though the Big Five studios only owned and ran about one-sixth of the nation's movie theatres in the 1930s and 1940s, these theatres included many of the all-important "first run" theatres that screened the top, A-list feature films. These movie palaces seated hundreds, if not thousands of theatre-goers, and generated well over half of the total industry revenues. [1]

At a time when up to 100 million people per week attended the movies, the Big Five were hard put to keep up with product demand. This heavy demand for film product allowed room for the "major-minors," which included Columbia, Universal, and United Artists (UA), to find a niche in the marketplace and also prosper. These studios were considered "major" because they turned out A-class features with major contract stars and had their own distribution arms. The other "smaller" studios were deemed "minor" because they did not own their own theatre chains. Other "minors" who could not compete on the same scale as the major or the major-minors, such as Monogram and Republic, also thrived during this time by providing a menu of low-budget B-type movies.

Rise of the New Hollywood

Taking a firm hold in the 1920s, this system of vertical integration filmmaking (the studios controlled product, talent, distribution, and exhibition), became the standard during a climate of national uncertainty and crisis that continued through the Great Depression and World War II. During this time period, government officials, busy fighting other more important battles at home and overseas, unofficially sanctioned and tolerated the studio's monopolistic control of the film industry. This averting of the governmental eye allowed the studios enough revenue flow and subsequent financial leverage to maintain both their factory operations and the all-important "star" contract system that directly tied talent to the studio.

The mainstay of the old studio system was the A-class feature film, usually a "star vehicle" with solid production values and a guaranteed market. Besides this first-run feature mainstay, the studios from time to time, made a few big budget "prestige" pictures, and regularly turned out a steady supply of low-budget formula quickies. These studio "quickies" made up as much as half of the total output of some of the major studios during the Depression. Thomas Schatz explains, "The key commodity in classical Hollywood was the routine star-genre formulation—an MGM costume romance with Greta Garbo, a Warner Bros. gangster saga with James Cagney or Edward G. Robinson, a Fox swashbuckler with Tyrone Power, and so on." [2] Accordingly, "Each studio's stable of contract stars were product lines unto themselves, and thus, the basis for each company's distinctive 'house style.'" [3] "These trademark star-genre formulas," Schatz elaborates, "gave each studio a means of stabilizing marketing and sales, of bringing efficiency and economy to top feature production, and of distinguishing the company's output from its competitors." [4]

For the most part, studio management during the vertically integrated era operated via a classic top-down hierarchical arrangement. Power flowed from distribution and exhibition (sales) executives in New York to the "front office" of the West Coast studio. Although it was true that the New York office controlled the movement and direction of capital, including sales, budgeting, and marketing, many of the studio moguls during the classic era in the West oversaw actual production and hence, controlled the actual filmmaking. Movie-moguls such as Irving Thalberg, Darryl Zanuck, and David Selznick created and ruled the empire known as the studio system in Hollywood's "Golden Age." It soon became clear though that the more entrepreneurial style of doing business developed by the movie moguls on the West Coast was soon out of synch with the corporate dictates coming from New York as more and more studios and East Coast offices were gobbled up by larger corporations that had begun to watch the bottom line. As the 1940s came to a close, the less efficient, self-made West Coast moguls began to pose a threat to the East Coast corporate need for greater studio profits and control. Not only was the division between the East and West Coast film offices a fiscal one, but over time became an ideological one as well. While the West Coast moguls were predominately Jewish, the East Coast corporate owners were for the most part, decidedly not.

Although the Hollywood studio system flourished during World War II, it quickly fell into a downward slide by the end of the decade. For many inside and outside the industry, the decline in studio revenue came as no surprise. For corporations, this decline allowed them to pick up studio stock (and ownership) at a discount, adding further value to their already diversified portfolios. As early as 1941, sociologist Leo Rosten observed:

> Other businesses have experienced onslaughts against their profits and hegemony; but the drive against Hollywood is just beginning. No moving picture leader can be sanguine before the steady challenge of unionism, collective bargaining, the consent decree (which brought the Justice Department suit to a temporary armistice), the revolt of the independent theatre owners, the trend toward increased taxation, the strangulation of the foreign market, and a score of frontal attacks on the citadels of the screen.[5]

The onslaught against Hollywood described by Rosten that had begun earlier in the decade resumed with even greater force after the war.

Along with the many factors listed above, and by far the most problematic for the studios, was the *Paramount* decree put forward by the Supreme Court in 1948. This decision by the court radically changed the way the studios were doing business. The anti-trust ruling effectively disintegrated the old studio system by forcing the studios to sell off all their theatres (and with them, a source of easy and sustaining capital).

THE PARAMOUNT DECREE: THE 1940s AND 1950s

By controlling the first run movie houses, the Big Five were guaranteed a return on their investment and therefore controlled a large share of the ticket-buying market. Even the Little Three (Columbia, Universal and United Artists) who did not own theatres, but created and distributed films, were in a much better position than others to negotiate booking for their product. Needless to say, the independent theatre owners objected loudly to this set-up and eventually the government listened. On July 20, 1938, the government filed an anti-trust suit against the Big Five and the Little Three[6] charging them with monopolizing the film trade via theatre ownership, block-booking, blind-bidding, as well as price fixing.[7] This decree became known as the Paramount decree which stated that the defendants, (a) set minimum prices for movie exhibition, (b) they "imposed unreasonable clearances," i.e., the length of time that second run houses and others had to wait before opening newly released films, which constituted a "conspiracy to restrain trade," and (c) block-booking which promoted non-competition and monopolistic practices: "Whereby a high quality film greatly desired is licensed only if an inferior one is taken, the latter borrows quality from the former and strengthens its monopoly by drawing on the other. The practice tends to equalize rather than differentiate the reward for the individual copyrights." Upholding much of the District Court's ruling, the Supreme Court further decided that "competitive bidding" by theatres was not a satisfactory solution and the court would settle for nothing less than the entire divestiture of theaters owned by the studios.

Unrelated to the antitrust decision, but just as important to the future of the New Hollywood, was the Court's concurrent ruling that, "moving pictures, like newspapers and radio, are included in the press, whose freedom is guaranteed by the First Amendment."[8] Interestingly enough, at the same time, the Court ruled "under the First and Fourteenth Amendments, a state may not ban a film on the basis of a censor's conclusion that it is 'sacrilegious'." The Court also addressed the issue of film's greater capacity for evil, particularly among the youth of the community.

The decision by the Court to protect film under the First Amendment fully opened the door for formal review of the constitutionality of film censorship which came in 1952 when the Supreme Court ruled on Burstyn v. Wilson, a case where the film, *The Miracle,* had been censored by the Commissioner of Education in New York. It was decided that the censorship of the film was completely unconstitutional. The Miracle case greatly weakened the power of the local boards to force or influence censorship decisions. Even though the fall of the Production Code would not happen for another fourteen years, the entire studio's power to regulate film content in affiliation with other organizations had been successfully challenged.[9] So although the studios were stripped of their theatres and a steady source of revenue and leverage with one hand, on the other, they were granted the ability to self-regulate their own film product and gain more control of their products. Taken separately, both the Paramount decree and the courts' ruling on the studio's ability to self-regulate film censorship signaled big changes in the film industry. So how best to capitalize on this ruling? The studios began their search for a solid business strategy.

While the studios were looking for a solution to their immediate fiscal problems, they were also involved in a politically charged labor crisis and were battling with labor unions for control of the Hollywood workforce as well as with the growing ranks of freelance talent and independent producers for control of the movie marketplace. A catalyst of these labor conflicts was the official formation of Hollywood's top talent guilds. During the 1930s, Hollywood had rapidly evolved from an "open shop" to a "union town," leading Variety to speculate in January 1939 that "the major studios are now 100 percent organized." [10] David Prindell noted, "because Los Angeles was the least organized large city in America [in the early 1930s], and because the motion picture was a rapidly evolving technology, Hollywood was a union battleground during these decades [the 1930s and 1940s]."[11] The formation of the Screen Actor's Guild (SAG), the Screen Directors Guild (SDG) and the Screen Writer's Guild (SWG) all posed immediate threats to studio filmmaking and control.[12] It was only with the allegations of communist infiltration of these guilds brought forward by the House Committee on Un-American Activities (HUAC) in the late 1940s that these previously strong labor unions began to lose some of their bargaining power. Although these same unions and guilds had been accused by the Dies Committee of leftist sympathies early in the decade, it was only at the end of the 1940s that these seemingly trumped up allegations began to stick—and stick with a vengeance. Interestingly enough, these charges of communist infiltration of the unions and guilds which targeted well-known talent began occurring at the same time as the studios were contemplating how to take back control and profit from the Paramount decrees and censorship rulings. In examining these seemingly unrelated events, film scholar Jon Lewis found a fascinating common thread.

While at first glance one might not see the House Committee on Un-American Activities (HUAC), the black list, the Paramount case, and the later establishment of the MPAA (Motion Picture Association of America) as related to the survival and reestablishment of Hollywood after divestiture, Lewis convincingly argues otherwise and to good cause, going so far as to suggest that together these events helped shape what is currently known as the New Hollywood.[13] While I agree with Lewis that these combined factors paved the way for today's new Hollywood structure, I do not think these are the only factors involved. My thesis throughout this book suggests otherwise. It is my opinion that Lewis leaves a very important factor out of the mix—Lucas.

To better understand the new Hollywood we need to begin to think in terms of the shift from "old" to "new" having two phases. The first phase, as Lewis points out, which will be discussed in detail in this chapter and others, is a combined result of business strategies put into place by studios after the Paramount decision. To protect their interests the studios (gradually taken over by corporations) teamed up with HUAC and the MPAA. The result of this collusion, I believe, is the rise of the auteur in the 1960s and 1970s. Corporations, unacquainted with how Hollywood worked, looked for a silver bullet to offset declining revenues. Grittier, more adult fare-type films that exploited the youth market (*Easy Rider*, as an example) now approved during these years by the MPAA helped to differentiate film product from television product and as a result gradually boosted film attendance. Corporations that bought a studio, but sold soda, for example, as its primary product, were decidedly "out of touch" with the younger film market and began to rely on young directors out of film school to help them make money. The New Wave, an independent talent pool, coupled with a corporate lack of understanding helped forge the first, or auteur, phase of the new Hollywood. The first phase came to a close after the corporations became more conglomerated and the new high concept blockbuster mentality began to permeate the industry—first with *Jaws*, then with *Star Wars*. Only the large conglomerates could afford to play in this high-stakes game. When Lucas creates the first franchise with *Star Wars*, as discussed in later chapters, the second or entrepreneurial phase of the new Hollywood begins. The film industry is now experiencing this second phase.

But many years before either the New Wave or a *Star Wars* film was ever conceived, the studios in the late 1940s were faced with difficult decisions, foremost among them "how do we regain control of and manage the industry workforce in such a volatile environment" and secondly, "how do we recoup the money lost in theatre divestiture?"

The House Committee on Un-American Activities (HUAC) in particular, became an unlikely studio ally and soon helped answer some of these more difficult questions.

In 1947, the House Committee on Un-American Activities (HUAC) convened its first session. It handed over lists of unionized writers, actors and directors, and despite overriding National Labor Relations Board (NLRB) protections, these individuals could, it was argued, for reasons of national security, be suddenly fired without any just cause or severance, and in a few cases, without any earned wages or option fees.[14] By acting in this way, HUAC helped the studios take control and manage an uncertain labor situation. It also helped studios cut payrolls and expenses in preparation for a widely predicted postwar box office decline. In his book, *Hollywood v. Hard Core: How the Struggle Over Censorship Saved the Film Industry*, Lewis maintains that the:

> so-called free market got a whole lot less free during the blacklist era because the studios discovered that they could circumvent the spirit of various antitrust decrees, keep production costs down, and control the industry guilds if they just learned to work better together. The new Hollywood we see in place today—a new Hollywood that rates and censors its own and everyone else's films, flaunts its disregard for antitrust legislation and federal communications and trade guidelines, and has reduced filmmaking to a science of market and product research is very much the product, the still-evolving legacy, of the blacklist.[15]

Lewis explains that to completely understand the complexities of regulations in the postwar film industry, we must first see the blacklist as not merely an ideological struggle.[16] It goes without saying that the Red Scare was politically motivated, but in Hollywood it is difficult, if not impossible sometimes, to separate the ideological from the fiscal or industrial. While the blacklist might not have originally been written as a complex and collusive business strategy, it gradually seems to have evolved in that direction. The blacklist helped the studios combat the unions, develop a new way of doing business that diminished the threat of further federal regulations in the business of making movies and at the same time promoted larger changes in the management of the industry, in particular, the mostly Jewish West Coast studios. During the Hollywood Ten hearings, HUAC and those who shared its politics often tied communism with unionism and antiracism. Based on a shared belief that the civil rights and union movements plaguing the country were Jewish causes, they further equated communism with Jewishness. Lewis contends that,

> When HUAC began is investigation of the movie industry, a new Hollywood seemed imminent. In concert with the forth-coming decision in the *Paramount* case, this new Hollywood promised or threatened to be a place in which talent, suddenly organized, seemingly radicalized, and soon to be further empowered by the free market engendered by divestiture, held significant power. It was thus in the best interests of the studio management to find a way to control the industry workforce before it controlled them."[17]
>
> In the final analysis the blacklist did not shelter America from films that promoted communism, humanitarianism, or liberalism. Instead it supported studio ownership to develop and adopt a corporate model that would lend itself to a future new Hollywood—one where studio ownership, exploiting stricter self-regulation, could maintain more control and, thus, profit. [18]

Not only did HUAC and the subsequent blacklist help the studios take care of their labor problems, the fledgling Motion Picture Association of American (MPAA) also emerged during this time as a strong studio ally. The MPAA was chartered in 1945 at the very same time that the Justice Department had revived its antitrust suit against the studios. "The studio membership of the MPAA used the Waldorf Statement in 1947 (which made public their intention to cooperate with HUAC) to establish an identity and moreover to assert studio unity in the face of a seeming ideological and very real fiscal crisis." States Lewis, "Over the years the MPAA [which today wholly supervises the regulation of film content] has done well to downplay its roots in the Red Scare. But its power today seems very much indebted to rightwing congressional support at its inception and the collusive strategies it, by necessity, developed in the late 1940s and 1950s."[19]

Gordon Kahn, one of the original nineteen brought forward by HUAC for questioning, tried to explain that the Hollywood Ten were sacrificed as part of an extremely complicated deal between studio ownership and the federal government. The MPAA, Kahn contends, overturned their decision to protect and defend the Ten against government regulation because they made a deal with HUAC that, in return for turning their backs on the defendants, HUAC would promise to call off any further investigation of Hollywood.[20] While Kahn's allegation was never proved, it is clear that the industry-wide panic, which grew out of the hearings, ran much deeper and was fueled by much more than the mere politics of patriotism.[21]

At about the same time that HUAC, the MPAA, and the studios were working to control the film workforce, television arrived on the scene. This was the second factor that radically impacted the studio system. Studios, contrary to commonly held beliefs, actually were actively involved in the evolution and exploitation of the new television medium. It is typically assumed that resistant and hostile Hollywood executives either vilified the new medium or took another stance and "dug their heads in the sand," while wishing that television would disappear and go away. There is historical evidence that suggests otherwise. In 1938, Paramount purchased half ownership of DuMont, which owned two television stations (KTLA in Los Angeles and WBKB in Chicago) including the DuMont Laboratories where television experimentation was being actively carried out. Many other studios, including Warner Bros., Disney, MGM and Twentieth Century Fox all vied for early television stations.

By the time television was introduced to the public in the 1950s, most of the studios had not only shown an active interest but had actually participated in the technological development of television—including helping to create a basis for pay television. [22] Paramount, for example, experimented with pay television and purchased fifty percent of a company called Telemeter, which eventually offered three channels using a scrambled broadcast signal. Movies could be viewed after placing coins in a box on the television set which descrambled the picture. Theatre owners challenged this set up and claimed violation of the recent anti-trust against the majors. Before shutting down under the threat of government restriction, Telemeter claimed a subscriber base of 2,500 homes primarily situated in an "experimental" area of Palm Springs, CA. Fox experimented with a system developed by IBM called Subscribervision, which instead of coins, used a punch-card to descramble signals. Broadcast and theatre forces lobbied to shut down pay television and a statewide California referendum (in 1964) was directed against a system called Subscription TV. Although declared unconstitutional, the referendum drew enough attention to put an end to pay television in the 1960s. [23]

Even though attempts were made in these directions to dominate the television hardware market or create a pay television subscriber base, Hollywood companies and studios failed or gave up in the attempt to dominate this aspect of the television industry. It was only later in the century with the conglomeration of the New Hollywood and the purchase of established television stations, pay-per-view systems and cable companies by the studios that this became a much fuller reality (e.g., ABC/Capital Cities Disney). However, direct involvement in the development of television technology was not the only area where studios were active. They became involved with "software" as well.

By the mid-1950s, studios were actively examining new distribution and promotional outlets for potential programming; including the leasing, or selling of the rights to old movies in their libraries to the companies that controlled many of the independent stations. By the early 1960s, most studios joined with local networks to provide prime-time airing of their older major features, which could be viewed in color by the growing television audience. But the ultimate involvement and response to television by Hollywood came about with the creation and development of product directly for the smaller screen. Columbia Pictures was the first to make the foray into this new territory in 1952 when it formed the first of many subsidiaries—Screen Gems—among the majors. First, half-hour entertainment programs were developed, then hour long shows, until finally Screen Gems was producing product on par with the old "B" features cranked out by the studios which, due to a more specialized audience at the movie theatres, were no longer profitable for the majors. By the mid-1960s, Hollywood began to make features directly for television, as well as for the theatres and became actively involved in creating and developing series for television to cover their losses in the declining theatrical market.[24] And as television became more and more established, both people and product began to move from it into film and visa versa.[25]

The third reason for the decline, which put an end to the old studio system, was not so much a single factor, but rather a number of things in amalgam that steered individuals away from the theatres. Overall changes in the American lifestyle after the end of the war—an increase in discretionary income, as well as a movement toward other recreational activities, and most notably the rise of affordable education and housing for servicemen and their new, growing families—began the migration from the cities to a suburban utopia. This migration helped to speed up the increasing decay of downtown and the decline of the centralized movie palaces built there. The cost of transportation to these downtown palaces increased, while the ease of access decreased. There were also many new ways to spend leisure time and the leisure dollar. Newly televised professional and collegiate events, stimulated by the exposure, drew larger and larger audiences. Mast explains, "Golf, tennis, and skiing attracted more middle-class enthusiasts than ever before—not only taking them away from the movie theatres, but taking plenty of their dollars for clothing, equipment, and travel."[26] By 1960, the DC-8 and 707 jets made long-distance travel easier, more accessible and more affordable. People continued to spend money on new technological developments in the music industry, including 33 1/2 RPM long-playing microgroove phonograph records (1948) and later, on new stereophonic systems which improved upon the mono players. A strong music industry diminished revenues on par with that of the booming television industry. The selling of newer feature films to television by the studios and other factors cited above (e.g., the development of viable product for television, etc.), including the advent of color television, and the building of "drive-in theatres" in the suburbs also helped to keep audiences at home (or at least, if not home, then nearby). It was not long before watching TV soon replaced going to the movies as the new form of mass entertainment and national habitual pastime.[27]

Douglas Gomery further argues, along with the reasons cited above (in particular, suburbanization and the radio), that the baby boom that coincided with suburbanization, was an important factor in the decline in theatre attendance. In fact, Gomery adroitly dispels any simple causal explanation of the substitution of television viewing for movie going, and considers the baby boom a key factor. After World War II, the two-child family gave way to families with three, four or five children. By the end of 1946, an all-time record of 3 1/2 million babies had been born in the United States. Gomery states, "nearly everyone who was in the eligible category had children . . . [and] families went out and acquired children as fast as they could."[28] During the late 1940s, suburbanites with small children looked for mass entertainment narratives at home, thereby eliminating the need to spend money on babysitting or transportation. Radio filled the immediate bill; television—a superior alternative to radio—which appeared on the scene in the early 1950s, gradually replaced radio as families quickly abandoned radio narratives for televised ones.[29] Whatever the reason, and there were many, the movie-going audience— along with studio dollars, experienced a decline during the late 1940s and 1950s.

In 1946, the American film industry grossed a total of $1.7 billion domestically—an all time high for revenues in the fifty-year American film industry. The following year revenues began to decrease. By 1958, that number dropped to just below a billion dollars, and by 1962, it plummeted even further to a ghastly $900 million. Even though by 1968, when many studios began to breathe a sigh of collective relief and watched as revenues rose to $1.3 billion, much of the damage had been done.[30]

FOUNDATIONS FOR A "NEW HOLLYWOOD" SYSTEM:

THE 1950s AND 1960s

During the next two decades, the studios struggled to make ends meet without benefit of vertical integration. Furthermore, the lack of talent contracts along with the strengthening of entertainment unions and talent agencies, the increase of run-away productions to Europe, and the downward spiral of theater attendance, pushed many of the studios to the brink of financial disaster.

Although the Hollywood studios saw audiences fade and their revenues plummet during the 1950s, they managed to survive by radically changing they way they did business. In doing so, they changed the very nature and structure of the movie industry. Without the theatre chains, the studios realized they lacked the necessary cash flow to sustain their factory system as well as their contract talent. The strategy was to lease studio facilities to the growing ranks of independent producers and provide a portion of a film's financing in return for distribution rights. Only quick thinking by a few of the remaining moguls and other corporate executives watching for opportunities to increase the bottom line, evidenced in financial decisions such as renting out sound stage space to independent producers and licensing of film libraries to television studios (such as Howard Hughes's decision to sell RKO's films to TV—a move he regretted later),[31] creating tour rides, as evidenced by Universal, or creating television product, kept the studios afloat.

The more "corporate" studios started nursing what would turn into a "blockbuster" mentality—realizing that releasing fewer, bigger, more spectacular films—wide-screen and Technicolor "spectacles" such as *Ben Hur*, *The Robe*, and many others, developed in reaction to the desires of the "old" movie going crowd, helped bring in the audiences. In addition, this business strategy of the studios (becoming everything TV was not) was not only more practical and profitable in the 1950s marketplace, but was an effective means of competing with TV.[32]

By the mid-1950s, this new financial strategy was paying off. *The Ten Commandments* and *Around the World in 80 Days* redefined the profit potential and even the event status of Hollywood movies. But the financial fiasco of *Cleopatra* in 1963 (bigger is not always better) all but put an end to the "old" blockbuster era.

Both economics and the *Paramount* decree favored the growth of independent production at the time and can be credited with the rise of independent producers into the market place. The effect of the decline in total output of the majors was to create excess capacity in the form of idle studios and underutilized systems of nationwide distribution. Even while the studios were trying to control the labor force, aspects of the labor force which were not directly tied to the studios took advantage of the situation and prospered. Paradoxically, the very firms that had created barriers to independent production in the prewar period were by 1950 vying to lease studio space to the independent producers and to distribute films for them. By 1951, all of the *Paramount* case defendants, with the exception of Universal, were distributing some independent pictures where rental charges by a major to an independent to make an A-class picture varied between $100,000 and $150,000. Many believe that this rise of the independent or "indy" producer was the final blow to the old system that had tried so desperately to protect itself against such competition.[33]

Beginning with United Artists, many studios shifted from a monopolistically integrated business into much less powerful, yet more diverse "corporate" companies that began to depend on contracting for individual products, works and/or jobs. Since space was rentable on the lots, contract studio producers and directors began to covet the autonomy of the independents they saw all around them. The studios decided that the only way to hold onto these people was to sweeten their studio contracts/deals by offering greater creative license to any studio directors and producers who could show their films actually made money. In the early 1950s, United Artists seized upon the idea of independent production as a natural way of overcoming a competitive disadvantage—a lack of production facilities into an asset that would help increase the studio's market share (e.g., United Artists retained the distribution rights, but handed over the creative decisions to their producers and directors—further sweetening the deal by giving away final cut rights and a percentage of the profits).[34]

This new division of responsibilities notably marks the beginning of a New Hollywood system of doing business. Studios now—for the first time—had to negotiate with producers (independent or otherwise) before the film went into production. After that, producers and the production for the most part was "on its own" (except for watching the budget bottom line, etc.). It stands to reason that many film crews were more favorably predisposed to this kind of independent set up.[35] As independent filmmakers were more easily able to gain a foothold in Hollywood, whether on a film lot or in a television studio, the center of power gradually shifted in favor of this new cadre of producers and directors. Eventually, gaining in reputation and financial backing, the independents soon began creating their own small-scale studios—effectively gaining and controlling their own means of production.

Nothing ever happens in a vacuum. This new mode and system of production sent out a ripple effect that allowed not only more independence for film crews, but also the actors who had lost contracts with the studios and the agents that represented them. The further abundance of independents in Hollywood led to the rise of larger and more powerful talent agencies. Lew Wasserman's MCA (Music Corporation of America) served as the model for others to follow. From the late 1940s and throughout the 1950s, Lew Wasserman's MCA had no rival as a talent agency and television producer.[36]

Competitors like William Morris Agency & MCA agencies filled the void. The new talent agencies became even more powerful later in the 1970s and 1980s—working hard to increase the bargaining power of their clients and likewise their own prestige, power, and profits. Filmmakers and actors benefited greatly from their work with these agencies, having moved as a group from being paid employees to free agents with tremendously increased power within the industry.[37] "Stars" were finally able to economically trade on what the studios had "made" of them.

NEW PRODUCTION CODES

Now the *Paramount* antitrust decision came full circle. Earlier developments, which dealt with issues centering on censorship, signaled a "sea change" in the new Hollywood industry. Film style and content—as a result of these changes—saw the break-up and decline of self-censorship epitomized by the gradual replacement of the old Production Code with a newer rating system. Compared to 1930, Hollywood in 1960 was a vastly different place from what it was when the original code was set in place. On October 7, 1968 Jack Valenti, a former LBJ administrator and ad man, announced a radically new motion picture production code and movie rating system. This rating system has been in place ever since.

By the 1960s, Hollywood box office revenues had been stuck in a twenty year decline. "Studio executives," Jon Lewis explains, "who had learned to work together to establish a new working relationship with exhibitors after the *Paramount* decision and reestablish control over the Hollywood workforce during the blacklist era, broke ranks and began to explore short term solutions to their box office problems."[38] The breakup of the institutional constraints that accompanied the old studio system soon contributed to greater artistic freedom for filmmakers and led to a transformation of Hollywood as a business and cultural machine. For instance, it has been suggested that, "Part of the explanation of why Hollywood movies changed so greatly in a relatively short time in the 1960s, involves the sudden loosening of restrictions over what Hollywood moviemakers could and could not show the public."[39] The new Production Code adopted officially acknowledged the need for artistic freedom and the defeating nature of censorship. This new code put forward the following objectives:

> 1. Encourage artistic expression by expanding creative freedom,
>
> 2. Assure that the freedom, which encourages the artist, remains responsible and sensitive to the standards of the larger society.[40]

Albert Einstein would be the first to suggest that "responsible" and "sensitive" are relative terms and mean different things to different people. This new code rather than excluding or "censoring" unseemly material, asked for responsible and sensitive inclusion of the products into mainstream society. The new aim of the newly adopted code was geared more to describing this previously unmanageable product than to judging it. Based on this new system, sex, violence and strong language —which seemed to titillate and draw an audience—became tied to the success or failure of a film at the box office (as a PG-13, R, and/or X rating). The studios had been looking for some kind of gimmick that would distinguish their product from that which was being screened on the small screen. Jon Lewis points out that, "a more liberal code promised to encourage the production of films that looked and sounded different from the strictly censored programming on television."[41]

It was Gerald Mast who noted in *Movies in Our Midst*, that the issue is a difficult one at best:

> Because the movies have sold sex and violence from the beginning (what extremely popular and public art ever sold anything else?), and because they were created within and supported by a society that condoned neither the doing nor the display of sex and violence,

> the motion picture industry has been in the paradoxical position of trying to set limits on how much it would let itself sell. The primary principle for regulation seems to have been "all that the market will bear," and when the market gets angry and will bear no more, curtailing its expenditures at the box office, the film industry repeatedly catches a severe case of moral fever.[42]

Mast clearly hits the nail on the head. A release from censorial restrictions, while allowing for more freedoms of expression—both what might be considered positive and negative—also has contributed to greater incidents of "what the market will bear" in terms of explicit sex and gratuitous violence that titillate the viewing audience. This trend has added greatly to a general de-sensitization of the public. What was considered alarming or shocking not that many years ago today is considered blasé and has been incorporated into the film narrative (or genre, etc.) that certain acts or figures of speech—for example—have become not only commonplace, but expected. Under the new rating system, strong language, extreme violence, and sexually explicit representations have all become part of the formula for box office success. The Clinton administration (1993), concerned about the rise in murder rates across the country began to question the amount of violence on television and in videos (taking an especially long look at children's television). Filmmakers have also questioned the extent of violence in the medium, especially as it relates to television programming.[43]

The Incorporation of Hollywood: The Late 1960s

Despite their growing rapport with the TV industry (created product and utilized active libraries), the studios were hard pressed to overcome not only a fall in film attendance and a succession of big budget flops, but also film imports notably surged during this time and represented almost two-thirds of all total U. S. releases.[44] Unprecedented, this trend and interest in foreign films became more and more prevalent as independents began to gain power in Hollywood. The eager new independents looked toward the New Wave French directors and their films and their way of filmmaking—an apotheosis of the director in the creative work of film—as the new ideal. As a result, in the 1960s the American version of the New Wave cinema was born.

At this time, along with the rise of television and the trend toward adults staying home to watch it, the bulk of the movie audience shifted and was soon comprised of primarily young adults without children and adolescents. Because it appealed directly to these groups, New Wave cinema was able to gain a foothold in the American market, where the "baby boom" audience was now younger, more affluent and better educated. Therefore, the fourth factor that led to the financial woes of the studio, along with 1) HUAC and the unions, 2) TV, and 3) American lifestyle changes at the end of WWII was, 4) the nature and composition of the film-going audience. Filmgoers were increasingly hip, cool, politically aware, disenfranchised, and disillusioned youth who clearly preferred films like *Bonnie and Clyde* (1967), *Easy Rider* (1969) and *M*A*S*H* (1970) to the mega-"blockbusters" the studios were trying to peddle without much effect.

From the beginning, the strategies of the studios remained intact: domestic box office of each film served as the main income. A lack of diversification made the studios vulnerable. By the late 1960s, Wall Street took further advantage of the studios' weakened position and started to purchase more of them (i.e., National Kinney), solidifying the trend toward deep pockets and diversification. The volatile income of motion picture studios, due to the uncertainty of audience reception of each film, and the distributor's increasing need for various sources of risk capital made them likely targets for takeover by conglomerate corporations.[45] As a direct result of these factors and overproduction in the 1960s, all the studios, except Columbia, Disney and Twentieth Century Fox, had been gobbled up by corporations by the end of the decade. Cook states,

> Beginning with the purchase of Universal by MCA in 1962, extending through Paramount's sale to Gulf & Western Industries

in 1966, the acquisition of United Artists by Transamerica Corp. in 1967, and the sale of Warner Bros. to Kinney National Service Corporation and of MGM to Las Vegas financier Kirk Kerkorian in 1969, the studios were one-by-one absorbed by larger, more diversified companies.[46]

THE NEW HOLLYWOOD, PHASE ONE: DISILLUSIONMENT, ANTI-HEROES, AND EASY RIDERS

The studios still had to make viable pictures even with the new infusion of capital big corporations provided. Looking at the cultural revolution exploding around them (i.e., the civil rights movement, women's rights movement, the Vietnam War protests, militant black power, the sexual revolution, etc.), where the credo of the day was "do not trust anyone over thirty," the aging studio executives began to take note and respond to viewers' needs and make "grittier," socially relevant or youth oriented pictures. However, in this revolutionary climate, nothing was a "sure bet"—old genres, and old ways of telling stories were no longer relevant. Anything that smacked of an old regime or of "tradition" was highly suspect and closely scrutinized for "establishment" ties and lies. Overall, the 1960s constituted a powerful break with the past and the film industry shifted to accommodate the burgeoning "youth market."

An astonishingly successful road picture *Easy Rider* (1969) was only made for $375,000 while it returned $19 million to the BBS Productions company that produced it. This film was a variant of the many Corman-produced exploitation biker films cranked out by AIP workers. The AIP-Corman strategy (according to Cook) was to ignore the mass audience and focus on target specific demographic segments of the film-going market (in this case the teens) so as to exploit their tastes (sex, drugs, rock n' roll, anti-heroes, etc.) with over the top, sensational, extremely low-budget material. Taking this approach to the market, a producer cannot lose. Cook further suggests a swift delivery of the "goods"— as with pornography, the ultimate exploitation genre—overcame other inherent low-budget problems with the picture's packaging and form. In fact, low budgets meant low risk—a high rate of return, and hence, success at the box office. The success of *Easy Rider* convinced Hollywood that inexpensive films had the potential to create a blockbuster overnight and could (or should) be made targeted specifically to the "youth market." This deluded desire to tap the youth market paved the way for an abundance of low-budget "youth culture" movies and the founding of many short-lived independent companies modeled on the "Easy Rider" BBS Productions prototype.

Unfortunately, this foray into the youth market and culture was not nearly enough to stave off an industry-wide recession from 1969-1971, which totaled $500 million in losses for the major studios, and by 1970, had left a whopping 38 percent of filmmakers unemployed. Of all the youth cult films, only *Woodstock* ($16.4 million) and *Joe* ($9.5 million) met with any kind of box office success, while *M*A*S*H*'s success and larger box office ($36.7) was clearly based on its appeal to a larger mass-market audience.[47] In any event, the studio's foray into the youth-cult market began to help in the blurring of distinctions between mainstream and exploitation genres that would characterize the early 1970s until mid-way through the decade when distinctions completely disappeared. Once Hollywood began the slide down this slippery slope, the authority enjoyed by classical mainstream film genres (and the security it provided filmgoers) was first diluted, then lost entirely, and with it, the good overcomes evil, happy-ever-after hopes of an entire generation.

David Cook best sums up this state of cultural despair and hopelessness in his book, *Lost Illusions: American Cinema in the Shadow of Watergate and Vietnam, 1970-1979*, while discussing the revision of the Western genre:

> Traditionally associated with conservative cultural and political values (in the hands, of John Ford, say), the Western became a vehicle for antiwar protest and social criticism in the early years of the decade. Six months before the release of *Easy Rider*, Richard

Nixon had been inaugurated as the thirty-sixth president of the United States, and three months later the toll of Americans killed in Vietnam reached 33,641 and exceeded that of the Korean War..."[48]

Cook adroitly points out that, "The hopelessness and romantic fatalism that pervades so many of Hollywood's 1969-1971 youth-cult films, starting with *Easy Rider* and continuing through *Zabriskie Point*... and *Joe*, can be traced very specifically to this despair and the Nixonian politics of division that produced it."[49] Hollywood Westerns during this time, for example, were not merely genre films, but for a brief historical American moment, were steeped in the politics of the time and functioned as symbolic vehicles for larger themes and issues, including, but not limited to, anti-military, anti-imperialist, or anti-colonial sentiments. The studios were in a win-win situation. They could subsidize and promote "safe" genre films, while at the same time supporting subversive themes which feed audience interests and concerns.[50]

Although many films were strictly marketed to the youth market ("hippie" values of sex, drugs, rock n' roll, and radicalism), many others were targeted to the new urban professionals and young adults who flocked to films that focused on themes of sexual revolution, coming of age and sexual awakening, marital angst, search for self-fulfillment, meaning and a sense of personal identity, as well as those which played on the fears of urban unrest, evoking a general tendency toward urban paranoia. This more adult fare was part of the studio's desire to differentiate film from television product. The changes to the production codes during this time favored this more "gritty" film product.

The desire for more and more of these type of "youth" movie blockbusters, also drove the studios to recruit a new generation of directors, producers, and writers from the ranks of film schools like USC, UCLA, and NYU. Sarris's and Truffaut's New Wave of "auteurs" approach to filmmaking, which firmly positioned the director as the central creative force of the production, was formally inscribed into the production curriculum at many of these film schools and became the creative and political mantra of the day. Auteurism beautifully coincided not only with the rise of film schools, but with the individualism inherent in the 1960s, the loosening of the production code restraints, the new wave of independent film producers, and independent productions working on studio lots. The New Wave, by foregrounding the auteur as the central creative force of the film, supported self-reliance and made it attractive for independent individuals to write, shoot, direct, and edit their own film. Likewise, many American studios and independent producers looking to break away from union control in the industry found this style equally attractive.

The idea of authorship in filmmaking was first formally defined or "coined" by Francois Truffaut (a member of the "New Wave" movement in France) in his seminal 1954 *Cahiers du Cinema* essay, "Une certaine tendance du cinema francais." His was a political essay (the term was originally 'politique des auteurs') that privileged and promoted the interest of certain filmmakers over others. The auteur was not simply a film director of better-than-average abilities. The auteur, as put forward by Truffaut and *Cahiers*, was someone who could achieve a personal form of expression while working within the impersonality of the studio system. As such, auteurism spoke to the predicament of anyone trying to live as an individual within a society based on mass-production. The film of an auteur, furthermore, should be a means of personal expression for the director, or director-writer, and should bear his or her "signature"—a personal artistic fingerprint or personal style—instead of being the work of an impersonal, artless, and soulless corporate factory."[51]

Truffaut's description spotlighted directors in Hollywood the likes of Welles, Huston, Curtiz, Ford, Hitchcock, and Hawks, who had worked within the studio system, but as Jon Lewis points out, had "transcended it to achieve a cinema of personal vision."[52] The French directors themselves respected these older Hollywood directors. They realized in the works of these directors the seeds of their own theories about directorial authorship, even though it had been produced within the studio system.[53]

Truffaut's "New Wave" of 'auteurs' did not really stick in America until nine years later, when in 1962, Andrew Sarris wrote his seminal essay, "Notes on the Auteur Theory in 1962."[64] By dropping the 'politique' from the title, Sarris set up auteurism, for the most part, to be an aesthetic proposition—weighing one director's talents against another—promoting one to the Pantheon, demoting another. Sarris began to build his case for the auteur theory around the likes of Hitchcock, et al.—evaluating a particular director according to three concentric circles: the outer circle representing technique, the middle circle representing personal style, and the inner circle representing interior meaning. According to the auteur theory, the author of the film (usually but not always the director) has complete control over his film (its images, camera angles and movement, lighting, dialogue, editing, sound) and use that control to express his (or her) vision to produce a work of art which directly and indirectly communicates "meaning" to the viewer, a meaning unchanged and unchallenged by the passage of time or presentation before audiences of different cultures. While a director like Hitchcock is famous for his control over a project, this was not normally the case with other "auteurs." As such, one can quickly see that the auteur theory as put forward by Sarris had some inherent problems. The corresponding roles of the director may be designated as those of a technician, a stylist, and an auteur, emphasizing the body of a director's work rather than isolate masterpieces. However, soon other critics followed Sarris's suit. By the end of the 1960s, even the most hostile toward the critical approach, had begun to, if not wholeheartedly, accept the premise of director-writer as author, and then tried to locate authorship in film—somewhere.

The New Wave in America (or what might be considered the American New Wave, or New American Cinema by others, or, more specifically the first phase of the New Hollywood,) was not an entirely foreign-born artistic movement, as Hollywood was not only filled with its own form of mavericks (independent-minded directors heading independent productions), but economically was struggling to please the new youth market, and in doing so, inevitably broke away from old genres and experimented with new ideas. Many of the films these "new" independent directors were unsurprisingly characterized by inventive camera work (the inventiveness, in many cases, occurred out of necessity when filmmakers and film students driven by economic necessity used handheld cameras left over from the war), self-reflexive style and play and a rambling compositional style epitomized in the New Wave films of Truffaut and Godard.

Many scholars and historians have argued over the years that the reason the films of the New Wave directors appealed to younger Americans was due to the correlation between the revolutionary techniques in the medium with counter-culture imagery. Neal Hurley in *The Reel Revolution* writes, "In a sense, he [Godard] is always making the same film which centers on: western people impaled on the 'throw-away-able' comforts of a synthetic civilization with an escalator standard of living, either socialist, or capitalist."[55] For younger directors in the 1960s who were eager to follow in the creative footsteps of the European New Wave and create an American New Wave, or New Hollywood of their own, the key to success seemed to be to exploit the widening gaps in industry control over filmmaking while capturing a large enough young audience for the film to make some money. The social turmoil of the 1960s and early 1970s certainly provided enough politically charged dramatic material for young Hollywood artists to work with while guaranteeing a good box office draw. Coupled with this climate in filmmaking was an audience that was increasingly disillusioned with particular stories and genres that were the cornerstone of the "old" Hollywood way of doing things. Old-fashioned stories, so "fashionable" and contemporary a few years before, no longer spoke to the political and social developments and upheaval in which people found themselves. The old stories and old attitudes that helped inform them had been thrown into extreme doubt. Michael Wood, sums it up by saying:

> The sixties were a decade that made life hard for a lot of old stories, an age that was full of an awareness of ugly, unavoidable realities:

> racism, torture ... assassination ... and the war in Vietnam; drugs, muggings, and turbulent, unmanageable cities. It was not that popular films had suddenly become false, for they had always been false. Just that they had become too false, false enough to upset the old, carefree truce between wishes and facts.[56]

Axel Madsen agrees with Wood stating, "that the new movies were an inevitable response to social and political developments:

> The post-Vietnam, post-Watergate seventies have produced a numbness to pain and corruption that has rubbed off the screen. The Vietnam war, the explosion of street crime and of government intrigue at the highest level, seem to mock middle-class gentility and to make despair and cynicism more than fashionable. More than ever modern heroic acts seem to be possible only as schemes of fools and lunatics. Makers of formula mine new veins for popular moods and come up with screen fare that accepts corruption and sentimentalizes defeat.[57]

Other genres and subgenres that typified this era of hopelessness are of some note—the gangster film, the detective film or film noir. Gangsters were for the most part portrayed sympathetically, usually martyred by unjust lawmen, thus reversing the moral order of the classic universe. These sacrificial gangsters (modern day saints and saviors)—whose murderous tendencies were tempered by winning personalities or mitigating circumstances—were set up as romantic revolutionaries who went up against a corrupt system and ultimately lost—like the Kent State Four. In most of these films, the corruption of the system was magnified.

The detective film took on vigilantism with a vengeance. The film noir detective was in the past a paragon of courageous individualism—tough, resourceful, and heroic in combating the moral anarchy surrounding him. Not so in the 1970s. During this era of skepticism and cynicism, the film noir detective was portrayed as inept, vulnerable, and usually victim of an anachronistic code of honor. *Dirty Harry* is a perfect example of this tired, alienated private eye/cop that needed to operate outside a law that was no longer valid or so entangled in the political and economical realities of corporate capitalism that justice could not be adequately carried out in such an impotent judicial system. Taking vigilantism a step further, *Death Wish* centered on a decent man who had been wronged, but could not hope to get justice under the law and as such is forced to seek it by violating it. The motivating factor underscoring this man's move from pacifist to vigilante is revenge for his wife's rape-murder. Not surprisingly, this rape-revenge theme ran thorough out many films of the 1970s (*Taxi Driver*, *Godfather* opening scene, *Deliverance*, etc.), clearly reflecting the culture's desire for retribution for a crime that will not be punished by those in power. Again, the implications of Watergate and Vietnam on the collective unconscious of America becomes clear. Many revenge films took the rural South as a base—the South being a place of civil unrest, enhanced violence and isolationism/elitism.

David Cook points out that, "The populist impulse of these rural revenge films is clearly related to the ideal of working-class purity enshrined in urban films like *Rocky* whose heroes overcome impossible odds to rise above their "betters." Cook continues, "At the core of both is the resentment of wealth, sophistication, and high culture that informs all populist mythologies of the little man, spiked with Watergate-Vietnam mistrust for institutional authority." [58]

Other genres of the period were: (a) the paranoid conspiracy film, (b) the revisionist musical, (c) parody film noir, (d) the disaster film, and at the end of the decade, (e) Dolby-driven musicals, and of course, (f) science fiction (both dystopian and utopian). The psychodynamics of the American family also came into focus as horror moved from Saturday matinees to more violent fare (R and X ratings) in what many consider the Golden Age of the American Horror Film. On the fringe and center stage came the subgenres of allusion (genre parodies, memorialization, biography pictures, hybridization), divorce, and feature length pornography.

Relying on the new independently contracted star system to create mass appeal, young directors consciously diverged from tried and true formula pictures and genres of the Old Hollywood system such as the western, cops and robbers, war stories, and glamour romances. Instead the young filmmakers undercut the old genres radically in the shift to a New Hollywood and instead of John Wayne as hero getting the girl and defeating the Indians (or whomever), Paul Newman and Robert Redford in *Butch Cassidy and the Sundance Kid* or Dustin Hoffman in *Little Big Man* as anti-heroes helped to parody and undercut the western genre. Jon Voight's anti-hero portrayal in *Midnight Cowboy* further serves to elaborate this genre shift.

But these films, with their undercutting of traditional genres and formulas, helped to perpetrate the turbulence prevalent in 1960s society. While "housekeeping" was necessary and certain truths needed to be revealed and shared as a collective society, the difficulty comes when that same society is numbed by the bleakness of the revelation, no matter how timely or important. The old stories had always served a purpose and allowed audiences to not only "feel good," but also believe in the overthrow of evil and the triumph of good—a happy-ever-after—no matter how absurd. These old stories and the myths which underscored them helped to put things into a recognizable and understandable order. When the old stories were lost, so went the myths that helped make sense of a chaotic world. If the myth no longer exists for the hero to slay the dragon, then the dragon will not only eat the hero, but everything else in its way. It was not until the very late 1970s that the dragon was finally defeated and the hero triumphed. Lucas clearly felt the lack and with the opening of *Star Wars: Episode IV: A New Hope* helped fulfill this societal need which was finally rectified then carried through to an extreme during the following "Reagan" decade.

And although mainstream genres found solid expression in television (taking over the B film function of the Old Hollywood—which might account for some of the audiences' following), many of these traditional genres became debased and diluted even further (exhausted, trite, limited, and boring). For the mass audience, Cook elaborates, "the constant diet of genre-based TV shows and classical Hollywood genre films bred something like contempt for traditional generic conventions, reinforcing a sense that they had become old-fashioned, "unrealistic" and culturally irrelevant."[59]

Although this infinite repetition created either an exhaustion of genre or an examination of its quaintness, it also by virtue of the studio's archiving of classical cinema onto the small screen (using film libraries as TV fodder and filler) helped to build a historical film consciousness of those up and coming in the New Hollywood. Like Spielberg, or Lucas for instance, who both grew up watching the old films with a unique sense of retrospection that informed their own films at a later date. Not only that, but the income and profits derived by film library sales also helped to subsidize and hedge the bets on blockbuster budgets.

Since the studios were a literal ghost town (due to a lack of production), and there were no people working at the studio below the age of fifty-five (most were now unemployed or lacked the connection to the "youth market" Brigadoon), the studio executives looked to the younger film school filmmakers to give them the magic formula—the silver bullet and philosopher's stone—to attract younger audiences (by 1974 the average age of people employed in the industry had dropped to thirty-eight—today that number is much lower).

Interestingly enough, this speculation in the youth driven film market motivated Warner Bros.-Seven Arts to hand Francis Ford Coppola $600,000 for the creation of American Zoetrope (and with it the funding for Lucas' *THX 1138*, including rough drafts and beat sheets for *Star Wars* and *Raiders of the Lost Ark*). This speculation also prompted Columbia to make a six-film deal with BBS (*Easy Rider* producer) that led to Bob Rafelson's *Five Easy Pieces* in 1970 and Peter Bogdanovich's 1971 hit, *The Last Picture Show.* These collective actions on the part of the studios all helped to usher in a new age of filmmaking in Hollywood.[60]

Power was soon divided between the independent producers who were bringing projects to the studios and renting out studio space (if the studios could not vertically integrate—then independent producers were the next best thing) and the young film school directors (agents were also beginning to gain ground). These young filmmakers were deemed acceptable because they had been trained at a film school. The studio executives were betting that university training would ensure responsibility when it came to budget and schedule. This tactic also kept costs down and helped shift the blame if the movie bombed. For a few years, the door of opportunity opened at the studios then, saturated with new talent, closed. George Lucas was one of the few who not only got his foot in the door during the first phase of the New Hollywood, but was one of the few who walked right through.

Notes

1. ENDNOTES For a comprehensive overview of the "studio system," see Thomas Schatz, *The Genius of the System: Hollywood Filmmaking in the Studio Era* (New York: Pantheon, 1988). Other notable studies of the subject include David Bordwell, Janet Staiger, and Kristin Thompson, *The Classical Hollywood Cinema: Film Style and Mode of Production to 1960* (New York: Columbia University Press, 1985); Douglas Gomery, *The Hollywood Studio System* (New York: St. Martin's Press, 1986).
2. Thomas Schatz, "The Return of the Hollywood Studio System," *Conglomerates and the Media*, Erik Barnouw, ed. (New York: The New Press, 1997), 77.
3. Ibid.
4. Ibid.
5. Leo Rosten, *Hollywood: The Movie Colony* (New York: Harcourt, Brace, 1941), 78.
6. *United States vs. Paramount Pictures Inc.* (131: 141-142; 131:146-147; 131:158, 1938).
7. Michael Conant, "The Paramount Decrees Reconsidered," *The American Film Industry*, ed. Tino Balio (Madison: University of Wisconsin Press, 1985), 537.
8. Stephen Powers, David J. Rothman, and Stanley Rothman, *Hollywood's America: Social and Political Themes in Motion Pictures* (Colorado: Westview Press, 1996), 20.
9. Ibid., 21.
10. *Variety*, 4 Jan 1939, 51.
11. David Prindell, *The Politics of Glamour* (Madison: University of Wisconsin Press, 1988), 153.
12. Thomas Schatz, *Boom and Bust: American Cinema in the 1940s, History of the American Cinema, Vol. 6: 1940-1949* (Berkeley: University of California Press, 1999), 31-32.
13. Jon Lewis, *Hollywood v. Hard Core: How the Struggle Over Censorship Saved the Modern Film Industry* (New York: New York University Press, 2002), 11.
14. Ibid.,11.
15. Ibid., 12.
16. Ibid.

17. Ibid., 17.
18. Ibid., 12.
19. Ibid.
20. Ibid.
21. Ibid., 14. The Production Code Administration (PCA), the MPAA's predecessor, was founded by individuals, Joseph Breen, in particular, who held anti-Semitic assumptions about the dangers of movies and the men who made them.
22. Janet Wasko, *Hollywood in the Information Age: Beyond the Silver Screen* (Austin: University of Texas Press, 1994), 11.
23. Ibid., 12-14. Also see Michelle Hilmes, *Hollywood and Broadcasting: From Radio to Cable* (Urbana, IL: University of Illinois Press, 1990), 118-119; Douglas Gomery, "Failed Opportunities: The Integration of the U. S. Motion Picture and Television Industries," *Quarterly Review of Film Studies*, Summer 1984, 219-227. For more research directed at the interaction between film and television, also see Thomas H. Gruback and Dennis J. Dombkowski, "Television and Hollywood: Economic Relations in the 1970s" *Journal of Broadcasting, 20,* Fall 1976; Fredric Stuart "The Effects of Television on the Motion Picture Industry: 1948-1960," and Barry R. Litman, "The Economics of the Television Market for Theatrical Movies" in Robert Allan, ed., *The American Motion Picture Industry* (Carbondale: Southern Illinois University Press, 1982).
24. David J. Londoner, "The Changing Economics of Entertainment," *The American Film Industry*, rev. ed., Tino Balio, ed. (Madison: University of Wisconsin Press, 1985), 608.
25. Jack C. Ellis, *A History of Film*, 2nd ed. (New Jersey: Prentice Hall, 1985), 273-274.
26. Gerald Mast, *A Short History of the Movies*, 5th ed., revised by Bruce Kawin (New York: McMillian Publishing Co., 1992), 278.
27. Michael Conant, "The Paramount Decrees Reconsidered," *The American Film Industry*, rev. ed., Tino Balio, ed. (Madison: University of Wisconsin Press, 1985), 539.
28. Douglas Gomery, "The Coming of Television and the Lost Motion Picture Audience," *Journal of Film and Video* (Summer 1985): 298. George Lucas, born on May 14, 1944, is a baby boomer.
29. Ibid., 297-300. For more information on the effects of the baby boom and the substitution of television for radio on movie-going, also see Landon Y. Jones. *Great Expectations* (Washington, DC: The Brookings Institution, 1982); and Louise B. Russell, *The Baby Boom Generation and the Econ-*

omy (Washington, DC: The Brookings Institution, 1982); Robert Sklar, *Movie-Made America* (New York: Random House, 1976); Fredric Stuart, *The Effects of Television on the Motion Picture and Radio Industries* (New York: Arno Press, 1976); Eric Barnouw, *The Golden Web, A History of Broadcasting in the United States, 1933-1953* (New York: Oxford University Press, 1968).
30. Gerald Mast, *A Short History of the Movies*, 5th ed., revised by Bruce Kawin (New York: McMillian Publishing Co., 1992), 275-278.
31. Douglas Gomery, "Hollywood's Business," *Wilson Quarterly 10*, Summer 1986, 43-57.
32. Stephen Powers, David J. Rothman, and Stanley Rothman, *Hollywood's America: Social and Political Themes in Motion Pictures* (Colorado: Westview Press, 1996), 21.
33. Stephen Powers, David J. Rothman, and Stanley Rothman, *Hollywood's America: Social and Political Themes in Motion Pictures*, 21.
34. Ibid.
35. Ibid.
36. Tino Balio, ed., *United Artists: The Company That Changed the Film Industry* (Madison: University of Wisconsin Press,1987), 77. In 1962, MCA, under investigation for antitrust violations—as Paramount had been little more than a decade earlier—was obliged to choose between talent and production and bought Universal Pictures after it gave up money contracts as a talent agency.
37. Stephen Powers, David J. Rothman, Stanley Rothman, *Hollywood's America: Social and Political Themes in Motion Pictures*, 22.
38. Jon Lewis, *Hollywood v. Hard Core: How the Struggle Over Censorship Saved the Modern Film Industry*, 135.
39. Ibid., 23.
40. Gerald Mast, ed., *The Movies in Our Midst: Documents in the Cultural History of Film in America* (Chicago: University of Chicago Press, 1982), 704.
41. Jon Lewis, *Hollywood v. Hard Core: How the Struggle Over Censorship Saved the Modern Film Industry*, 111.
42. Gerald Mast, ed., *The Movies in Our Midst: Documents in the Cultural History of Film in America*, xix. The exposure of Janet Jackson's breast during the 2004 Super Bowl half-time show and the subsequent regulatory backlash across media outlets (e.g., pulling the Howard Sterns radio program from certain markets) illustrates this point.

43. Stanley Rothman, and S. Robert Lichter, "Personality, Ideology, and World View: A Comparison of Media and Business Elites," *British Journal of Political Science* 15, 1 (1984): 29-49.
44. Stephen Powers, David J. Rothman, and Stanley Rothman, *Hollywood's America: Social and Political Themes in Motion Pictures*, 22.
45. Michael Conant, "The Paramount Decrees Reconsidered," *The American Film Industry*, Balio, Tino, ed., rev. ed. (Madison: University of Wisconsin Press, 1985), 554.
46. David Cook, "The Film Generation," *American Film History*, Jon Lewis, ed. (London: Duke University Press, 1998), 14.
47. Ibid., 171.
48. David Cook, *Lost Illusions: American Cinema in the Shadow of Watergate and Vietnam, 1970-1979* (Berkeley: California University Press, 2000), 173.
49. Ibid., 173.
50. Ibid., 174.
51. John Caughie, ed., *Theories of Authorship* (London: Routledge and Kegan Paul, 1986), p. 9.
52. Jon Lewis, ed., "The Corporate Era," *The New American Cinema* (North Carolina: Duke University Press, 1998), 11.
53. Paul Monaco, *Ribbons in Time: Movies and Society Since 1945* (Bloomington: Indiana University Press, 1987), 37.
54. Andrew Sarris, "Notes on the Auteur Theory in 1962," *Film Culture*, no. 27, Winter 1962/1963. Also see Andrew Sarris. "Notes on the Auteur Theory in 1962," *Film Theory and Criticism*, Gerald Mast, Marshall Cohen and Leo Braudy, eds., 4th ed. (New York: Oxford University Press, 1992), 585-588.
55. Neal Hurley. *The Reel Revolution: A Film Primer on Revolution* (New York: Orbis Books, 1978), 133.
56. Michael Wood. *America in the Movies: or Santa Maria, It Had Slipped My Mind.* (New York: Basic Books, 1975), 194-195.
57. Axel Madsen. *The New Hollywood: American Movies in the '70's* (New York: Thomas Crowell, 1975), 23.
58. David Cook. *Lost Illusions: American Cinema in the Shadow of Watergate and Vietnam, 1970-1979* (Berkeley: California University Press, 2000), 197.
59. Ibid.
60. Jon Lewis, *Whom God Wishes To Destroy: Francis Ford Coppola and the New Hollywood* (Durham, NC: Duke University Press, 1995), 13. For more on this subject, see also David A. Cook. *Lost Illusions: American Cinema in the Shadow of Vietnam and Watergate, 1970-1979*; Peter Biskind. *Easy*

Riders, Raging Bulls: How the Sex-Drugs-Rock'n'Roll Generation Saved Hollywood (New York: Simon & Schuster, 1998); Michael Pye and Lynda Myles. *The Movie Brats: How the Film Generation Took Over Hollywood* (New York: Holt, Rinehart and Winston, 1979); Jon Lewis. *The New American Cinema* (London: Duke University Press, 1998); Robin Wood. *Hollywood: From Vietnam to Regan* (New York: Columbia University Press, 1986).

CHAPTER 2

NEW HOLLYWOOD MAVERICKS

If young people were to be entrusted with the millions to make a movie, they'd better be people with a strong conservative streak. And who better than kids from a University? They've learned their craft, they've delivered on time, they've worked under supervision—they've grown up watching old movies. They'll do just what we want: make new old movies.
--Richard Corliss, "The Seventies: The New Conservatism," *Film Comment*, no. 16, 35

Francis' personality was larger than life. You knew Francis was around even if he was a block away. George, though, he would stand right behind you and unless he'd speak, you'd never even notice he was there.
Bonnie Koehler, Editor to Lucas and Coppola, personal interview

Universal Studios, July 10, 2002

We were taught, it was the credo of film school, that nobody would ever get a job in the industry. Then Francis did it, clearly and indisputably, and this happened just when we were in school.

> He was about five years ahead of me, and he was working on his second film already, his first big feature.
> George Lucas, "An Interview," *Take One*, 5/79, 4

> We were going to be the new Godards and Kurosawas. Francis was gonna lead us. We wanted to ride in the car, but he was still at the head of the parade.
> John Milius, cited in Peter Biskind, *Easy Riders, Raging Bulls*, 142

At this same time, throughout Hollywood, a new generation of directors made a foray into the business. Unlike their predecessors who mostly hailed from Broadway theatre or Europe, this breed of directors were trained not only in film schools, but on low budget films or television. During this time, most television studios were not as rigidly unionized as the film studios and provided a fertile ground for up and coming writers, directors, and others needed on the crew. Steven Spielberg falls into this camp. Gary Kurtz, who went on to become Lucas's producer and partner, went to USC from 1959 to 1962 and had focused on working as a cameraman. Jobs during those years were less than plentiful, and it was more or less impossible to break into the industry in any of the guilds or unions (or perhaps rather the process and requirements of eight years of hard apprenticeship, in a given craft, asked patience from a group of young filmmakers who were used to making films of their own and not willing to wait the required time as an apprentice—which probably led to the demise of this particular practice).

Television work often led to low budget and nonunion film jobs. These jobs further led to coveted apprenticeships at American International Pictures (AIP) with producer-director Roger Corman—the king of schlock and low budget, youth culture, exploitation genre films that were so much in demand. This association with Corman came as no accident. He had been noted for scouring the film schools throughout the Los Angeles area for talent and struck gold, especially with the likes of Francis Ford Coppola, writers Willard Huyck, and John Milius, and producer Gary Kurtz, all of whom were more than happy to give it a go for nonunion wages. Corman, ever industrious, further scoured the television studios for talent as well, coming up with the likes of Spielberg.

The New Hollywood "mavericks" or "movie brats" as they are sometimes lovingly (or not so lovingly) called, most notably by the old Hollywood regime they were replacing, Lucas included, came onto the filmmaking stage during a time when "corporate" Hollywood was adrift and looking for a quick answer to their fiscal woes. As mentioned earlier, what these new filmmakers offered was a fresh, new creative talent that easily adapted to a system in chaos. They had studied film as film more thoroughly than any generation that had gone before them at the University—taking film aesthetics, film history, and production as academic subjects while learning the technical aspects of production (including film finance, budgeting, marketing, and distribution). They thrilled to the new and innovative films of the European New Wave auteurs, challenged old Hollywood myths and narratives and soon patterned their work off of that of their new filmmaking "heroes." These new directors didn't just study film; they immersed themselves in it and they learned it from top to bottom.

Film schools, with their heavy diet of classic Hollywood cinema, are natural dispensers of film history. Just as the French critics of the 1950s consumed a decade's worth of classic Hollywood cinema following the end of World War II, (having been presented with an unparalleled opportunity to view an artificially compressed history of 1940s films), so did American film school students consume fifty some odd years of Hollywood film while pursuing degrees.

In film school, these new directors acquired knowledge of serials, B Westerns, adventure movies—all of which had become "de-familiarized" genres by the mid- to late 1970s. This allowed these students of film to invoke these genres' long lost stylistic and narrative elements. Obviously, one side effect of seeing so many films from different eras back to back, day in and day out, is to begin to experience a blurring of the lines between the styles, genres, techniques, and subjects—blurring the distinctions between high and popular culture postmodern theorist Fredric Jameson and others have spoken of.[1] Seeing the likes of *Citizen Kane* followed by the *Nutty Professor* followed by *Rio Bravo*, *The Rules of the Game*, and *A Day at the Opera* can be simultaneously vertiginous and liberating.

Perhaps because of this enthusiastic immersion in the films of older directors like Kurosawa, Lean, Hitchcock, Ford, and Welles, the fledgling filmmaker's inspirations seem to have come less from literature, theatre, and politics, those things which inspired many of their idols, than from the films themselves. Many years later after the success of *Star Wars*, George Lucas, Paul Schrader, and Francis Ford Coppola met with their "hero," director Akira Kurosawa. Tellingly, after the meeting, Kurosawa told Lucas and the others, "If I think of John Ford as a father, I guess that makes you my children."[2]

The youth and age of these new filmmakers guaranteed their ability to tap into the needs and desires of the younger film-going audience who, like themselves, had grown up on a steady diet of television and rerun old movies. They spoke the same film language. They self-reflexively called upon devices such as parody, paying homage to, and using the same film references as those who watched what they made. Their inexperience as seasoned directors not only meant that they could be hired for much less than their contemporaries, but since they had mounted at least one film production and had experience holding various positions in others, they were at least familiar with a film set and could be trusted to finish a project. Since they had some training, they knew more about motion pictures than many of the non-film executives making the decisions and made the new corporate managers feel more secure in their choice and investment. Likewise, these whiz kids could also be used as scapegoats and could be blamed for any failure, taking the heat off the politically sensitive (and usually aging) executive. Lucas has a long history of taking the blame for a jittery executive's lack of vision, fear of failure and lack of trust in those he had hired to do what he himself could not.

In the book, *The New American Cinema*, Jon Lewis explains how Francis Ford Coppola was the vanguard figure of this new generation of "auteur" filmmakers, quickly becoming the mentor and figurehead around which they all rallied. Prominent members of "Club Coppola" included George Lucas, Steven Spielberg, Martin Scorsese, and Brian DePalma. Writer-directors John Milius and Paul Schrader rounded out the group.[3]

According to Lewis, Francis Ford Coppola graduated from Hofstra College (University) with a degree in drama, and promptly was accepted and enrolled in the graduate film program at UCLA. Early in his career, Coppola worked on the fringes of the industry, paying his dues while performing un-credited second-unit direction work for Roger Corman; eventually leading to a directing job on *Dementia 13* in 1963. The film was an extremely low budget horror film shot entirely in Ireland over a difficult three-day period with a crew that had been held over from *The Young Racers*, another of Corman's films. Before Coppola had even finished his postgraduate degree at UCLA he had already directed two soft porn films, *The Peeper and the Belt Girls* and *The Playboy*. He had also written both the lyrics and music for a musical, finished a feature screenplay, worked extensively in Roger Corman's film "factory," and had turned around foreign science fiction films into screenable drive-in fare.[4]

Producer Ray Stark recognized Coppola's talent and offered him a job as a script fixer at Seven Arts, where Stark was then head of film production. Coppola, enticed by promises of a future directing credit and Stark's assurances of his genius, accepted the offer. The day he took the job, it is reputed that an anonymous sign went up on the UCLA film school bulletin board simply stating "Sellout." A born writer, amazingly prolific, in his spare time when not fixing problem screenplays for Ray Stark, Coppola also worked collaboratively on several major feature scripts during this period—some with credit (*Is Paris Burning?*, 1966; *This Property is Condemned*, 1966), some without (*Reflections in a Golden Eye*, 1967), in the hopes someone would finally give him a break to direct one. But Seven Arts always assigned the plum position to someone else.

Eventually, he would write two original films for Seven Arts, including *The Conversation* and *The Rain People*, and one adaptation, Hawthorne's *The Scarlet Letter* (*The Conversation* would pop up later as a product of American Zoetrope), but that came later.

After awhile though, Coppola caught on and optioned his own directing vehicle for $1000, a British comic novel, *You're a Big Boy Now,* written by David Benedictus. Highly influenced by the style of the New Wave, half flower-power, half pop-art musical, all done to the rhythm of a handheld camera, Coppola made an American version of Richard Lester's innovative *A Hard Day's Night* released in 1964 without the Beatles. Seven Arts was impressed enough with the outcome to sign a new deal with him. Warner Bros.–Seven Arts distributed the film and Phil Feldman produced it for $800,000. Coppola also submitted *You're a Big Boy Now* to UCLA as his Master's thesis—a film school graduate's dream. "It was unheard of for a young fellow to make a feature," Coppola recalled. When the film opened, the *Los Angeles Times* stated that it was, "one of those rare American things, what the Europeans call an auteur film." [5]

Even though the film did not make much money according to normal studio standards (and in fact lost all of the $800,000 it took to make) until it was sold to television, Seven Arts was too busy with the new purchase of Warner Bros. studios to take much notice. Since *You're a Big Boy Now* received good enough reviews, Seven Arts-Warner Bros. decided to dust off an old 1947 musical, *Finian's Rainbow,* to strike some quick gold, and assigned this dubious film with a budget of $3.5 million dollars to their hungriest, youngest, and cheapest director—Francis Ford Coppola. The film, starring an aging Fred Astaire and Petula Clark, featuring the song, "How Are Things in Glockamora," was a far cry from *A Hard Day's Night* and the New Wave. Coppola was at first reluctant to come aboard. But persuasive studio executives were hoping to cover their bases—bet on a young director to appease the youth crowd and the pull of Fred Astaire to lure in the older audience. The film did neither. Coppola, though, with his usual flamboyance and flair for the artistic and his ability to put production values on the screen was able to make the $3.5 million box office flop feel like a big budget spectacle that appealed to Warner Bros.

About this same time, Coppola noticed a thin young man of twenty-three who was watching him during the shoot. Day in and day out, the "kid" wore the same thing: a white T-shirt, black chinos and white tennis shoes—the "kid" in the chinos was George Lucas. It was the beginning of a long relationship between the two men.

George's Early Years

Up until Lucas's life-changing meeting with Coppola, he had enjoyed an idyllic, "Norman Rockwell," middle-class, American upbringing.[6] Born on May 14, 1944 to parents George Walton Lucas, Sr. and Dorothy Ellinore (Bomberger) Lucas, he grew up surrounded by a loving family —two older doting sisters, Ann and Kate, a younger sister and constant companion, Wendy—as well as a community of close-knit friends. Living in a typical small town, George was raised in a modest ranch house at Ramona Avenue nestled amid a row of tall Modesto Ash trees.[7] On any given afternoon, you could find him walking to the "Little Market" around the corner, playing with his little black cat, Dinky ("Dinker"), riding his bike to the Scenic Drive-In for hamburgers and a coke with his younger sister, Wendy, or just running along the alley behind the house playing with childhood friends.[8] There was always something to do in the neighborhood. It was on Ramona Avenue where George forged many friendships that would last a lifetime.

He used his creativity to do many things that showed his talents and gifts at an early age. When he wasn't creating elaborate Lincoln Log cities and landscapes for his Lionel train set, building an ornate dollhouse for the girl across the alley, or making 8mm war movies or stop-motion films with one of his friends, he was thinking up new ways to entertain the neighborhood with backyard carnivals and by designing spooky houses rigged with special effects in his friend, Melvin "Mel"

Cellini's, garage. Throughout his childhood, George's vivid imagination and unlimited creativity found fertile ground and blossomed on the quiet, suburban street. When he was eight years old George and his friends, John Plummer and George Frankenstein, took a cart, nailed on some wheels, appropriated a giant, abandoned wooden telephone spool, laid down a wooden track, and built their own child-sized roller-coaster to the delight of the neighborhood kids. Plummer, whose father knew people in construction, procured additional lumber. [9] John Plummer reminisces,

> George had an idea about putting on a circus. So we decided to put on a circus. So we first made a little puppet theatre then all of a sudden somehow George came up with the idea we were going to build a roller-coaster, and so I got a wheel from a cable roll that the telephone company used and Freddie got all the lumber, and we build a crazy roller-coaster. You know, it went down one level and in the middle it had a turn table where you could turn and go down to the next level. Now you think about it, it was dangerous as Hell, but it was his [George's] drive that made it all come together. [10]

When he was young, weekdays for George were typically spent at the "New" John Muir Elementary School on Lucern Avenue. [11] As he grew older, he attended Roosevelt Jr. High School, and finally Downey High School on Coffee Road. During the summers he worked at the LM Morris Co. store helping his father out with the family office supply business. Although bored by the routine, George learned a lot from his successful businessman father who had been born during the depression. "He [our dad] taught us the value of the dollar," Wendy Lucas explains, "and inspired us to have a great work ethic, and to persevere no matter what, and to stand up for what you believe."[12] These values would often serve George later as a filmmaker to stay on budget, hit his deadlines, and stand up to the studios who wanted to re-edit or change his films. What George did in his free time, away from school and the drudgery of his father's business, was a different story altogether.

His dad's store was ideally located downtown and was only a short walk to Nichol News, where he, Wendy, and friends would pool allowances to buy the most recent issues of favorite comics "for 10 cents each," adding to his growing comic book collection. "These adventures sparked George's imagination years later as he started his *Star Wars* movies," said his sister, Wendy, "They also sparked his interest in drawing, which he had a great talent for. That gift helped him later sketch out ideas for films." [13] George's time was also spent in reading biographies, histories, and *National Geographic* magazines, listening to adventure and comedy on the radio (*The Whistler* and *The Shadow*), participating in Cub Scouts, or spending time seated spellbound on a bleacher in the garage of his friend, John Plummer's house, watching the only TV in the neighborhood. When George was 10 years old, the Lucas family finally purchased a TV of their own. Favorite television shows included, fast-paced, non-stop action cliffhangers like *Adventure Time* featuring *Crusader Rabbit*, or *Don Winslow of the Navy*, and Westerns, mysteries, cartoons and science fiction fantasies like *Flash Gordon Conquers the Universe*—genres which would later influence his award-winning work in cinema, most notably his *Star Wars* saga and *Indiana Jones* films.

Also downtown, near his dad's store, were two movie theatres where George would happily spend many of his Saturday afternoons. Most of the "big" films came to the beautifully designed art deco, State Theatre, but the Disney films, George's favorites, were shown a few blocks away at The Covell Theatre.[14] When not watching films on the big screen at the neighborhood theatre, George often enjoyed spending "movie nights" at his Grandfather's house (Paul Bomberger) on Helen Avenue where he watched 16mm movies and cartoons projected in the garage. He loved it. George also enjoyed going to the Children's Library that was once located in the basement of the McHenry Library at 14th & I Streets (now the McHenry Museum). His love of reading quickly translated into a love of stories and storytelling in print and on screen. Even when he was very young, George loved to tell stories. In 1955, the Modesto Bee (H Street)--where George worked as a paperboy--ran it's first article about

George when he was only 11. In the photo alongside the article, you can see an 11-year-old George, next to his neighborhood pal, Mel Cellini, proudly holding up a copy of his neighborhood newspaper, *The Weekly Bugle*. It was apparent even then that George had a knack for turning his dreams and ideas into fantastic stories.

That same year, when George was 11, he flew out of Modesto Airport to spend time with a close friend who had recently moved to the Los Angeles area.[15] It was during this memorable stay that he visited Disneyland for the very first time and attended the second day of its opening weekend in 1955. They also visited Knott's Berry Farm. George later looked forward to the family trips to Disneyland where he could spend a few days experiencing the wonders and magic of the Disney kingdom—a love that would translate later into the adaptation of two of his films into theme park rides (*Star Wars* and *Indiana Jones*) and weigh heavily in the sale of Lucasfilm Ltd. to Disney years later.

During the long summer evenings in Modesto, George and his family would pack a picnic dinner and head out to Graceada Park to listen to exciting musical concerts conducted by band director, Frank Mancini, a teacher at Modesto High School. Mancini had played in John Phillip Sousa's Band and was a talented musician. Every night, Manicini thrilled the audience with the passion of his music—a passion George translated into all his films—most notably, his *Star Wars* and *Indiana Jones* epics.

From 1956 to 1962, George attended Roosevelt Jr. High, then matriculated into Downey High School. In 1959, when George was 15 years old, the family moved from Ramona Avenue to a 14 acre walnut ranch on Sylvan Road, located far on the northern outskirts of Modesto. Away from the action, unhappy with the move, missing his friends, Lucas spent most of his time either experimenting with trick photography with a 35mm still camera that his grandfather gave him in his newly converted darkroom, reading *Mad Magazine,* or listening to his ever-growing collection of 45 and 78rpm rock and roll records featuring the electrifying sounds of musical heroes such as Elvis Presley and Chuck

Berry. [16] The music was new, exciting and transformational for a 15-year-old boy stuck on "The Ranch." [17] A year later, in 1960, his dream to spend more time with his friends became a reality when his dad bought him his first car—a Fiat Bianchina. "When George got his own car, his life changed. For him, it was his freedom," recalls Wendy. [18] No longer confined to the Ranch, he traded his old style for a new look, slicked back his hair, put on his dark "chino" jeans and white T-shirt and began "cruising" the popular 10th and 11th street "loop" with friends. [19] Overnight, George became the epitome of "cool."

In the evenings and weekends you could find George hanging out with friends and looking for girls while blasting rock and roll on his radio--providing inspiration for his *American Graffiti* soundtrack later. George tinkered and modified his tiny "sewing machine" Fiat motor until he made the car fly—beginning his lifelong love affair with speed, both on the street and on the screen.

When he wasn't cruising, he was working on his car after school at the Foreign Car Service on Scenic Drive (located across from the Scenic Drive-In), getting it ready for gymkhana races and autocross (where he won many trophies), or venues like Laguna Seca, where he worked for other racers as a member of the pit crew with the Ecurie AWOL Sports Car Competition Club. Suddenly, however, on June 12, 1962, George's amateur racing career came to a crashing halt. Heading home, about to turn left toward his house on the corner of Sylvan and Rexford, another student, traveling at high speeds, smashed his Chevy Impala broadside into Lucas's small Fiat Bianchina, flipping the car three times before it crashed into a tree. His seatbelt broke on the second flip, and he was thrown from the car, helping to save his life. Because he sustained critical injuries to his chest and lungs, he had a long recuperation period—two weeks in the hospital, followed by weeks of daily physical therapy sessions. About the wreck, John Plummer remembers,

> Oh that was awful. I remember driving out and looking at the tree and everything and thinking 'Oh, Gosh, this is really bad.' I went

to the hospital when he recovered and bought him a racing car helmet that we had taped and glued a roller-skate to on the top... just to kind of bring some levity to such a horrible situation. His lung was punctured and it was *really* awful. When you looked and saw that it was a jet seat-belt he had in there, a military jet seat-belt—and it [the crash] literally just popped it. That's how bad the impact was.[20]

Having been given this second chance, George decided he needed to do something meaningful and significant with this life—and made a decision to focus on less dangerous career goals—quickly trading racing for photography. "The accident made me more aware of myself and my feelings," George has been quoted as saying, "I began to trust my instincts. I had the feeling that I should go to college, and I did." He enrolled in the local Modesto Junior College, and became fascinated with anthropology and the mythological teachings of Joseph Campbell—concepts that would forever inform his storytelling style. George graduated from Modesto Jr. College with an Associate of Arts degree in 1964. It was during this phase of his life, while photographing race cars around Modesto and at racing events at the Laguna Seca Raceway, that Lucas met Haskell Wexler, a film cinematographer, who befriended him. In Wexler's own words,

I met George on a race track. At the time, I had Haskell automotive and was racing a Lola T 70 and a guy named Erikson brought a kid over and said, 'Look it, he's interested in movies and he's helping in the pit, I'd like to introduce you to him.' When he [George] said he was interested in movies he had that look in his eye. He wasn't just interested in 'movies' in Hollywood, but had that cameraman's look in his eye and so I got to meet him and talk to him. I happened to know the head of a very small cinema school at USC, Mel Sloan, an editor, and I told him about George. I don't know if I was the final guy who got him in or not. I think on the basis of the little stuff he was shooting that he would have gotten in any way, but for history, that's how George got into USC.

George's friend John Plummer had been accepted to the University of Southern California's Business School at about this same time (following in George Frankenstein's footsteps, another childhood friend) and also suggested that Lucas apply to the film school there. Lucas did, and was accepted, despite low high school grades. [21]

If fast cars and cruising were a defining moment in George's life, then attending USC was another. At USC, George admits he "realized he had found himself." [22] The University, whose motto is "Reality Ends Here," provided a rich environment for George's quick mind, creative spirit and ever-growing love of photography and cinema. George loved being a film major in a school where the emphasis was on experimenting and doing rather than on traditional academic learning which he had always found boring. He learned how to use a camera and how best to communicate his ideas on film. Lucas said, "I was trying to create emotions through pure cinematic techniques. All the films I made during that time [and after] center on conveying emotions through a cinematic experience." [23] He was not only becoming a filmmaker, but also a talented film artist. During USC, as well as afterward, George thrived and quickly forged lifelong friendships with like-minded talents who shared a passion for making films. The list of his USC film school peers reads like a "Who's Who of Hollywood" and included dorm roommate director Randal Kleiser, editor Walter Murch, producer Howard Kazanijian, writer-game designer Hal Barwood, writer-director John Milius, producer Chuck Braverman, writer-director Bob Zemeckis, director John Carpenter, and writer-director Willard Huyck. Other local student filmmakers, most notably Steven Spielberg from Long Beach, and later, Francis Ford Coppola from UCLA rounded out the young filmmaking group, or what they called themselves, "The Dirty Dozen." Eventually, East Coast notables Brian DePalma and Martin Scorsese would add their names to the elite group. Like those of his childhood, Lucas would treasure and nurture these friendships for a lifetime. Prompted by Lucas's love and dedication to his friends, Ron Howard, being one of them, wrote,

> I've known George and we talk all the time, so I've come to understand his many innovations and endeavors are all born out

> of a personal sense of what's right and what's wrong, both in the film industry and in the world. When people ask me what George Lucas is like, I say he is truly the most honorable person I've ever met. His word is his bond. That's been my experience. Ultimately, George's pioneering spirit comes from a very developed sense of integrity which also makes him a great friend. The kind of friend everyone hopes for in a lifetime. [24]

While at USC, George made several award-winning short films that pushed the boundaries of storytelling and style, most notably, *THX 1138:4EB*. His other experimental and narrative films included, *Look at Life, The Emperor, Freiheit* (Freedom), *Anyone Lived in a Pretty (how) Town*, and two short films, *Herbie* and *1:42:08*, the last two both about cars and racing. He particularly enjoyed making abstract visual films that created emotions purely through cinema. Whenever a Lucas USC film was ready to screen, a buzz of excitement and anticipation would fill the theatre. One time, when George's parents came to visit Los Angeles for a screening of several student films, his father remarked,

> Every time one of George's films would come on, the kids would whisper, 'Watch this one, it's George's film.' We went out to the car and all over the campus all they were talking about was Lucas's films! Now I had been against his thing of his going to the cinema school from day one, but we guessed he had finally found his niche. As we drove home I said to Dorothy, 'I think we put our money on the right horse'. [25]

Spielberg came from Long Beach State to see George's films as well to meet the man who made them. Later Steven said, "I never had seen a film created by a peer that was not of this earth—*THX* created a world that did not exist before George designed it." [26]

Lucas graduated from USC with a Bachelor of Arts degree on August 6, 1966. During this time in American history, graduate film students faced an uneasy future. The Vietnam War was in full swing, and the draft, for most students, was not just a possibility, but a looming reality.

Lucas, like most college students, had been politically active during his years on campus. In fact, it was hard not to be. He supported civil rights and other liberal causes, and was against the war in Vietnam and the policies of Lynden Johnson. Too late in the year to apply to USC graduate school, Lucas was caught in a unenviable dilemma—wait to be drafted or enlist. Since the 1940s, USC had sponsored filmmaking training programs for the military, including the navy, army, and air force, and supported a large military student population. Armed with a college degree and filmmaking skills, some military students suggested that Lucas enlist as an officer in the service's photography unit. Eventually the draft caught up with him and, resigned, Lucas reported for his induction physical in downtown Los Angeles. Surprisingly, he was rejected. He found out he had diabetes, a disease that Lucas would continue to live with, and battle, throughout the rest of this life. A free man, Lucas eventually found a job with veteran female editor, Verna Fields, who put him to work cutting United States Information Agency (USIA) documentaries which included President Johnson's trip to the Far East. Lucas's final cut of Johnson's trip to South Korea drew criticism from officials who thought he portrayed the South Korean's as "too fascist." This criticism of Lucas's work by those "in charge," would foreshadow other, more invasive censure by studio executives later. It was during this time, while working for Fields, Lucas started graduate school at USC. During the day, he took classes at USC and cut documentaries for Fields, while at night worked as a teaching assistant to a class of navy film students. It was at this time two important things occurred—he met Marcia Lucas, whom he would eventually marry, and he conceived his film, *THX 1138:4EB*.

Lucas's work with the USC navy students proved to be a significant moment in his career—showing both his talent for filmmaking and business savvy. Lucas had been brought in to the class by his undergraduate camera teacher, Gene Peters, to ostensibly teach the military students basic film techniques, but also to potentially get a futuristic film idea which Lucas had been kicking around in his head on to the screen. It was an ambitious project "based on the concept that we live in the future and that you could make a futuristic film using existing stuff." [27] These military students, typically lacking in imagination, Peter's believed, needed a project that would stimulate their creativity, while furthering their understanding of filmmaking. To do both, Peter's suggested Lucas shoot one of his own films, using the navy students for cast and crew. Facing antagonism from the navy students, who were twice as big and older than he, Lucas decided to turn the project into a contest—something the navy students understood---and divided them into two teams to see which could make the better film. Lucas headed up one group, while the other team worked with the highest ranking navy officer in the class. A brilliant move that not only diffused any dislike of their younger, scrawny teaching assistant, but bred a healthy rivalry among classmates that pushed the typical boundaries of a student film. Lucas had hit the jack-pot. Not only did he have a dedicated crew willing to do most anything to turn his complicated short script into a professional film, but suddenly he also had navy access to unlimited amounts of color film, camera equipment, and locations he would have previously been denied —the USC computer science department, an underground parking lot at UCLA, and the Los Angeles and Van Nuys airports. [28]

Charles Champlin, a critic for the *Los Angles Times*, touted the film as one about a Huxleyian man inadvertently given free will who tries to flee the nightmare world of tomorrow. The debt owed (or homage paid), and references made to other nouvelle vague films, such as Godard's *Alphaville* and Chris Marker's *La Jetee*—a short science fiction film comprised almost entirely of stills in which memory carries a man between a dystopic future and a past of lost opportunities—is clear. The story was fresh and timely. Says Champlin, "It was a period when there were a lot of good people at USC, but THX was an astonishing piece of work. It wasn't brilliantly absorbing drama, but the whole sense of paranoia and freedom in a bleak, uncertain world was very, very impressive. It was obvious that Lucas was someone to watch." [29] It was also clear, even at this early stage in his career, that Lucas had his finger on the pulse of the American zeitgeist. John Baxter mentions in his book, *Mythmaker: The Life and Works of George Lucas,* that:

> *THX 1138 4EB*—the subtitle *Electronic Labyrinth* was added later—was included in a program of USC films at the Fairfax Theatre in Hollywood. One party who went to see it included Fritz Lang... George Pal, producer of *When Worlds Collide* and many other science fiction films; and young film journalist Bill Warren. 'Among the films shown that night,' recalls Warren, 'Were *Glut, The Resurrection of Bronco Billy*, by John Carpenter, and *THX 1138 4EB*.' Afterwards, we're all standing on the sidewalk outside the Fairfax, and Fritz says, "All right, which one was the best?" Forry and George Pal look at each other, and Forry says, 'I think we liked the *Resurrection of Bronco Billy* best.' George Pal agreed with Forry. And Fritz says, 'That is why your films all stink, George. The best one . ..was *THX 1138 4EB*... If I ever meet that young director, I want to tell him how great that film was.' [30]

The THX production at USC wasn't always smooth sailing. As John Plummer, Lucas's friend explains,

> He fought cats and dogs with them. He thought he was going to get thrown out just because of the fact he fought them. When he made THX, basically he was going to use color film come Hell or high water. And the professors said, 'No. You are not,' and he did. At the time the school was more egalitarian. You had all these military people and they couldn't do anything like that, but George didn't want to be a technical person, even though he became the genius of film technology. He didn't just want to be a cameraman, he wanted to do more. [31]

After twelve grueling weeks shooting the film on weekends, working at Field's editing political footage during the day, and cutting THX sometimes until 4:00 a.m. in the morning, he was finished. It was a tour de force by any student film standard. Lucas's artistic vision and persistence paid off. The film contained computer graphics, traveling shots, and film optical processes never before seen in a college film. Pollock notes, "The student screening where it was finally shown turned into a madhouse, the cheering beginning when the opening title flashed on the screen: the USC logo turning from yellow to blood red." [32]

After the screening, word spread to Hollywood, and the success of THX soon translated into a student scholarship (he shared with three other students) at Columbia Pictures headed by producer Carl Forman to work on the set of *McKenna's Gold*, a Western starring Gregory Peck, Omar Sharif, Telley Savalas, Lee J. Cobb, with J. Lee Thompson directing. In exchange for expense money, equipment, and film stock, Forman asked the scholarship recipients to go to film locations in Utah and Arizona and make four, short, ten minute, 16-millimeter films to promote *McKenna's Gold* in theatres and on television. While the other three students quickly chose producer Forman, director Thompson, and the horse wranglers of *McKenna's Gold* as topics, Lucas took a different route. "I thought the whole thing was a ruse to get a bunch of cheap, behind-the-scenes documentary films made, and they were doing it under the guise of a scholarship," Lucas said, "Well, if they were going to give a scholarship to make a movie, then I wanted to make a movie. I wasn't going to do some promo film to advertise the picture." [33] Lucas called his visual poem of the desert, 6-18-67, named for the same day he completed filming it.

> The film begins with soft-focus pictures of desert wildlife and displays an acute awareness of the sights and sounds of the wilderness. There is the unearthly hum of giant power lines and transformers, the slow turning blades of a watermill, and speeded-up footage of clouds racing over a landscape. The contract between the reality of nature and the artifice being created by the move crew (which is seen only in long shots of the camera under an umbrella) is clearly established. The film ends with a glorious sunset. [34]

Although Forman eventually warmed to Lucas's film and understood his poetic vision ("...a lot of things were going on in the desert we weren't paying any attention to. Life went on before us, and life went on after us, and that's what George's film was all about."), Lucas was not impressed with what he saw going on in Hollywood.[35] For a recent graduate from film school used to budgets of a few hundred dollars, the waste of hundreds of thousands of dollars every day on the large set was ridiculous at best, and asinine at worst.

Soon after his work on *McKenna's Gold*, Lucas entered his films into three categories of the "Third" National Student Film Festival (1967-1968) —the major showcase for student film work. He entered *THX 1138:4EB* as a dramatic film, *The Emperor* as a documentary, and *6-18-67* as an experimental film. His film, *THX 1138:4EB* won first prize as dramatic film, while the others took honorable mentions. Lucas's USC friend, John Milius, won the animation award for his film, *Marcello, I'm So Bored* (that Lucas edited). Past winner of the National Student Film Festival Award, Martin Scorsese (from New York University film school), as well as John Milius, and Lucas were prominently featured in a *Time Magazine* article that highlighted their creative achievements.

The first place recognition of his film in the National Student Film Festival helped Lucas to secure a six-month Samuel Warner Scholarship that allowed him both an $80 a week intern salary and carte blanche on the Warner Bros. lot—doing what he wanted, learning what he could.

The Beginning Of A Beautiful Friendship

In his book, *Skywalking: The Life and Films of George Lucas*, Dale Pollack states that in 1967, "the day George Lucas walked onto the Warner Bros. lot to begin his apprenticeship with Francis Coppola was the day Jack Warner cleaned out his office and left."[36] A bit of embellishment. In truth, Jack Warner's departure from the lot was anything but sudden, and had been going on since he sold his stock to Seven Arts in November 1966. He was encouraged to stay in his offices and take the role as an independent producer. Even after Steve Ross's Kinney Services bought out Seven Arts a few years later in 1969, Warner remained on the lot. It was only when Kinney let him know that his offices were going to be turned into private dining rooms, did Warner leave the lot and move over the hill to Century City and set up Jack L. Warner Productions.

Although the truth runs counter to the romantic myth, Lucas did find Warner Bros. a very desolate place when he arrived. Only one film was being shot on the entire lot and that happened to be *Finian's Rainbow*. Lucas has been cited as saying as he walked through the empty lot, "This is the end"—fully believing the industry had been taken over by people who knew how to make deals and operate offices, but had no idea how to make movies. It was clear to Lucas at that time, according to some sources, that the old Hollywood was dying—if not already dead. The time was ripe for the maturation of the New Hollywood that had been going through its birth pangs for the past ten years. From Lucas's point of view, states Baxter, "the film industry had died in 1965 . . . it just took a while for people to realize that the body was cold. The venerable Warner Bros. studio, started in 1922 . . . had been sold to a television packaging firm, Seven-Arts, hastening the departure of the last of the moguls."[37]

Because it was the only game in town, and he was intrigued by the legend of Francis Ford Coppola, the first film school student of his generation to enter the Hollywood arena, Lucas, according to Pollack, decided to watch on the sidelines of the *Finian's Rainbow* production.[38] Impressed with Coppola's confidence on the set, Lucas quietly stood at the back and took it all in. After two days, Coppola went up to Lucas and asked who he was. Lucas told him about the Warner Bros. Scholarship and asked Coppola if he could work on the film with him. After a few weeks, Lucas grew bored on the sidelines watching Coppola struggle within the confines of the insipid musical, and decided to leave the set and try to get some film stock to fulfill his scholarship and make his own short movie while at Warner Bros.. Coppola, though, had grown used to having someone of his own generation on the set that he could talk to about the film and enjoyed Lucas's camaraderie. Coppola is reported to have said to Lucas when he mentioned leaving *Finian's* to make his own film, "What do you mean you are leaving? Aren't I entertaining enough? Have you learned everything you're going to learn watching me direct?" [39] On the spot, Coppola offered Lucas a permanent job on the production of *Finian's Rainbow* and his next film, *The Rain People*, and Lucas took it--making him on July 31, 1967 one of the first new employees of Warner Bros.—Seven Arts. Lucas signed a six months contract as Coppola's "administrative assistant" for a total of $3,000.

Lucas learned a lot from Coppola during the next ten years while they worked together; first as Coppola's assistant on the Fred Astaire musical, *Finian's Rainbow*, then as a documentary filmmaker/jack of all trades/PA on Coppola's, *The Rain People* (Lucas made a documentary film about the "making of"), and then as a Vice-President of the Warner Bros. financed experiment, American Zoetrope in San Francisco. On *Finian's Rainbow*, Lucas learned that a young filmmaker could "make it" in the industry, that to be a filmmaker you had to write, and on *The Rain People* he saw that Coppola, rather than asking the studio's permission to make the film —"just did it"—and would argue with the studio (or ask forgiveness) later. Coppola knew at the time that the studio needed him—and Lucas learned from that too. But in learning from Coppola, Lucas reacted. Lucas says, "My life is kind of a reaction against Francis's life. I'm his antithesis."[40]

Coppola was large and bulky, Lucas was leaner and lanky. Coppola was flamboyant, gregarious; Lucas reserved and reflective. Coppola was collaborative to a fault, Lucas—not as much—he truly enjoyed the challenge of doing everything—write, direct, produce, shoot, and edit— by himself. Where Coppola was irresponsible with cash and mortgaged himself to the studio, Lucas tried not to spend money and saved. Whereas Coppola considered himself a soulful poet, Lucas countered by being a strong businessman. No matter how little money Coppola had, he always acted like a man who had more. No matter how much money he had, Lucas, on the other hand, always acted like a man who did not need any. And where Coppola wanted to take over the game, Lucas just concentrated on redefining the rules. One followed the path of the auteur, while the other took the road toward entrepreneurship. Coppola always referred to Lucas as the "seventy-year-old kid." But of Coppola Lucas said, "All directors have egos and are insecure ... but of all the people I know, Francis Ford Coppola has the biggest ego and the biggest insecurities."[41] Even so, the two men became close friends and shared a similar vision. Lucas responded strongly to Coppola's auteuristic dream of creating a studio environment away from the interference of any "suits." Lucas recommended they move their operations to the San Francisco Bay area.

With four unimportant films to his credit, Coppola in November of 1969 asked Warner Bros. to finance his and Lucas' dream. Coppola envisioned an "*Easy Rider*" kind of avant-garde, alternative studio that was based on the Roger Corman AIP model. It appears that while Coppola negotiated the details of American Zoetrope with Warner Bros.--Seven Arts, the deal was finalized on December 12, 1969 while Warner Bros.—Seven Arts was being acquired by Kinney National Company (who dropped the hyphenate and reclaimed the Warner Bros. brand), a corporation run by Steve Ross who knew more about parking lots than the making of movies. Ross, had taken Kinney out of the mortician business into car hire by renting the limos out at night used by funerals during the day. He then moved into parking lots, despite, or in light of, the fact it was a territory associated with organized crime.

Ross then diversified into movies. He hired Ted Ashley, a "hot" talent agent, to take over as new head of the Warner Bros. studio and John Calley as head of production.

Regardless of the reason, it is possible that the cash strapped, Warner Bros.—Seven Arts, or new Warner Bros. executives accepted Coppola's proposal, not so much based on his auteuristic studio pitch, or his interest in setting up an alternative filmmaking studio, but because the studio executives were looking to accept anything that could make a profit and/or shift the blame for any box office failure away from themselves. Using a particular filmmaker's name would not only help in selling the finished film product as a packaged commodity (the corporations understood this tactic), but would provide a good way of placing blame. Hedging their bet on the possibility of success, but shifting all responsibility of failure on Coppola et al., Warner Bros. financed American Zoetrope to develop movies for the youth market in response to *Easy Rider*, and, in exchange, Warner Bros. would be guaranteed the "first look" on any material. Coppola also guaranteed the studio seven films, none costing over $1 million. In early negotiations, he pitched Lucas's feature version of *THX 1138* and offered other potential scripts, including *The Conversation* and Lucas and John Milius's *Apocalypse Now*.

Warner Bros. financed the project, but not without some concessions. They offered to lend (not invest or advance) $3.5 million, much of it in the form of a weekly $2,500 seed-money draw to help Coppola get started. Warner Bros. made Coppola promise that he would supervise the entire project. If they liked Lucas's *THX 1138*, then this draw would become a down payment on the entire package. If they did not like *THX 1138*, then Coppola would be responsible to pay back the entire draw.

Coppola and Lucas shot *THX 1138* for $800,000 and Lucas did all his own editing, accompanied by Marcia Lucas in his attic in Mill Valley. In May 1970, Coppola and Lucas screened the film for the Warner Bros. executives. After the screening, Warner Bros. not only confiscated Lucas's film and re-edited it —intensifying Lucas's distrust and anger toward studios in general ("It was like watching them cut the fingers off my baby"), but effectively put an end to American Zoetrope. Warner Bros. demanded their money back and sent the company spiraling toward bankruptcy, adrift without any financial backing.[42]

Devastated, at the darkest hour, with Warner Bros. demanding repayment of a $300,000 loan, Coppola got a message about a project called *The Godfather*. To pay the debt to Warner Bros., Coppola, on Lucas's advice, agreed to direct the seminal 1970s film, *The Godfather* for Paramount (which up until that point in film history became the biggest grossing film of all time in January of 1973), while Lucas began work on his next project, *American Graffiti*.[43]

Auteur, Auteur, Where Art Thou?: End of the New Hollywood, Phase One

While Zoetrope was in its death throes, the "auteur" (in its New Wave-American form) began to suffer the same fate—or at least a gradual mutation in form. During the 1960s and into the early 1970s, the unstable environment of the failing studio system allowed for independents and first time directors to take over the reins of creative control and create films imbued with their own personal "signature." In fact, due to the burgeoning "youth market" and culture saturating the United States, these reins of creative control were thrust into their open, eager hands. But it was not long before these reins were drawn back into the hands of the studio. At the end of the 1960s, the studios combined losses totaled roughly $41 million. As the studios saw it, the youth market boom had crashed in a blaze of rising debt. Of all the films geared to the youth market in 1970, only the youth film, *Easy Rider,* made any money.

Just a few years later, by the early 1970s, new corporate owners who used the industry as a means for corporate high-stake speculation and tax-sheltering had reversed this negative trend and earned profits totaling over $170 million—in large part due to the heavy marketing blitzes of a few blockbuster films. These new studio owners were not looking for the artistry in film so much as the revenue return. Auteurism rose with the rise in college-level film education among the industry's most lucrative audience segment and gradually became a marketing tool instead of a way of filmmaking. A well-known name of a director (who had been studied in school by college students, for instance) could sell a picture. Actors still had the power to sell, but were now coupled with "from the director of." Auteurism as "branding" came to the fore.

An interesting mutation seems to have taken place when looking at the differentiation of studio product or the "signature" of a studio (a way to categorize) and the marketing of a film. In the 1960s, auteurism seems to have taken the place of genre and studio style, whereby the quality and artistry of the earlier films were the product not simply of individual human expression, but of a melding of institutional forces. Thomas Schatz explains in *Genius of the System*, "In each case the "style" of a writer, director, star—or even cinematographer, art director, or costume designer—fused with the studio's production operations ad management structure, its resources and talent pool, its narrative traditions and market strategy. And ultimately any individual's style was no more than an inflection on an established studio style." [44]

One only needs to think of Jimmy Cagney in *Public Enemy*, staggering down a dark, rain-drenched street after a climactic shoot-out with rival gangsters, looking past the camera and muttering "I ain't so tough," then falling face down into the gutter . . . that was a signature Warner Bros. moment, what can best be described as a narrative-cinematic epiphany when star and genre and technique coalesced into a single ideal expression of studio style, circa 1931. Previously, as a marketing tool, one only had to mention the name of a particular studio and you knew the kind of film genre (and the star brand due to contracts) that would be made and shown. Studios thrived on routine star-genre formulations. Star, genre and technique coalesced into an ideal expression of studio style. Universal was home to the horror film, MGM the musical, etc. When the studio system fell into disarray, so did the means of easy studio recognition, product differentiation and signature.

With the rise of auteurism, certain directors affiliated with certain studios allowed for another kind of signature. Eventually, product reference back to the studio fell away and only the auteur remained and as a brand helped sell the picture. In the 1970s, the genre came back into play, but only as part of a larger "package" that helped to sell the film. This easy sale or use of a quickly identified film package branding still works today and has been "enhanced" by use of sequel and franchise.

David Cook points out that:

> . . . from the cinema of rebellion represented by films like *Bonnie and Clyde* (Arthur Penn, 1967), *The Wild Bunch* (Sam Peckinpah, 1969), and *Easy Rider* (Dennis Hopper, 1969), America's youth

> transferred its allegiance to the "personal" cinema of the seventies auteurs without realizing how corporate and impersonal it had become. Between the speculation of the new studio owners and the entrepreneurship of enterprising agents and managers who picked up on the selling power of the brand and began "packaging" talent for "big" Hollywood films (raising the cost of the film ... making them "bigger" in cost for marquee value than they were in fact or subject matter), the whole concept of the auteur underwent a drastic sea change. The auteurs themselves were transformed from *cineastes* into high-rolling celebrity directors (many of them) with their own chauffeurs, Lear jets and body guards." [45]

"In 1968," Cook continues,

> "Coppola had said, 'I don't think there'll be a Hollywood as we know it when this generation of film students get out of college,' accurately forecasting the enormous impact his generation of filmmakers would have on the industry. What he could not foresee was how the change would boomerang on the new auteurs and recast their films as branded merchandise to be consumed." [46]

Fast forward twenty-plus years. Since the 1990s (and now into the millennium) the auteur brand is widely used to help sell "director's cut" DVD's.

Coppola's dream of attaining easier access to film financing for auteurs turned into a creative quagmire as auteurs became more and more dependent on the studios to make a success of the "bigger-type" films. But this reality was still a few years in the offing. The blockbuster as we know it today in the early 1970s had just begun to take shape and with it phase two of the New Hollywood.

Notes

1. Fredric Jameson, "Postmodern and Consumer Society," *The Anti-Aesthetic Essays on Postmodern Culture*, ed., Hal Foster. (Seattle: Bay Press, 1983), 112.
2. Audie Bock, "Kurosawa," *Take One*, March 1979, 34.
3. Jon Lewis, ed., *The New American Cinema* (London: Duke University Press, 1998), 13-14.
4. Ibid., 14.
5. Biskind, Peter, "The Young Lions: Raging Days, Boogie Nights," *Vanity Fair* (April 1998): 220.
6. *Local Lucas History: Where Were You in '62?*, narr. Wendy Lucas, prod.Patti McCarthy, dir. Erik Howell (PMC Productions, 2013). http://www.youtube.com/watch?v=P18CDWvttZA . Situated in the Central Valley of California, Modesto, was a typical small town whose close-knit community embraced the fundamental small town values that distinguish it today. Fifteen years before George, Jr. was born, Modesto, in 1929, had a population of only 13,800. It was at this time that George's grandmother, Maude Lucas, a widowed woman (her husband, Walton Lucas, a oil worker, died in 1928 from diabetes), moved from Merced to Modesto to raise her 16-year-old son, George Walton Lucas (George's dad) and two older daughters. George, Sr. soon enrolled in Modesto High School (located on Paradise Road). A serious student, a member of the debate club, he became class president by his senior year. His vice-president and senior play co-star, a pretty, dark haired girl, named Dorothy Bomberger, caught his eye. They both graduated from Modesto High in 1931, and were married in 1933 soon after at the First Methodist Church (16th & I). The couple were very happy, but George, Sr., at the age of 20, needed to find a job. After working a few months in Fresno, he was offered a job in 1934 at L.M. Morris Co..(I Street near 9th), where he excelled at selling office supplies, furniture, typewriters and other business related products. The same year, Ann, their first child was born (George's oldest sister), and 18 months later, their second daughter, Kate arrived. Armed with a strong work ethic, George, Sr.'s dedication paid off and the family prospered and in 1947 he became sole proprietor of the L.M Morris Co.. George Sr. eventually moved the L.M. Morris Co. to 1107 I Street in 1956. A true Horatio Alger success story and brilliant businessman, George

Sr., later opened a second store, the George W. Lucas Co., where he sold 3M copy machines, service and supplies. A highly respected member of the Modesto community, George Sr. was an active member of the Rotary Club throughout his life. George Sr. wanted his son to take over the extremely successful and profitable family business, but George, Jr. had other plans. Today, viewed from Highway 99 in Modesto, you can still see a fading George W. Lucas Co. sign painted on the side of what was once one of the large warehouse buildings George, Sr. used to store his inventory.

7. Ibid. George Sr. purchased a lot on Ramona Avenue and built a charming one story home. It was a perfect place to settle down and raise children. The community was close-knit. It was here, to the little white house, on this shady, suburban street, that George Walton Lucas, Jr. was brought from the County Hospital where he had been born on Mother's Day, May 14, 1944. Two and a half years later, Wendy, George's youngest sister was born. Soon thereafter, George's mother's health faltered. During this time, George's father hired Mildred Shelly, nicknamed "Till," who moved from Missouri to help with the children and housework. Much loved and respected, Till remained with the family for many years. She would sometimes take George and Wendy to church (Dunkard Brethren Church/Old German Baptist) located at Dakota & Beckwith Roads. Both children enjoyed attending the elaborate church services. Across the road from the white plank board-sided church was the Dunkard graveyard. Wendy recalls how Dunkard mourners would sing religious songs as they walked in a processional with the deceased from the church to the graveyard on the way to the burial plot that the family had dug themselves. Till's brothers and sisters lived nearby the church and George and Wendy spent a lot of time with her family—eating great meals, enjoying homemade ice cream, and having fun playing outside.

8. Ibid. George grew up in what can be called an alleyway culture. The alleyway that ran behind George's house on Ramona Avenue was an amazing thoroughfare that fostered a strong sense of community, supported unlimited creativity, exploration, and collaborative play. Many homes and backyards could easily be accessed via the fence doors and backyard gates that were left open along the hidden street and the kids used it to full advantage to ride bikes, share materials to build forts or roller-coasters, swap comic books, or just hang out and have fun and play. If you visit the site, it's easy to imagine George and his friends--John Plummer, Melvin Cellini, and George Frankenstein, to name a few--run-

ning down the alley--playing, happy and free. The "Little Store" where George and Wendy often walked for treats and groceries was a short walk from Ramoma Avenue and was/is located at the corner of El Vecino Avenue & Lucern (called *Sam's Food Mart* today). Gene's Market, another frequent haunt, where George and Wendy would often buy comics, was located at the corner of High Street & E. Morris (called *PJs Market* today). The popular Scenic Drive-In was located on Scenic Drive near Coffee Road. Growing up on Ramona Avenue was a perfect slice of Americana--the kind of place milkmen delivered to the door and fresh vegetables were sold out the back of a truck by a neighborhood produce deliveryman (Mr. F.Y. Yuen).

9. *George Lucas: The Early Years*, prod. Patti McCarthy, dir. Andy Crete (PMC Productions, 2013). https://www.youtube.com/watch?v=c4Edj29BObs
10. John Plummer interview, for *Historic Graffiti Cruise Route*, Modesto, 14 September 2012. See also, *George Lucas: The Early Years*, prod. Patti McCarthy, dir. Andy Crete (PMC Productions, 2013). https://www.youtube.com/watch?v=c4Edj29BObs
11. *Local Lucas History: Where Were You in '62?*, narr. Wendy Lucas, prod.Patti McCarthy, dir. Erik Howell (PMC Productions, 2013). http://www.youtube.com/watch?v=P18CDWvttZA . Following in his older sisters' footsteps, George began attending the "Old" John Muir School on E. Morris near the Modesto City Cemetery. His friend John Plummer lived in a white house down the alley (between Ramona and El Cajon Avenue) and across the street from the graveyard (E. Morris). As Modesto grew, so did the need for new schools. In 1951, when George was in second grade, the "New" John Muir School opened on Lucern Avenue. On October 6, 2001, George and Wendy both attended the 50th Anniversary of the "New" John Muir School. At the event they visited with three of their "New" John Muir teachers—Mrs. Annette Bright Rasmussen (George's 6th grade teacher), Mrs. Dorothy Elliott (George's 2nd grade teacher), and Mrs. Hazel Ackors, (George's 1st grade teacher).
12. Ibid.
13. Ibid.
14. Ibid.
15. Ibid. The Modesto City-County Airport is located on Mitchell Road on the outskirts of Modest. Even today, the airport resembles the airport seen in George's film, *American Graffiti*.
16. Ibid. George's grandfather not only gave him a 35mm still camera, but a 8mm movie camera as well. "Our grandfather [Paul Bomberger] gave

George an old movie camera in high school and George experimented with it," Wendy Lucas remembers, "He made a short film about a car going around a race track to a popular Jazz tune, Dave Brubeck's *Take Five*. At this point, his meticulous attention to detail when making a film emerged. He tried to coordinate the sound track with the car going around a track. It had to be perfect; he took the phone off the hook for hours and played the song over and over again to get the timing perfect. It was his first try at film editing, and he thoroughly enjoyed it." See also *Dave Brubeck: In His Own Sweet Way*, exec. prod. Clint Eastwood, dir. Bruce Ricker, co-prod. Patti McCarthy (University of the Pacific/Derry Music, 2012).Many Downey High School students, including George, frequented Harley's Records on J Street. At Harley's, teenagers could pick up the latest 45 and 78 rpm records of their favorite artists. "This is where George and I bought most of the "45s" that were later featured in the *American Graffiti* soundtrack," Wendy Lucas recalls (interview, 2012).

17. Ibid. George's experience of being "stuck on the Ranch" during this time of his life clearly parallels that of his young protagonist, Luke Skywalker, who, at the beginning of *Star Wars: A New Hope*, is frustrated at being stuck on the farm. A bit of trivia: Luke was named after his creator, George Lucas. George was frequently called "Luke," a nickname given him by friends based on the shortening of his last name—Lucas.

18. Ibid.

19. Ibid. Any Modesto local could tell you at that time that "dragging," or cruising (the "loop") took place on a two-way turn around at Burge's Drive-In at 10th and O streets, and then around the block between F & G Streets. Burge's Drive-In was a popular stop on the "loop" and a favorite of George and his family. It featured roller-skating car hops and was the true inspiration for Mel's Diner in *American Graffiti*. The roller-skating car hop tradition currently lives on in Modesto at the A & W Root Beer Drive-In at 14th & G Streets where you can still see car hops balancing frosty mugs of root beer, hamburgers, and a side of fries on a tray. You can also visit the Modesto Historic Graffiti Cruise Route. The Modesto Historic Cruise Route was dedicated by the City of Modesto on June 8, 2012. Twenty-five permanent kiosks were strategically placed around the original cruise route that, in prose and photographs, recount the history of Modesto and tell the story of the people who originally participated in the cruise, inspired *American Graffiti*, and made Modesto what it is today (http://www.modestocruiseroute.com/about/). There are also kiosks specifically dedicated to Lucas' life and work (#2, #29, #20, #22). Many of

the kiosks are linked (on-site or via internet, i.e., *youtube.com*) to short films and/or interviews that tell these stories in greater depth and detail (www.modestocruiseroute.com; https://www.youtube.com/watch?v=c4Edj29Bobs; https://www.youtube.com/watch?v=Dn5jPjgpP7g; https://www.youtube.com/watch?v=P18CDWvttZA). See also https://www.modestogov.com/newsroom/releases/prdetai; http://www.modestoview.com/george-lucas-grand-marshall-2013-cruise-parade/; http://www.modestogov.com/newsroom/releases/prdetail.asp?id=1962; http://www.nytimes.com/2013/06/12/us/george-lucas-visits-modesto-for-american-graffiti-parade.html?pagewanted=print; http://www.modbee.com/2013/06/07/2752888/celebrated-return-to-modesto-for.html; http://www.modbee.com/2013/06/05/2749165/come-to-parade-welcome-lucas.html; http://www.mercedsunstar.com/2013/06/07/3059622/celebrated-return-to-modesto-for.html; http://www.news10.net/video/default.aspx?bctid=2454267700001&odyssey=mod%7Cnewswell%7Ctext%7CFRONTPAGE%7Cfeatured. At the time of the Historic Graffiti Cruise Route dedication on June 8, 2012, plans were announced for a "Walk of Fame" to celebrate *American Graffiti* and those people ("Legends of the Cruise") who inspired or appeared in the film. The following year, on June 6, 2013, George Lucas was the first to be inducted into the "Walk of Fame" and a replica of the sidewalk marker was presented to him during his appearance as Grand Marshall at the Kiwanis Graffiti Parade & *American Graffiti* 35th Anniversary celebration in Modesto. On June 4, 2014, permanent sidewalk markers were installed and the "Walk of Fame" was unveiled (on 10th Street in front of the Brenden Theatres). Current "Legends of the Cruise/Walk of Fame" inductees include George Lucas, Leroy Applequist, Bart Bartoni, Chuck Billington, Candy Clark, Pete Hischier, Bo Hopkins, Paul LeMat, Terry McGrath, and Gene Winfield (http://www.modbee.com/2014/05/29/3352006/modesto-historic-cruise-route.html)

20. John Plummer interview, for *Historic Graffiti Cruise Route*, Modesto, 14 September 2012.
21. Ibid., 220. For more on Lucas's early years, see John Baxter, *Mythmaker: The Life and Work of George Lucas* (New York: Avon Books, 1999); Howard Maxford. *George Lucas Companion: The Complete Guide to Hollywood's Most Influential Film-maker* (London: B. T. Batsford LTD, 1999); Sally Kline, ed., *George Lucas: Interviews* (Jackson: University Press of Mississippi, 1999); Marcus Hearn. *The Cinema of George Lucas* (New York: Harry N. Abrams, Inc., Publishers, 2005). See also short biographical films at: www.modestocruiseroute.com (*George Lucas Bio & History:*

Early Years, George Lucas Bio & History: Later Years, Lucas Locations in Modesto) or visit the *Historic Modesto Graffiti Cruise Route* kiosks #2, #19, #20, #22 along the 10th & 11th Street loop in Modesto, CA.
22. Dana White. *George Lucas* (Minneapolis: Lerner Publications Company, 2000), 23.
23. *Dave Brubeck: In His Own Sweet Way*, exec. prod. Clint Eastwood, dir. Bruce Ricker, co-prod. Patti McCarthy (University of the Pacific/Derry Music, 2012).
24. Marcus Hearn. *The Cinema of George Lucas.* New York: Harry N. Abrams, Inc., Publishers, 2005, Foreward, Ron Howard. See also, *George Lucas:Visionary Filmmaker*, prod. Patti McCarthy, dir. Andy Crete (PMC Productions, 2013). https://www.youtube.com/watch?v=c4Edj29BObs
25. Dale Pollock, *Skywalking*, 59.
26. Dana White, *George Lucas*, 30.
27. Dale Pollock, *Skywalking*, 67.
28. Ibid., 67.
29. Ibid., 68.
30. John Baxter, *Mythmaker: The Life and Work of George Lucas* (New York: Avon Books, 1999), 75.
31. *George Lucas: The Early Years*, prod. Patti McCarthy, dir. Andy Crete (PMC Productions, 2013). https://www.youtube.com/watch?v=c4Edj29BObs
32. Dale Pollock, *Skywalking*, 68.
33. Ibid., 69.
34. Ibid., 70.
35. Ibid., 70.
36. Ibid., 80.
37. Dale Pollock, *Skywalking*, 72.
38. Ibid., 73. Also see John Baxter, *Mythmaker*, 81.
39. Dale Pollock, *Skywalking*, 74.
40. Peter Biskind "The Young Lions: Raging Days, Boogie Nights," *Vanity Fair* (April 1998): 220.
41. Ibid., 220.
42. John Baxter, *Mythmaker*, 95.
43. John Baxter, *Mythmaker*, 109.
44. Thomas Schatz. "The Whole Equation of Pictures," *The Genius of the System: Hollywood Filmmaking in the Studio Era* (New York: Pantheon, 1988), 656.

45. David Cook, *A Lost Illusions: American Cinema in the Shadow of Watergate and Vietnam*, 1970-1979 (Berkeley: California University Press, 2000), 157.
46. Ibid., 157. Timothy Corrigan in his essay, "Auteurs and the New Hollywood," in the book, *The New American Cinema*, Jon Lewis, ed., (Durham, North Carolina: Duke University Press, 1998), 63, points out that John Caughie noted that how the author is constructed by and for commerce has been overlooked since Brecht's 1931 *Threepenny Opera* trial in which Brecht brilliantly exposes the contradiction in cinema between the commercial need to maintain the ideology of the creative artist and the simultaneous need to redefine ownership in terms of capital, rather than creative investment.

Chapter 3

The "High Concept" Blockbuster

> There's no message or long speech, but you know that, when the story ends, America underwent a drastic change. The early sixties were the end of an era. It hit us all very hard.
>
> George Lucas, *Interviews*

> Graffiti is an Italian word meaning a drawing or inscription on walls, glib, funny, immediate. Everybody has a different way of checking out a culture. Some look at clothing, others at cars. My way is to examine rock radio, which is an American graffiti.
>
> George Lucas, cited in John Baxter, *Mythmaker*, 107

The general malaise, incoherence and confusion that were part and parcel of the 1960s and early 1970s culture, was reflected in theatre-going practices as well. In 1971, the studios lost millions and ticket sales were at an all time low.[1] The old studios continued to connect themselves to corporations who could help with growing debts and the rising costs of production (the cost of production had risen to an average of $2.2 million). The newly incorporated studios began to watch the bottom line and put their money on "sure bets" that catered to the "post-television" youth market, age twelve through twenty-six years. Coppola's film, *The Godfather* set the tone of the Vietnam/Watergate 1970s whereby corruption and destruction of the American Dream seemed to run rampant as a theme. As a culture, we had certainly lost something—something irreplaceable (innocence, trust, etc.) amid the War, assassinations, general political deceptions, and social upheavals. In stark contrast to Coppola's darker vision that demythologized the American dream and family, Lucas' take on American life in *American Graffiti* was completely different. Lucas returned to the warm glow of a pre-Kennedy past ("Where were you in '62?") to a place he loved and knew very well —Modesto, CA. Universal wasn't sold on the idea, but agreed to finance the film if Francis Ford Coppola would produce it having just swept the Oscar nominations in 1973 with the highest grossing film of all time, *The Godfather*. The studios, as well as the agents who had started "packaging" talent, were beginning to appreciate the value of the auteur's brand name, and decided to further capitalize on the tag—"From the man who brought you *The Godfather*...". Coppola fully supported the project.

> When he conceived *American Graffiti*...I told him that the thing was to write, and write about what he knew about...and be a writer. He really didn't think of himself as a writer really. He realized on that production that he was a writer. [2]
>
> "It all happened to me, but I glamorized it," George said. "I spent four years cruising the main streets of my hometown in Modesto and did it all. I drove the cars, chased the girls...I think a lot people did, which is the whole idea behind the title--a very American experience." [3]

American Graffiti opened on August 1, 1973 and rapidly became one of the most successful movies of its time, earning more than $100 million dollars. It was filmed in 28 days at a cost of $750,000. The production schedule that demanded Lucas prep filming during the day and shoot all night, drained Lucas of every bit of his energy, but it was the only way he could get the film in on time and on budget and maintain control of the production. Amid the many production difficulties and seemingly superhuman challenges faced by cast and crew, *American Graffiti* eventually won the Golden Globe Award for Best Motion Picture--Comedy or Musical in 1974. It was nominated for the Academy Award® for Best Picture, Best Director, Best Film Editing, Best Supporting Actress, and Best Original Screenplay. Building on experiences from his youth, George made a film that depicted an experience that had been common to teenagers across America. He raced cars, listened to rock 'n roll on the radio, chased girls, and grew up with childhood pals whose friendships he maintained for a lifetime.

American Graffiti has been described as a return to an idealized time-- as a popular look at the last days of America's innocence. George Lucas has said, "three eras were coming to an end...it's about the end of a political era, a sociological era, and the end of rock 'n roll...the people and the country had to change. You go from a warm, secure life into the late '60s which forced social and anti-war involvement and a different kind of rock 'n roll." [4] George tuned into the country's need to believe in something. People at the time of the film's release were tired of what they were seeing on the screen--a world without clearly delineated values, morals, or images of right and wrong. During this time, America lost something irreplaceable amid the war in Vietnam, the assassinations of Martin Luther King, Jr., and the Kennedy brothers, the civil rights movement, and the deceptions of Watergate. In stark contrast to other films of the time, *American Graffiti* recaptured the small town values and way of life George had experienced while growing up in Modesto. People wanted to believe again in the good and innocence in themselves—Lucas gave it to them on a silver screen platter.

Successful Hollywood cinematographer, Haskell Wexler, who George had met on the racetrack before going to USC and had hired to shoot THX 1138, worked not only as a visual consultant on the film, but flew up each night from Los Angeles to work on the film after shooting commercials during the day, stylistically giving the film the neon look of a classic 1950s jukebox. Not only was the film nostalgic to see, but also to hear. A trailblazer, George called *American Graffiti* a "musical," but the film wasn't a typical musical. "Instead of people," George said, "the dancing is created by cars performing a fifties ritual called cruising." [5] The film's soundtrack, the foundation on which the rest of the story is built, was inspired by George's time spent cruising the popular loop between 10th Street and 11th Street in Modesto. The film's classic rock 'n roll soundtrack covers at least a decade's worth of popular tunes, from the '50s sound of Buddy Holly to the '60s sound of the Beach Boys, and has become one of the most popular soundtracks of all time. George gambled ten percent (10%) of his film budget on acquiring the music rights, and it paid off--the audience loved it.

American Graffiti is the story, during a pivotal night in 1962, of four teenage boys--Curt, Steve, John, and Terry--aged 17 to 20 who cruise through the streets of town, picking up girls and racing cars. Steve and Curt are about to leave their small hometown for college. Both have doubts. The common theme of these experiences and the soundtrack's rock 'n roll music allowed viewers who hadn't grown up in Modesto to identify with the film. George said, "I was telling the story of a group of kids during their last days in high school, a world that most didn't realize would soon change dramatically as the realities of the larger world and adulthood intruded." [6] Some of the characters in the film, George admits, are partly portrayals of himself, as well as a combination of different people he knew. Clearly, *American Graffiti* struck a chord with the American public. The film's popularity, many suggested, was due to its nostalgic ability—via music and image, to recreate a "happier," less tumultuous past.

American Graffiti was the "quintessential fifties nostalgia movie—a comprehensive recreation of the world of sock hops, drag races, cherry cokes and Eisenhower complacency."[7] It was a culmination of a process that had started with films in the 1940s that exploited cross-selling of film and film music ("buy the music, see the film")—a trend and successful money-making formula that would set the tone for films produced later in the decade (*Saturday Night Fever, Grease*, etc.). Lucas' integration of "classic" rock n' roll music into the *American Graffiti* soundtrack brilliantly played on the emotional memories of the film-going public, deepening it's nostalgic tone.

Interestingly enough, Fredric Jameson, a contemporary cultural analyst, singled *American Graffiti* out as a prime example of the "nostalgia" film.[8] Jameson divided the nostalgia film into four categories: "1) films that are about the past and set in the past (*Chinatown, American Graffiti*), 2) films that reinvent the past (*Star Wars, Raiders of the Lost Ark*), 3) films that are set in the present but invoke the past (*Body Heat*), 4) Films such as *Chinatown* and *The Conformist* which take place in "some eternal Thirties; beyond historical time."[9] In reference to Jamesons' remark, Freidberg comments, "The 'nostalgia film' is described in stylistic terms here—these examples represent cases where a film's narrative and its art direction confuse its sense of temporality."[10] The classic nostalgia film, writes Jameson, "while evading its present altogether, registered its historicist deficiency by losing itself in mesmerized fascination in lavish images of specific generational pasts"[11]—the privileged generational moments being the 1930s and 1950s. Postmodern pastiche is symptomatic, contends Jameson, of a general loss of historicity, and our incapacity to achieve aesthetic "representations of our own current experience."[12] In other words, we retreat to the past when we are unable to define our historic present, but in doing so we replace true history (and our presents and possible futures) with our idealized images of it. He suggests that, "the formal apparatus of nostalgia films has trained us to consume the past in the form of glossy images."[13]

Friedberg takes this a step further and posits that cinema spectatorship is itself based on a nostalgic desire that is deferred in endless secondariness—the nostalgia for nostalgia—in a seemingly endless return to specific, but secondary, representations.[14] It could be, she suggests, the reason for the endless supply of sequels we experience today—the sequels express a nostalgia for the earlier, original film (as if the commodity-experience were a guarantee for profit). Perhaps we long for a past that, with the "end" of history, no longer exists.

Friedberg further picks up on Jameson's definition of the nostalgia film, stating, "Nostalgia (from Greek, *nostos* = a return; *algos* = painful) means a painful return, a longing for something far away or long ago, separated by distance and time...An etymological history of the word nostalgia demonstrates that its first usage in the late seventeenth century was to describe the longing for a space, a technical term for "homesickness." By the late nineteenth century, as the discourses of history produced a concomitant idealization of the past, nostalgia also came to mean a longing for a time past. Late nineteenth-century revival styles and museology encouraged a return to the past, to compensate for the threat of the 'modern' and the shock of the new. Nostalgia can hide the discontinuities between the present and the past; it falsifies, returning the past to a safe, familiar place.[15]

> Nostalgia comes from the Greek. It literally means the pain from an old wound. It's a twinge from the heart far more powerful than memory alone...it's a time machine. It goes backwards and forwards and takes us to a place where we ache to go again...It lets us travel the way a child travels, around and around and back home again to a place where we know we are loved. [16]

The nostalgic desire to return to an idealized past can also take a utopian turn. The desire to return to the 1960s might help recall a radical moment of awakening, growth, political activity, and engagement to those who were involved, and, as such, constitutes a return to a past youth and lost vitality. Through the gauze of Maya's veil the past becomes idealized.

Lucas explains about the nostalgia label. "I didn't have the West or gangsters, or anything, so I used what I grew up with. I'm doing what filmmakers have always done...it's just that now they've made it a classification, so any time you do a film that's five years in the past, it's a nostalgia film."[17]

Taking a different approach to the film, Marc Le Seur remarked that *American Graffiti's* use of nostalgia reflects Lucas' familiarity with popular culture, especially cruising and rock and roll: " This verism pertains to surface details only, elements such as dress, cars, settings, etc., for what is being enacted on the screen is often...wish fulfillment expanded to the magnitude of myth. Lucas makes a distinction between the realism of *Graffiti's* style and the unrealistic nature of many of the character's actions...The period detail which is so characteristic of nostalgic art serves to further confuse the viewer's clouded memory of his clumsy teenage years...It never really happened."[18]

Critics have observed that *American Graffiti* in its use of nostalgia contains some similarities to *High School Confidential, Rock Around the Clock,* and *Rebel Without a Cause* (the climactic drag race). Whether the quotes were intentional or not, *Graffiti* does contain elements of the nostalgic style. It is very clear that more than any other, however, *American Graffiti,* set the standard for the retro-trend that continues today, and, in its evocation of nostalgia, stokes the desire of the masses to return to a "happy, nostalgic" past. People just couldn't get enough of the film, and it ignited a world-wide resurgence of retro '50s and '60s culture, reintroducing the drive-in, cruising, and poodle skirts to a world ready for small town authenticity. More than a film, *American Graffiti,* was a cultural phenomenon. The hit television series "Happy Days," featuring such memorable characters as "The Fonz," and "Richie Cunningham," spun off from *American Graffiti,* as did "Laverne & Shirley," and the movie, *Grease.*

At a negative cost of $750,000 and with a return of over $100 million after opening on August 1, 1973, *American Graffiti* still can boast being one of the highest profit making movies of all time. In his book *Mythmaker,* John Baxter explains that, "Only Ned Tanen at Universal conceded that it [*American Graffiti*] might have some remote possibility of success [since almost everyone in town conceded that the youth market was finished]." [19] When Lew Wasserman, the head of Universal, launched a youth division to make low-budget films by new young directors in 1969, he put Tanen in charge. His edict was clear. No film could cost more than $1 million, and ideally only $750,000. Everyone involved would receive the minimum union rate, or "scale." They would be given no studio space, no facilities; they could shoot on location, and if they had problems, solve them there. On the other hand, they would receive a generous share of the profits, and, in theory, the final cut, though the small print gave Universal the right to make almost any changes it cared to in the interest of better sales.

Yet, after the film's first preview screening on January 28, 1973 in San Francisco, Universal was ready to pull it, completely ignoring the overwhelming response from the cheering audience. For Lucas, it brought back bad memories and paralleled the disaster of *THX 1138* all over again. According to sources, if not for Coppola's angry demand to buy the movie from Universal on the spot, the picture would have been immediately shelved or directly sent to television. It is reputed that Coppola shouted at Ned Tanen, the studio executive at the screening who was overseeing the project, saying, "You'll see if you can release it? You should get down on your knees and thank George for saving your job. This kid has killed himself to make this movie for you. And he brought it in on time and on budget. The least you can do is thank him for that! If you hate it that much, let it go. We'll sell it some place else and get you all your money back!," Coppola said, taking out a checkbook to better make his point. Lucas was angry with Universal's reaction, but reputedly pleased with Coppola's performance.[20]

American Graffiti was the only picture at the time aimed at a young audience, the studios having changed their position on the youth market, and, as such, the film stuck out amid a long list of green-lighted crime and violence films starring established brand name stars and directors (these included *The Exorcist, The Day of the Jackal, Enter the Dragon, High Plains Drifter, Serpico, The Sting,* and the big money maker, *The Poseidon Adventure*). But because Coppola argued so strongly for it (and had an

The "High Concept" Blockbuster   81

Oscar for writing *Patton* and Oscar nominations for direction to his credit for *The Godfather* the year before), Universal changed their position and distributed on a platform—but not before they took the film away from Lucas and re-edited some scenes. (Even though the studio executives did not think it was a hit, they still bowed to Coppola's auteur brand name). It has been said that Lucas was absolutely livid. This was the second time a studio had tampered with his project, furthering his growing distaste for, and suspicion of, Hollywood and Hollywood types in general.

Of course, the picture, a classic sleeper, flying under the new Lucasfilm, Ltd. banner, was an overnight success and continued to make money even up until the Academy Awards where it was nominated for Best Picture, Best Director, Best Screenplay, Best Supporting Actress, and Best Editing; having previously won the Golden Globe and National Critics Award. The film broke all house records and earned over $100 million in rentals against $750,000 in direct costs, plus $500,000 for prints, ads and advertising, an astounding 4,300 percent return on investment.[21] It is interesting to note here that while some references, report that Lucas' take of the box office was roughly $4 million after taxes, Michael Pye and Lynda Myles in their book, *The Movie Brats*, publish a much more conservative number of $300,000—and some of that was used for seed money for *Star Wars*.[22] All in all, Lucas walked away with enough profit from *American Graffiti* to seed Industrial Light and Magic (ILM) and Skywalker Sound.

At twenty-nine, the success further ensured Lucas of a "brand name." He did not need the selling power of Coppola's name any more. He now had his own. Now, more than ever, with the star system in disarray and the branding of directors and producers (touted as the new "stars") by agents and corporations, many people were just as inclined to go to a "George Lucas" or "Coppola" movie as see a "Jimmy Stewart" picture.

Coppola soon began work on *Godfather II*, and according to sources, tried to talk Lucas into directing *Apocalypse Now*, a screenplay he (Lucas) had written while at American Zoetrope. Lucas worked toward getting the screenplay into shape for production, but while Lucas was rewriting the screenplay with Milius, the climate in Vietnam changed radically. Previously cooperative, the South Vietnamese army no longer welcomed cameras into a country to witness the rout and the steady retreat of the army that would later culminate in the disaster of refugees scrambling onto the roof of the American Embassy in April of 1975. Due to this state of affairs, Lucas gave up any thoughts of making *Apocalypse Now*. Walter Murch has suggested that Lucas took some of the material from *Apocalypse Now* and transformed it into what would later become *Star Wars*, a kind of Vietnam in space. Interestingly enough, Lucas agreed with Murch's assessment saying, "I was interested in the human side of the war and the fact that there was a great nation with all this technology which was losing a war to basically tribesmen."[23] And so, Lucas, busied himself with a science fiction film first called *The Story of Mace Windu*, then *The Star Wars: From The Adventures of Luke Starkiller*, and better known today as *Star Wars: Episode IV: A New Hope*.

THE HIGH CONCEPT BLOCKBUSTER

> Director Steven Spielberg took a routing fish-bites-man story and transformed it into a show business phenomena [sic]. *Jaws*, a merciless attack on the audience's nerves, quickly established its creator as the reigning boy genius of American cinema and went on to pile up the largest box office take in the history of the movies.
> Frank Rich, "The Aliens Are Coming," Nov. 7, 1977, 102

> Whatever else [*The Godfather*, *Jaws* and *The Exorcist*] proved about the dream state of the national psyche, they proved without a shadow of a doubt, that a single picture could carry the entire industry for a year, and could carry the individual company that produced and distributed it, or the exhibitor who played it, for several years.
> Harlan Jacobson, *Film Comment*, 1980

While Lucas was writing *Star Wars* and Coppola was creating another installment in his *Godfather* trilogy, Hollywood was still undergoing considerable changes in its business practices as it tried to adapt itself to a new marketplace. The shakeout the film industry experienced in 1969-1971 forced the majors to see that a regular flow of product through the pipeline was no longer able to turn a profit because there was not a "normal," regular, or predictable audience for their films. *Easy Rider* in 1969 had returned $19.2 million in domestic rentals while lavish and expensively produced films like *Paint Your Wagon* and the even bigger budgeted *Hello, Dolly!* lost $14 million together.

In 1970-1972, however, a few big budget movies with a traditional appeal, like *Love Story* and *The Godfather* earned tremendous profits. Based on these film successes and failures, Hollywood (adrift without a reliable guidepost for production practices) used them as a map for future production. In doing so, Hollywood experienced a cataclysmic market shift.

In the past movie making environment, it was expected that only a few films each year would make big money, while the rest would show losses or break even at best. This was based on the idea that in a volatile market only the movies with big budgets had the best chance of succeeding, but there was no guarantee of which one of the big budgeted features would be a hit. Without any real way to predict a sure-fire "hit," the studios concerned themselves with aggressive marketing and promotion to help create better product awareness (read: "buzz") and sell their films as "special attractions." If movie-going had become less a routine and more a matter of choice then the studios believed they must pull out all the stops and sell the film as a "blockbuster"—a major event and thrilling, unique experience that was sold on a global scale. Then Columbia Pictures president David Begelman explained in 1974, "We feel we must put out special event films because no one goes anymore as a routine exercise."[24]

It is interesting to note at this time, as David Cook does in his book, *Lost Illusions*, that the 1970s blockbuster in general represented a shift back to a performative spectacle that had characterized the cinema's early, more "primitive" period—now of course enhanced by state-of-the-art, pre-digital special effects which by the end of the decade included high-quality Dolby stereophonic sound.[25] This earlier presentational mode of cinema, or a *cinema of attractions*—which capitalized on sensory stimulation (spectacle and shock), dominated the early years of cinema, after which narrative eventually took over as the major form of film expression. Various elements of this "cinema of attractions" remained as components of certain narrative genres states Cook, like the musical and the horror film where direct sensory stimulation (like spectacle, shock, and awe) remained a key element of viewer pleasure. Cook cites a reversion of the studio system to a pre-World War I industrial configuration in the 1970s as being in large part responsible for this backward filmic trend.[26] Stephen Farber speaking to the new wave of big-budget horror and disaster films being churned out by Hollywood in the 1970s wrote that: "Movies were a form of circus spectacle long before they began to tell stories—and long before they were considered an art . . . that is the backward direction they seem to be taking in the seventies."[27]

After the Paramount Decree, a bust-boom cycle could be traced to divorcement and the end to block-booking inasmuch as a small number of blockbusters carried the whole filmmaking economy on their backs. This business strategy resulted in the "hit-or-miss" mentality of the 1960s and early 1970s. (The downside of this was that a blockbuster flop could sink a studio just as easily.) But something changed in the early 1970s, something called "marketing." Previously, if a film did well early at the box office, the distributor's sales force (studio) would back it and create exhibitor demand; if it did not sell, both distributors and exhibitors effectively shelved the product. The past philosophy was simple: Why bother marketing a bad film? Present marketing philosophy changed all that. Perhaps if you could "dress it up," and market it well you might be able to pass the bad film off as something else, something fine, something that would not resemble a bad film anymore—maybe the audience would buy it?

In 1971, only fourteen of 185 major films—or a whopping 8 percent—generated 52 percent of the income. Out of the rest, fifty-four or 29 percent earned less than $250,000, and only seventy-one (38 percent) could expect to break even by earning $1,000,000 or more in the domestic market. The "blockbuster syndrome" evolved using this type of data which suggested that seven out of ten pictures would lose money, two out of ten would break even, and one would be successful. This blockbuster syndrome way of thinking caused a trend toward spending more and more on advertising and marketing to increase a film's success, which in turn, resulted in spending more and more production and development dollars on a smaller number of films made.

A studio has only so much money budgeted to make a certain number of films each year. The extra money spent to market and distribute a big film decreased the amount of money that could be spent on the development, production, marketing, and distribution of other films—reducing the total of films produced each year dramatically. Ironically, during the decade that the "movie brats" took over Hollywood, the industry actually produced fewer pictures than any decade before and witnessed a shift in filmmaking that forced the cost of film promotion to exceed the cost of production—usually twice the negative cost (or sometimes even more).

It is also ironic to note, as has been mentioned before, that this pervasive blockbuster syndrome type of thinking increased the power of the majors, because only they had the means and organization to distribute films at home and abroad and the resources to finance production in the context of rapidly escalating costs. This marked the end of the creative freedom previously available to the independent and freewheeling 1960s author/auteur. Economics had put an end to that way of thinking and solidified the use of American "auteur" as just another way to market a Hollywood film. [28]

This heavy use of marketing, something Lucas would adopt and refine, is tied strongly to what Barry Diller (or as others believe Michael Eisner) coined "high concept." According to some, Barry Diller, the king of programming at ABC in the 1970s, needed product that could be easily summarized and sold to an audience in a thirty second TV spot—and as such, only began to approve those shows that could be distilled to a single sentence (this single sentence became what is known in the industry as the "pitch" or "log line").[29] Not only did this approach of distilling a concept for a TV show into a sentence take over in television, but also caught on at the film studios and became "the pitch" in filmmaking and the ensuing "log line" of any self-respecting screenplay. Studio executives or presidents such as Peter Guber at Columbia Pictures, embraced the use of "high concept" and the subsequent "pitch" as a way of distilling narrative into a very straightforward, easily communicated, and easily comprehended sentence or form. Eisner's take was similar while working as a creative executive at Paramount and he used the term to describe a unique idea whose originality could be conveyed briefly ("A woman reminisces about her narrow

escape on the Titanic and the lover she lost on the ship.").[30]

The larger structural changes in the industry, like conglomeration, the development and use of new technologies, and the rise of marketing and merchandising that goes along with conglomeration, operate in such a way as to privilege movies that can be distilled, summarized and sold in a single sentence. If you could not distill the concept of a film into one line, then the film was not considered saleable by a producer or studio. Writers were paid for their pitch as well as the produced screenplay. It also cut down on the amount of time one needed to make a decision about whether or not to make the movie (the producer sometimes didn't even read the screenplay). Eventually, the pitching of films became distilled even further into using mere titles of films, such as "Big Foot meets E. T." (*Harry and the Hendersons*) which are currently used today—a further and further recycling and distilling of old, tried (read: tired) and true concepts. In turn, studios bought a film based on a high concept story pitch and, through smart marketing tactics, then pitched it in visual and narrative form to the public.

As such, the one sentence high concept pitch became nothing more than the ad line that would show up in the marketing campaign and on the one-sheet movie poster. If you want to pitch a story well, then it must be high concept. Steven Spielberg has been known to say that if a person can tell him a movie idea in twenty-five words or less, then he knows it's going to make a pretty good movie—fully endorsing the idea of high concept. In one sentence: High concept is a form of narrative that is highly marketable.[31]

Of course there are just as many critics of high concept as there are supporters. Many film critics, analysts, and journalists fall into the former camp. Frequently these critics of the phrase use the term against the contemporary film industry to suggest a total bankruptcy of creativity in Hollywood. Richard Schickel has pointed out that high concept, or at least the "high" in the phrase, really means a concept so low that it can be summarized and sold on the basis of a single sentence.[32]

While many creative executives, producers, and writers at the studios stress the originality of a high concept idea, media critics reply that high concept represents the ultimate zero point of creativity. Rather than coming up with new ideas, it is frequently pointed out that the industry relies too much on the replication, duplication, and combination of previously successful narratives—focusing on commerce rather than art, placing an emphasis on marketable stories rather than "original" stories. This tension between art and commerce in film is an old theme and will always be there. The very structure of the film industry is based on this dichotomy and constant push me pull you. It is apparent that the high concept film with its heavy reliance on marketing and box office potential seems to be more grounded in the economic versus the aesthetic. However, high concept—by its very nature—is highly reliant on recycling and recalling classical Hollywood style, narrative, genre and aesthetics. It calls upon the images and stories of Hollywood's golden (and not so golden) age and "plays" with them in a very postmodern way. Most of those who are pitching the high concept stories are film school graduates who, because they have studied them, are able to readily call to mind visual and narrative film and television references and use them sparingly. *The Searchers in Space* is certainly not an overly original, creative, concept, but its final product *Star Wars* arguably is.

Justin Wyatt points out that star power can also contribute to broader marketability of a film when the star persona links favorably with the film's concept. [33] For instance, Clint Eastwood in a crime thriller—as in the *Dirty Harry* series—implies a high concept. So does Arnold Schwarzenegger in a science fiction action picture like *The Terminator* franchise. Clint Eastwood in *White Hunter, Black Heart* as a crazy film director, though, does not. Oddly enough, stars that take a chance playing against type do help the film lend itself to high concept. Will Tusher brings up the example of a star playing against type as high concept in an announcement in *Variety* that stated that Columbia Pictures was considering starring Arnold Schwarzeneggar as the tooth fairy in a picture called *Sweet Tooth*.[34] While that picture never came to fruition, Arnold did play against type with Danny Devito in *Twins* as a gentle brother looking for his lost twin, a high concept film that did work.

High concept can be thought of as a product that can be differentiated by an integration of the film with its marketing, but also with an emphasis on style of production. As a matter of style, high concept films always take advantage of an abstraction of a key image from the film (e.g., image of the shark in *Jaws*) that can help sell the picture, keep it visible, and make it a part of the public consciousness. If you can compress the story into a sentence, why not compress it further into a saleable image? This image, replicated over and over through merchandizing, product tie-ins, one-sheets, and TV ads, etc., becomes probably the most commercial element of the high concept film—not to mention use of trailer saturation, sound tracks, and wide releases. Wyatt introduces what he calls the "look, the hook, and the book" as traits of high concept. "The look of

The "High Concept" Blockbuster 89

the images, the marketing hooks and the reduced narratives," explains Wyatt, "form the cornerstones of high concept." [35] Wyatt believes that all Hollywood films fall along the low-high concept scale and are easily categorized accordingly. As such, Wyatt goes on to explain, *Grease* (1978) along with *Jaws* (1975), *Star Wars* (1977) and *Saturday Night Fever* (1977), are of much greater significance to American film history than other less high concept films (but more highly critically praised and institutionally recognized films) of the period, such as *Network* (1976), *One Flew Over the Cuckoo's Nest* (1975), or *Kramer vs. Kramer* (1979). It is Wyatt's belief that by understanding the commercial "recipe" and economic determination of a film like *Grease* or *Jaws*, one can actually gain a better and true appreciation of the contemporary American film landscape that has privileged the high concept film.[36] Many films in the Lucas oeuvre clearly fall into this category.

Justin Wyatt and R. L. Rutsky further contend high concept movies rely "less on a well-developed story and characters than on a big name star, a commercial musical score, and high visual impact."[37] High concept movies, *Jaws* forward, tended toward becoming advertisements that could be easily abstracted to easily assimilable images and regenerated through multiple viewings and the ancillary sales of a multitude of tie-ins (T-shirts and the like). In just seven years, the cost of a Hollywood feature rose from $2 million in 1972 to $9 million in 1979 (when Fox's *Alien* cost $11 million to produce and $16 million to promote). By the end of the decade, marketing expenses often ran three times a films cost and, next to the cost of "stars," became the biggest cause of budgetary inflation (including the rest of the "package"—all above-the-line talent, including directors, producers and writers). Use of stars feed into the pre-sold identity of the high concept film and through advertising helped to establish an identity with the public by the time of opening. Tag lines such as "Arnold Schwarzenegger in *Terminator II*," "A new action adventure starring Harrison Ford," or "From the director of *The Godfather*" (using auteur as both brand and star) were worth their weight in gold.

Ever since the earliest moments of the star system, profits could be directly measured against the draw of the stars name. During the 1970s, though, the star system was in chaos and most films did not feature a star player, yet the studios and corporations (that owned them) were undaunted. Corporations who had made and marketed bread and cars saw no difference between those products and a film. A Chrysler car, the corporate mindset determined, was not very far from a Spielberg film and Spielberg was just as valuable as Jimmy Stewart if marketed correctly. It had worked with Coppola and some of the other auteurs, so the corporations saw no reason not to use the same sales tactics with more reliable "brand name" directors or producers. Accordingly, these film "commodities" now had a guaranteed seal of studio approval which helped to market and sell it more effectively to the audience. Thus, the most significant pre-sold property of the high concept film was, and still is, the star (in whatever form) and proved to be one of the best hedges against a bet in a volatile marketplace.

As market costs increased, however, so did the value and cost of a star or brand name. Not only did marketing help inflate the blockbuster budgets, but also the salaries of stars that were considered bankable (Table 2). This type of thinking also gave rise to the purchase of "pre-sold" properties such as best selling novels or plays whose reach to the audience could be guaranteed through publishing and recording tie-ins (record albums, books, etc.) and other ancillary merchandise. Using the promise to create a "synergy," the film built the book, which in turn built the album, which in turn helped to build and rebuild the film. Interestingly enough, dependence upon star power would later come to haunt the studios in the next decade when agents were able to grab power and raise the price of star contracts (and consequently the percentages paid to the agencies).

This shift toward synergy--book and movie tie-ins--in particular, became more and more valuable as more and more studios became linked via conglomerate ownership with publishers, pushing the cost of bestseller rights by the end of the decade to a whopping $2.5 million.[38] Merchandising in the form of apparel also helped to sell and resell and pre-sell a film. This tactic (if we can fast forward a few years) of exploiting various types of ancillary markets was used during the late 1970s and 1980s, and was especially evident when used in conjunction with films like *Saturday Night Fever, Urban Cowboy, Grease, American*

Gigolo, and *Flashdance.* This type of merchandizing not only created market awareness in its film-going audience, but also a desire for consumer products tied to

the film which further helped to impact both American culture and fashion for years to come (long after the film had played out). Book publishing was only one arm of the conglomerate octopus that profited from synergy. Music and the creation and use of music videos was another.

Music, especially when discussing the high concept film, became an area of intense marketing focus and tied into the mindset of the movie-going audience—namely the thirteen to twenty-five-year-old males who constituted the majority of film-goers.[39] Hollywood was finally able to harness and exploit the youth market they had been chasing since the 1960s with music. Lucas, as mentioned earlier, was savvy to this music-youth market link when he brilliantly exploited the use of music in *American Graffiti.*

Using popular music in the soundtracks of films was nothing new (or trading on the popularity of music artists of the day to sell a film or set a "hip" tone, as in the pairing of Simon and Garfunkel with *The Graduate,* for instance), but in the era of high concept, soundtracks, songs, and the ensuing MTV music videos developed in the early 1980s that were based on the songs and films were used more aggressively as a form of marketing, sales and a retelling (and sometimes reinvention or rewrite) of the narrative. All these factors contributed to the audience's need or desire to see the actual film for the first time or, even better, see the film over again.

Some films used the music to sustain and inform the narrative (*The Graduate*), others used it as a underlying motif or tie to a particular time period (*American Graffiti*), still others used it to set the tone (*American Gigolo*) and introduce characters, the story, and the world of the character (*Flashdance*), or use the musical numbers that appear in the narrative to help sell the film either in subsequent marketing campaigns (ads, music videos, etc.) or as a point of audience discussion and memory (word of mouth, tell your friends, go back and see the musical number again) as with *Batman, Risky Business, Ferris Bueller's Day Off*, etc.

The music video became another vehicle for promoting and pre-selling the film. It even had the unique capacity to fulfill a double function. It helped to promote the song (songs or soundtrack) for album sales while at the same time promoting the film in which the song was heard. Oddly enough though, rather than strengthening the narrative features of the film, the music video had/has the unique ability to undermine the narrative and offer a retelling or a rewrite of the actual film through an odd mixture of images (musical artist) and juxtapositions of song with actual film footage—either in proper context or outside of it. This use of images, soundtrack, and footage to re-convey and refigure the narrative helps to multiply the meanings in the narrative in order to multiply the marketing and audience base.[40] While one "cut" of a music video might appeal to young women, another cut might just as well appeal to older males. Wyatt explains, "the music video functions not just as an emblem/icon of the film, but also as a method which complicates the narrative. This process seems very much connected to the pleasure associated with repeat viewing of the high concept films, a pleasure based on the play between familiarity (of story, characters, and music in the original film) and discovery (of the story, characters, music as refigured in the promotional music video)... and encourages a re-reading of the film. [41]

In an unpredictable marketplace, another smart way to hedge a producer's bet was to drag out the tried and true—the genre, the series, the re-make, the prequel, and the sequel. If it worked once, then maybe it would work again. Genres were already established and easily marketed types of film categories in which audiences readily filled in the gestalt. Gangster films and horror films especially carried their own set of narrative expectations—the more easily distillable into a single saleable concept the better. It was good common sense that if *The Godfather* did well, then *The Godfather II* should do just as well, or even better. The first film in any sequence has a built in audience that could easily be sold on seeing the sequel. It was the closest to a "sure thing" you could get. The risk was minimal, the audience was guaranteed and the market established. Even better, you could release the first film again theatrically (or on DVD) to whet the appetite for the second and make some money on both (a tactic Lucas would later exploit with his *Star Wars* franchise, Warner Bros. *Harry Potter* franchise, or New Line Cinema's marketing of the *Lord of the Rings* trilogy).

To illustrate this point, Paramount and Disney, in particular, were able to mine this fertile genre ground. Paramount's movies for the most part have capitalized on the utopian, mainstream fantasy of the "everyman" struggling against all odds in order to realize their American dream. During the decades of high concept, Paramount adhered to specific genres that worked: the musical *(Flashdance)*, the action/adventure film *(Raiders of the Lost Ark)*, teenage comedy *(Pretty In Pink)*, and the "fish out of water" comedies *(Beverly Hills Cop)*. Paramount updated these genres by working with the viewer's understanding and knowledge of mass culture by playing off the filmgoer's recognition of various genre conventions—using them as a springboard, so to speak, or foundation on which to make the genre films hipper, cooler, trendier and gutsier. *Flashdance* is a perfect example of the contemporary, updated, hipper, high concept musical. Disney also followed suit by working within known genres.

It comes as no surprise, that Disney's approach to the market would parallel Paramount's, considering Jeffery Katzenburg, Michael Eisner and Richard Frank all worked at Paramount under the direction of Barry Diller. Disney continued to make high-end family entertainment and in order to keep up with the competition without confusing the Disney name or product, Disney set up Touchstone Pictures to develop adult-oriented fare. Paramount and Disney both keep a tight reign on budgets and projects and in doing so, were able to guarantee product consistency (a studio version of McDonald's) and audience recognition of their film products. Not only did the studios capitalize on the use of the genre (sequel, prequel, etc.), but used the audiences craving for more in the form of television spin-offs. *Happy Days* is a perfect example of this use of synergy spin-off.

JAWS: THE UR-BLOCKBUSTER

After Coppola had swept the Oscars for *Godfather II*, *Jaws* burst on the scene in 1975. A variety of factors, besides the conglomeration of Hollywood, led to this blockbuster environment, namely an increase in theater-goers, and hence, the building of multiple, cineplex facilities conveniently located in suburb shopping centers, and as previously discussed, an increase in advertising and marketing. Both the extra theatres and increase in theatre-goers helped the growth of profits as the studios learned to exploit, market and promote their products more effectively. Along these lines, Universal's *Jaws* (1975) directed by Steven Spielberg—is a turning point in the history of post-classical Hollywood. Not only does it present an interesting case study, but also demands closer scrutiny since the film and the way it was distributed, produced, and especially marketed lays the groundwork for *Star Wars* (and what would later develop into the *Star Wars* franchise) and all other films produced in the post-*Jaws* industry environment.

David Cook points out that *Jaws*, more than any other film, marked the arrival of the, "New Hollywood by recalibrating the profit potential of the blockbuster and defining its status as a marketable commodity...In terms of marketing, not only did the film's media campaign shape the direction of film marketing for a long time to come, but it was also the first "high concept" film whose conceptual premise and story was easily reducible

The "High Concept" Blockbuster 95

to a salient image, which in turn, became the basis for an aggressive advertising campaign keyed to merchandising tie-ins and ancillary markets, creating 'synergy' between film, products and related media. As a cultural phenomena, *Jaws* represented a revival and 'implosion' of the disaster cycle that had had its real-world correspondence in Vietnam and Watergate."[42] But it was also the paradigm for what Thomas Schatz calls "the high-cost, high-tech, high-speed" thriller that became the major Hollywood genre of the eighties and nineties.[43]

Jaws, like many other blockbusters, followed the prescriptive "pre-sold" mold. The film was adapted from a best-selling novel written by Peter Benchley and was shrewdly picked up in its galley stage by producers Richard D. Zanuck and David Brown for a mere $150,000. *Jaws* had been targeted for a summer release, due to the subject matter, in an era when the most important movies were released during the Christmas holidays. The producers, Zanuck and Sheinberg at Universal, had mounted an unprecedented marketing campaign with a budget of $2.5 million that was built around a massive network TV-ad extravaganza and the adapted film's best-selling novel (most likely motivated by the film's final budget overage of 150 percent, or almost $9 million, instead of the original $3.5 million production budget). By the time the film hit the theatres, the book was a runaway bestseller with over 7.6 million copies in print.[44]

Who can forget, even now, over thirty five years later, the *Jaws* print ad featuring the enormous shark ready to attack the hapless woman swimming alone. Accompanying the ad is the copy, "The terrifying motion picture from the terrifying No. 1 Bestseller . . . ". To keep costs down, it was decided that the film be shot on location at Martha's Vineyard on a budget of $3.5 million (which by the end of the production, due to logistic problems and special effects delays with the shark, came to roughly $13.5 million). This replication in both image and copy gradually made the ad instantly identifiable and recognizable to the masses. In this way, *Jaws* was easily reduced to a single image, and with it the idea of high concept was solidified. Along with better marketing, Universal also took advantage of the growing strength and importance of the talent agencies by using ICM to "package" the talent for the film—including Steven Spielberg (a new twenty-six-year-old director with a minimum of credits to his name including a TV movie, *Duel* in 1971 and a feature, *The Sugarland Express* in 1974) who was among the new generation of film school directors.[45]

On June 20, 1975, in another unprecedented move, Universal opened the film wide at 464 theaters in the U. S. and Canada.[46] Whereas in the past, this type of opening in a wide pattern of theatres had been reserved for films which the studios judged to have little playability, the opening of *Jaws* signified a new adoption of this type of release and marketing pattern for high-quality studio pictures. In later years, this strategy proved to work on both levels by maximizing the blockbuster film's status as a special event while protecting it against possible bad reviews and word of mouth. Since the multiplexes had been built, why not use them? Universal even pushed the producers and some of the crew to work the newly established talk-show circuit to create even more "*Jaws*-consciousness."

Just three days before it was scheduled to open wide in the U.S. and Canada on June 20th, Universal unleashed the biggest advertising blitz in film history via every conceivable media outlet within range of the theatres.[47] Using John Williams' ominous, pulsating theme in coordination with the print campaign designed around the single, striking graphic image of a large open-mouthed shark rising underwater toward the unsuspecting naked female swimmer, the public interest and awareness grew to a frenzied pitch. In its first weekend of release, *Jaws* took in over $7 million in receipts and attracted over thirty-eight million moviegoers in its first month of release. The media and marketing blitz was an unheard of success. By the end of the summer of 1975, the film, the book, and the tie-ins (everything from T-shirts to toys) had raised *Jaws* to the level of a national fetish. Over twenty-five million tickets had been sold, raising over $100 million in domestic rentals—the top grossing film of all time (until May 1977 when another blockbuster, *Star Wars*, burst onto the film scene). *Jaws* the first movie to ever gross over $100 million domestic, but also over a short amount of time, $200 million.[48] Not only did the producers take advantage of new marketing, distributing and advertising methods, but generated commercial tie-ins—from toys, to video games, to sequels, and soundtrack albums.

In this way, *Jaws* was not just a blockbuster, but was the precursor to Lucas's historic *Star Wars* franchise that would follow a few years later (If *Jaws* was to become the Ur-Blockbuster, then *Star Wars* would be the Ur-Franchise that would set the stage for the 1990s synergy paradigm). This break from moviemaking tradition represents a break with traditional star-genre formulas of the "old" Hollywood which were geared to produce a singular commodity, the feature film. As such, *Jaws* re-invented the previous "blockbuster" flops, such as *Cleopatra, Hello, Dolly*, etc. *Jaws* had become its own genre whose story could be reiterated in a myriad of media forms.

With *Jaws*, the blockbuster, albeit reinvented, was back with a vengeance and swept the film industry like wildfire. As Thomas Schatz mentions in his essay, "The New Hollywood, "*Jaws* marked the arrival of the New Hollywood by recalibrating the profit potential of the block-buster film and redefining its status as a marketable commodity."[49] It had also put an end to the post-1969 recession that had proceeded from the late-1960s strategy of diversification and conglomeration and established a merchandising sub-industry while cementing the direction film marketing would take in the future.[50] It has been noted by Michael Pye and Lynda Myles that the most salient feature of *Jaws* was "the transformation of film into an event through clever manipulation of the media."[51] It also solidified and permanently hooked the film industry on the blockbuster "syndrome" and the potential profits it promised. David Cook mentions in *Lost Illusions* that Richard Zanuck's monetary take on *Jaws* was more than what his father, Darryl F. Zanuck had made throughout his entire career. Considering this, it is no wonder that the film industry sat up and took note of what Universal had done with *Jaws*.[52]

Without a doubt, *Jaws* heralded the arrival of the "blockbuster mentality" that still permeates the industry today. Biskind explains, "*Jaws* whetted corporate appetites for big profits fast, which is to say, studios wanted every film to be *Jaws*. In a sense, Spielberg was the vehicle through which the studios began to reassert their power. Hollywood was thriving."[53]

As a result of all these developments, the motion picture industry arrived at a critical juncture in the late 1970s. One hit movie could mean the difference between a profit and a loss for the entire year, so studios—although cautious—were willing to risk large sums of money on production and advertising for a single movie if they believed it could gross $50 million or more. Along with the rise of the blockbuster (and its bigger budget) came the re-invention and rise of the producer. Someone had to watch the shop, control the profits, make sure that talent demands would not get out of hand (i.e., the Ur-disaster, *Cleopatra*) and make sure that the blockbuster, with its ever increasing budgets, would stay on schedule and on budget and turn a nice profit. High concept, blockbuster movies on tight budgets needed strong producers who would be accountable for the budget of these films. The high concept was a producer's cinema that had to be fiscally responsible, not self-indulgent. Since most of the studios had undergone a turnover during the 1970s and had very few good executives like Zanuck around, the studios had to go outside to the independents to ensure control. The rise of the talent agencies helped in this regard and further strengthened the producer's position at the negotiating table. Not only were these producers budget-savvy, but many had come out of television where they were required to have a "creative spark" and wrote or directed much of their own material. Spielberg was one of these who came out of the television environment.

Steven Spielberg was a self-taught filmmaker. He made his first film —a three and a half minute stagecoach robbery—as a young boy eager to earn his Boy Scout's photography badge. His passion for films and filmmaking continued through his early and teenage years, but it was not enough to win him a place in USC's film school. Low grades kept him from entering the prestigious film program. So, instead of a formal film education, Spielberg immersed himself in film lore, watched every old movie he could on television, read the daily trades, and entered California State University, Long Beach as an English student. He continued to study film on his own and began to work out his list of personal favorites —from Ford's *The Searchers* to Robert Wise's thriller, *The Haunting*. [54]

As an aside, it is interesting that many new directors from this period have quoted *The Searchers* in their own films. *The Searchers* resonates not only in the work of Spielberg, but also that of Paul Schrader, John Milius, Martin Scorsese, George Lucas and Michael Cimino. The Searchers theme finds resonance in *Hardcore, Taxi Driver, Close Encounters of the Third Kind, Dillinger, Mean Streets, Big Wednesday, The Deer Hunter, The Wind and the Lion, Ulzana's Raid,* and *Star Wars.* In these films an obsessed man searches for someone—a woman, a child, a best friend—who has been taken away to a strange place or fallen into the clutches of an alien people. But when found the rescued one does not want to be found. Clearly, with all these various renditions of this theme during this period there is a narrative need on the part of the filmmakers to tell a story about having lost "something" which cannot be recovered or found in the society in which they live—history, innocence, God, love, friendship, family, etc.— and once discovered that thing or whatever has been "lost" does not want to be found (or can't be), rather it leads back to "no thing" at all. In the words of Thomas Wolfe, perhaps not only was there a belief you couldn't go home again, but even more disturbingly, no matter how much you searched, you'd never find it. These sentiments are not surprising in the post-Watergate-Vietnam era of disillusion and disenchantment. No wonder nostalgia flourished. Today, like then, the theme of searching takes the form of Holy Grails, last crusades, and impossible quests, but with one distinction. The search takes the form not so much that of a lost object in the new millennium, but of a hole in the heart that won't heal.

In any event, it was during this period Spielberg became both an expert on film and American culture. He wanted to know what people wanted to see at the

movies and every month was known to read everything from *Tiger Beat* to *Playboy* to become expert on what was "hip" and what people were thinking, wanting.

While at CSULB, he wrote, directed and edited a short called *Amblin* which won him a number of awards, including some at the Atlanta and Venice film festivals. The short film also won the attention of Sid Sheinburg, head of television films for Universal/MCA who offered him a contract.

The urban myth surrounding Spielberg's hire at Universal is a bit more romantic. As Spielberg and others tell it, he put on a dark suit, walked into the offices of Universal and found an empty office to occupy and make his own. Persuading the switchboard to list his name and give him a phone extension, he eventually got acquainted with the lot and invaded a film set where Hitchcock was filming. He was said to have been eventually thrown out, but in his dark, unassuming suit, he received carte blanche in a studio that didn't question or take notice of a serious young man in a side office. Romantic, but true? In most likelihood, not. Spielberg also tells a story that one day, having nothing really to do on the lot, he happened to be in Zanuck's office and picked up a copy of *Jaws* in galley form, took it home and went back to Zanuck and asked to direct it. This account may be closer to reality and may, indeed, be true.

Over the next year or so, Spielberg worked directing television fare (one week a *Night Gallery* starring Joan Crawford, the next a *Marcus Welby, MD* or *Columbo* episode). "When I first heard about Steven Spielberg, he was already a Hollywood guy, absolutely part of the system without even a second thought, not a drop of rebellion in him," said screenwriter Matthew Robbins who became one of Spielberg's closest friends.[55]

Many were taken aback by Spielberg's obsession with film. He had no interest in anything else—not art, books, music, or politics. Auteurism was a foreign idea to Spielberg. He wasn't made aware of the treatises of Truffaut and the New Wave in any film school. The idea of making films as personal expression was novel, an oddity. You made movies because people wanted to see them. "He didn't want to be the son of Jean-Luc Godard, he wanted to be the son of Sid Sheinburg."[56] He was anathema to Coppola, John Milius, Scorsese and the others. "Steven was the one who ran out to buy the trades. He was always talking grosses," said John Milius.[57]

It is no wonder then, that Spielberg starts and eventually solidifies the trend toward auteur as brand and celebrity, a trend that ran counter to Coppola's original dream of auteur as author and creative force. As a recognized auteur, Coppola had the expectation from the studios that he could get more and more creative control over his projects. In direct contrast, Lucas, with his many run-ins with the studio, clearly understood how the winds of change were blowing in Hollywood and realized that to get control of one's project one needed to own the modes and means of production, not be indebted to it, hired by it, nor become a puppet within it. The latter kind of control was false. If you had to ask permission or fight over editing, then you never had true control in the first place—only illusory control. During this time the same winds of change were blowing right in Coppola's face, but he could not, or would not feel it. Coppola and others who believed in the most creative form of auteurism during the mid-1970s, and had been labeled as such (Scorsese, Coppola, DePalma, Schrader, Lucas, Spielberg, Bogdanovich, etc.) were unable to stop the push toward using American auteurs as a marketing ploy to promote a film (in fact many directors were only too happy to take on the mantle of a self-promoting celebrity). Some may have not been able to stop this trend, but Coppola tried to do what he could to at least slow it down. It was in the spirit of supporting auteurs and their creative vision that Coppola produced Carroll Ballard's *The Black Stallion* (1979), co-produced (along with George Lucas) Akira Kurosawa's

Kagemusha (1980), and distributed the restored version of Able Gance's silent epic *Napoleon* (1927:1980) under the American Zoetrope banner. He also continued to produce, distribute, and promote the work of an amazing group of eclectic filmmakers, including Wim Wenders, Hans-Jurgen Syberberg, Jean-Luc Godard and Paul Schrader until 1984 when the studio was finally sold. [58]

As suggested before, auteurs became defined more by their commercial status and not so much on the product they might produce. Interestingly enough, the reinvented auteur-star had the potential to carry any sort of film, often to the extent of making the audience forget the film altogether through the marvel of its existence. Timothy Corrigan states:

> promotional technology and production feats become the new "camera-style," serving a new auteurism in which the making of a movie . . . foregrounds an agency that preempts and forecloses the value of the film in and of itself. As Godard has parodied so incisively in films like *King Lear* (1987), in today's commerce we want to know what our authors and auteurs look like or how they act; it is the text and not its author that now may be dead.[59]

By the end of the decade, in 1980, Michael Cimino's *Heaven's Gate*, became a good example of this new auteur classification whereby a director and "his" event dramatize the major points and counterpoints defining celebrity auteurism. When United Artists (UA) was taken over by Transamerica Corporation, the company pushed UA to produce a "blockbuster." Cimino was hired as an auteur-artist: part epic genius and part promotional commodity. The executives built his blockbuster auteurism solely on the potential of his latest film—a study of Vietnam, *The Deer Hunter*. When they signed Cimino for $7.8 million, they gave him directorial freedom that hadn't been experience by many directors since the early to mid- sixties. To make an interminable story short, the budget ballooned to over $40 million and *Heaven's Gate* became one of the most horrible and notorious financial (not to mention critical) disappointments of all time. In the studio's haste and attempt to promote (exploit) a celebrity auteur it backed a blockbuster film that tried to appeal to everyone, but because it had no true target audience, appealed to no one. This disaster eventually led to a long succession of corporate takeovers of the studio and eventually foreclosure. In the world-wide hue and cry that went up about the film, Cimino became the poster boy and scapegoat for what was considered auteurism-out-of-control. Yet, oddly enough, the image of the auteur would survive the corporate (and later in the next decade, conglomerate) formulas of the New Hollywood via the redemption of the home video market which allows for revenue returns sufficient enough to turn a box office "bomb," into a "hit."[60] In an interesting twist on the original tenet, in whatever shape or whatever agency, auteurs are not so much dead or alive, but have been forced, willingly or not, in the New Hollywood to give up their authorities as authors and begin to communicate within the commerce of that image.

Spielberg, a product of the times, was not empowered by a celebrity of the auteur (until later when he paired with Lucas who learned how to leverage this new status) since he had contracted under the "old" conditions of the system. He received a fee and a percentage, but had less say than the producers when push came to shove. In the traditional studio model, the producer and/or studio owned the property (in this case the book, *Jaws*) and hired on a director (one that had box office appeal and celebrity) to realize the studio/producer's vision, help the writer with the script and turn it into a movie. So while *Jaws* changed the way films were marketed and distributed, as well as setting a new standard of production in the industry, the business practices between director and producer or studio reverted clearly back to "normal," pre-1960s auteur practice, with the control of the final product firmly in the studio's hands. Lucas, a few years later, would be the only one to challenge and shake this power paradigm from its foundations. The "power" given to the auteur during the 1960s and 1970s was an anomaly and was over.

But through it all, the corporations knew that there was a "value" to be had from a name. Peter Biskind, states, "after *Jaws* the business would never be the same. As the studios discovered the value of wide openings at hundreds of theatres and massive TV advertising, the costs of marketing and distribution rose. As costs mounted, the willingness to take risks dissipated. *Jaws* whetted corporate appetites for big profits, which is to say, studios wanted every film to be *Jaws*."[61]

With the popularity of the blockbuster, the studios were making money again, life was good and getting better. The war in Vietnam was finally over. Talent agents became even more powerful after the creation of CAA (Creative Artists Agency) in 1975, and "packaging" of brand names increased with the promise of "risk less" investment, while at the same time studios became ever more dependent upon independent producers who utilized the studios as a financial clearing house. With the rise of CAA, the packaging of movies became a fine art form (a practice originated by prior agent, turned Seven Arts Productions producer, then Warner Bros.–Seven Arts studio head, then Rastar Productions producer, Ray Stark). According to Frank Yablans who presided over Paramount in the 1970s, "During my era, you got the script, you hired the director, you hired the actors, you made a movie. Now they did it backwards. The package was put together before the movie was ready to get made, so the script became the slave to the process. It was the lazy man's way of making movies."[62] For those who know nothing of script development, Yablans statement (and prophecy) certainly rang true.

With the release of *Jaws*, the birth of CAA and the changing of the guard at Warner Bros. and Paramount, many consider 1975 a watershed year. Not far behind CAA in packaging power, were ICM and the William Morris Agency. All three agencies specialized in packaging New Hollywood media franchises and soon grew even more powerful during this time than many of the studios.

By the late 1970s, Hollywood's economic recovery was well underway, fueled by the revitalized blockbuster mentality. Total domestic grosses, that had reached an unprecedented $2 billion for the first time in 1975, surged 40 percent in the next three years, with hits like *Rocky* (1976), *Star*

Wars, *Close Encounters of the Third Kind*, *Saturday Night Fever* (1977), *Grease* and *Superman* (1978) all doing record business. Compared to the preceding ten years from the *Sound of Music* in 1965 through 1976, only seven pictures, including *Jaws*, had returned $50 million in rentals; in 1977-1978 alone, nine films surpassed that mark.[63]

STAR WARS: A NEW HOPE

> *Han Solo*: Here's where the fun begins!
>
> *Ben Kenobi*: How long before you can make the jump to light speed?
>
> *Han Solo*: It'll take a few moments to get the coordinates from the navi-computer.
>
> *Luke Skywalker*: Are you kidding? At the rate they're gaining . . .
>
> *Han Solo*: Traveling through hyperspace isn't like dusting crops, boy!
>
> Star Wars

> That movie is going to make $100 million and I'll tell you why—it has a marvelous innocence and naiveté in it, which is George, and people will love it.
> Steven Spielberg, cited in John Baxter, *Mythmaker*, 230

Jaws unequivocally helped re-invent the blockbuster, with its high concept, slick and fast-paced style, but it wasn't until *Star Wars* that the blockbuster-franchise was born, completely changing the way our movies look, the way they are made, how they are seen, and, of course, marketed. The success of *Star Wars* was the frosting on the cake and forever changed the studio's idea of what a movie should do in terms of investment versus return and proved that *Jaws* was anything but a fluke. A New Hollywood was beginning to take shape and as it did the film product became more and more valued as a commodity. In terms of both narrative and marketing, *Star Wars* was the ultimate New Hollywood commodity—a hip-ironic, high speed, male action adventure tale, whose characters are essential functions of plot, with the plot itself adaptable to hundreds of ancillary media and marketing forms. The Lucas designed "space epic" quickly eclipsed *Jaws* as Hollywood's all-time box-office hit, while securing the future for adolescent, by-the-numbers, male-action films. From *Jaws* to *Star Wars* and onward into the 1980s, Hollywood's dominant product would become increasingly plot driven, progressively more visceral, kinetic, fast paced, ever more fantastic and reliant on special effects, and more and more targeted to much younger audiences.

In an effort to broaden their appeal, however, these films were also strategically open to other formal and narrative possibilities. An important aspect of *Star Wars* and its myriad of successors (*Raiders of the Lost Ark*, etc.), was the amazing collection of genres, genre conventions and the elaborate play of cinematic references. J. Hoberman writes that *Star Wars*, "pioneered the genre pastiche."[64] As such, *Star Wars* does rapidly move from one genre coded episode to another—from western to war film to vine-swinging adventure, all reinforced by a nostalgic quality (again, as in *American Graffiti*) that evoked old movie serials and TV series which was lost on the younger set, but relished by their cine-literate elders. "*Star Wars* is a combination of *Flash Gordon*, *The Wizard of Oz*, the Errol Flynn swashbucklers of the 30s and 40s and almost every western ever screened—not to mention the *Hardy Boys*, *Sir Gawain and the Green Knight* and *The Faerie Queene*," *Time Magazine* noted. Lucas admits that he threw in everything from his readings and his childhood into his *Star Wars* drafts. "It's the flotsam and jetsam from the period when I was twelve years old," Lucas said.[65]

Lucas assumed that his audience had the same familiarity with the older films and cinematic conventions and genres that he had. Gary Kurtz, the producer of *Star Wars*, points out the *Star Wars*' story "advances, not by any orthodox storytelling, but by telling the audience what to expect. It depends on their cine-literacy."[66] It can be argued that the cine-literate (cineaste) audiences of today, as well as then, helped to complete Lucas' films by recognizing the elements taken from other films. Filmmakers, like Lucas, rely on what Jane Feuer calls a metatext. Feuer points out that the metatext is made of elements usually ignored by the traditional researchers in favor of the analysis of the primary text (e.g., reviews, fan magazines, fashion systems, and the general knowledge of the genre or subject matter). Bennett calls these "hermeneutic activators," popular readings of popular texts located within critical apparatuses.[67] Accordingly, Lucas' preteen and teenage audiences were, and are, with their knowledge of film history via TV and other modes of film distribution (pay-for-TV and computer downloads) as much attuned to his genre mixing as he and his fellow film-school graduates.

Reviewers, certainly as fluent with the popular culture mix that makes up *Star Wars* meta-text as filmgoers, were quick to pick up on Lucas' homages, especially to Kurasawa's films, in particular *The Hidden Fortress* (1958) which centers on a perilous journey by a young princess and her loyal general. They are assisted by two bumbling misfits (C3PO and R2D2 clearly fall into this category).

Since Lucas himself admitted that *Star Wars* has a lot of material lifted from Westerns, mythology, and samurai movies, we can list some of the sources he has quoted. James Monaco in his book *American Film Now*, points out that Lucas "recalls Tarzan movies (Luke and Leia's rope swing across a steel canyon), B Westerns (Han Solo's character, his western garb and his shoot out with a bad guy in the Cantina), *The Wizard of Oz* (a trio of unlikely heroes, one covered in fur [the cowardly lion/ Chewbacca] enters the Witch's castle/Death Star to rescue Dorothy/ Leia), *Forbidden Planet* (C-3PO's character is not unlike Robbie's; also "hyperspace"), *Silent Running* (Huey, Dewey and Louie, the little chirping and twittering "droids" who predate R2-D2), and just about any World War II or Korean War aerial dogfight movie ever made, for the final attack on the Death Star."[68]

When the similarities between the final awards scene in *Star Wars* and Leni Riefenstahl's *Triumph of the Will* were pointed out to Gary Kurtz,

Lucas' producer on the film, he said, "I can see why people would think that."⁶⁹ Another critic noted that the scene in John Ford's *The Searchers* when Martin discovers his family's ranch house burned to the ground and the one in *Star Wars* when Luke finds his uncle's moisture farm destroyed by Imperial Troops are almost identical. He also noted that 'the Tusken Raiders' intrusion into the left foreground of the frame as Luke and C-3PO fly through the countryside in search of R2-D2 is a shot right out of *Fort Apache*.⁷⁰ Other critics, such as Terry Curtis Fox weren't so complimentary, stating: "When it comes to extending the genre, Lucas hasn't done a thing. Consider Luke's return from the desert to find his surrogate parents blown away by an Imperial raiding party. The shot itself is a direct quote from *The Searchers* and...a particularly relevant quote at that. Martin Pauley's discovery of the massacred family...forces Pauley to begin the redefinition of his family which lies at the heart of that film. But the death of Luke's "family" causes neither pain nor a confrontation with difficult decisions. Rather than raising problems, it resolves them. With his old surrogate parents conveniently killed off, Luke can now go follow his new surrogate father to the ends of the universe. Between good and evil is an easy choice."⁷¹ Many argue that Fox misses the point and the scene described above does mark a significant story point. Kenneth Von Gunden counters Fox's argument, stating, "Lucas, is not interested in extending the genre, rather he is content to merely replicate the scene visually."⁷² Along with Von Gunden, another critic observed: "*Star Wars* doesn't work within or even in genre. He plugs in genre, flashing its proven elements at us as though they were special effects."⁷³

This notion of extending the genre, or better yet, extending the device is a postmodern stylistic. Lucas, from what we have seen, while being postmodern in his use of pastiche, parody and nostalgia, can also be classified as both classical and modern in his stylistic approach. Lucas, a product of USC, was taught and uses a classical Hollywood style for telling his stories—even though the films he made at USC were "experimental" cinema "poems," a more modernist type of film fare (an auteur signature or style; high art—a film vs. a commercial movie, subversiveness, disjunctive irony, etc.)—his student film, *THX 1138* being an example. Rather than relying on one particular style or another, Lucas, a postmodernist filmmaker subjected to the postmodernist characteristics of the cinematic apparatus itself, utilizes all three.

While some may argue differently, I believe that it is not uncommon for many films to exhibit any number of film styles, and as a brief digression, think it is worth the time to consider the aesthetic implications. To try and situate certain works in only one specific style (earlier modernist or late postmodernist) suggests a misunderstanding of the nature of style. A work need not be wholly one without an admixture of the other style indicators. This approach takes a commonality of properties to be the be-all-and-end-all of what it is to be a style when the locus of a style term involves a complex relationship of vectors, or elements. There is no incompatibility between the three various styles mentioned above: classical Hollywood, modernist, and postmodernist. Much of these films' historic stylistic boundaries are blurred (read: mixed) even among critics (they may look for "breaks," but will never find them). By its very nature, a postmodernist style would contain all the other styles as a description/reflection of itself. It is difficult even for postmodern theorists like Fredrik Jameson to decide where the stylistic breaks might occur: "It can be witnessed in film, not merely between experimental and commercial production, but also within the former itself, where Godard's 'break' with the classical filmic modernism of the great 'auteurs' (Hitchcock, Bergman, Fellini, Kurosawa) generates a series of stylistic reactions against itself in the 1970's and is also accompanied by a rich new development of experimental video (a new medium inspired by but significantly and structurally distinct from experimental film)."[74]

These assumptions beg a variety of important questions: if Jameson's classification of modernism includes the auteurs Hitchcock, Bergman and Fellini, is Godard a postmodern? Does this make classical Hollywood cinema pre-modernist? Is auteurism the only determinate of modernist cinema or are other elements such as foregrounding of the device, self-reflexivity, irony/black humor, juxtapositions of conflicting textures, moods and tones, shifts points of view, and manipulation of genre also modernist components? Are modernist and postmodernist problematic as stylistic terms?

On another level, cinema has been classified a "modern" apparatus, yet it is nonetheless a mass medium that, in many cases, was not considered "radical," subversive, or high art (except when used in that political capacity by avant-garde filmmakers such as the surrealists, Dada, etc.). However, the cinematic apparatus is a-temporal and stretches and condenses space. Cinema often involves citation and it is unique in its ability to exactly replay and repeat its exact same form (e.g., one film can be projected from many places at once, a film can be "remade" a million different ways and times, viewed at different times in history and be set in a different time period and, in doing so, can be a parody of its original while "being them and mocking them at the same time," creating a schizophrenic experience for the viewing subject confronted by subjective timelessness). As such, on many levels, cinema may be classified as "postmodern."

Lucas' films exhibit all three of these classification features, insofar as many of his films hide the device and allow the audience to be absorbed in the action/story. Viewers, with little sense of the presence of the cinematic apparatus, are able to become involved with the characters and become intrigued by the story while suspending disbelief, or submitting to the illusion of seeing "real" events. The presence of all these factors denotes a classic Hollywood style. Insofar that many of Lucas' films can be considered nostalgic, a pastiche of forms and genres, and filled with parody, they can be considered postmodern. That many of his films are self-reflexive and bear an auteurist signature, suggests they also have a modernist component as well. These various properties can be seen to be part of the cluster of concepts for classical Hollywood cinema, modernist and postmodernist cinema. It certainly can be argued that identifying the single presence of one of these concepts by itself is not enough to enable the audience to apprehend the presence of either the classic Hollywood, modernist or postmodernist style. These historical style-making properties mentioned above are only a few out of many concepts typically associated with being in those styles. For modernity, for example, there are also the properties of foregrounding the device, autonomy, disjunctive irony, and no doubt many others. So it follows that just to find that a particular film has seamless editing does not necessarily make it a classical Hollywood film. A weighted amount of properties from these various categories must be revealed before a determination can be fully made as to a film's historical style.

Regardless of aesthetic category, *Star Wars* began as fourteen pages of story that no studio was originally willing to touch. With the title, "The Story of Mace Windu," it then began: "Mace Windu, a revered Jedi-bendu of Ophuchi who was related to Usby C. J. Thape, Padawaan learner to the famed Jedi." The rest of the fourteen pages were not any easier to decipher, let alone, pronounce. Michael Blake, child actor, makeup artist, and biographer of Lon Chaney, relays an interesting account of his audition with George Lucas for the part of Luke Skywalker. In his words,

> In September of 1975, I had an interview at the old Goldwyn Studio on Santa Monica Blvd. Coppola had an office there (it was called "Coppola Cinema Seven") and that is where I had my interview for *Star Wars*. When I went for the interview, my agent had no title for the film. When I went in, there were two guys in the office. One I do not remember and the other guy was a slight figure, with a beard and horned-rimmed glasses. He is the one who I spoke with. This was Lucas. Lucas looked at my portfolio book of photos, clippings, etc.. I then read a brief scene for him (do not remember what it was) and mispronounced Obi Wan-Kenobi's name. Lucas corrected me right in the middle of the reading (something no other director had ever done during an interview in my 18 years of acting), which kind of threw me. Anyway, when I finished we shook hands, he thanked me for coming in and that was it. Two

years later, watching all the media coverage of the film, I realized what that interview was for and who this Lucas guy was. [75]

It was a difficult read, to say the least, especially for studio executives who were used to reading the trades and short deal memos, relied on one-line pitches, and run-of-the-mill scripts that made some sense and could suggest at least some audience interest. Even for the initiated who read comics and were savvy enough to navigate the fantasy worlds of J. R. R. Tolkien et al., the story line was baffling. [76] Had any readers of Lucas's early treatment been familiar with the work of either Joseph Campbell or Carl Jung, they might have recognized the archetypal "Journey of the Hero" paradigm from Campbell's book, *Hero with a Thousand Faces*, woven into the story.[77] J. R. R. Tolkien also follows this "Hero's Journey" paradigm in his *Lord of the Rings* trilogy. Watching either *Star Wars* or *Lord of the Rings* you can easily pick out chapter headings from Campbell's book which parallel narrative plot points in both films, including: the heroes call to adventure, the refusal of the call, the arrival of supernatural aid, the crossing of the first threshold, the belly of the whale, and the series of ordeals culminating in four possible outcomes, including the first, a show down with the angry father, when, Campbell points out, "the hero beholds the face of the father, understands—and the two are atoned"—which parallels Lucas' ending in *Jedi*. In *Lord of the Rings* the end result is a combination of the other three possible outcomes—a sacred marriage, apotheosis, or divination of the hero, and a theft of the boon the hero came to get. [78]

It may be that Lucas instinctively tapped into the popular culture fervor surrounding the Tolkien books which had taken off (as a trilogy, genre and collective myth) like wild fire in the 1970s. Gandalf the Grey and The Shire in the 1970s were discussed as hot topics then, as again, in 2001 to present. *Star Wars*, in borrowing heavily from Jung, and Joseph Campbell, may have inadvertently tapped into Tolkien's *Lord of the Rings* trilogy fan base—a built in demographic that would further help to make *Star Wars* a hit. Later, this trend and built in fan base would be reversed

The "High Concept" Blockbuster 113

when *Star Wars* fans would flock to *Lord of the Rings* screenings some thirty-plus years later.

It would take until 2001 for Tolkien fans to see their favorite books turned into feature films, but at the turn of the millennium, director Peter Jackson produced a stunning and accurate film version of *Lord of the Rings (LOTR)* which is worthwhile to mention here since it shares many characteristics with Lucas' *Star Wars film* series. Special effects and talent finally coalesced into a film that breathed life into the hero quest myth. During the weekend of December 18-22, 2002, LOTR's second installment, The *Two Towers*, broke all opening records at the domestic box office with an astounding gross of $101.5 million—($26m on opening day, the largest ever for a December opening), up 33 percent from the previous years opening grosses for the first LOTR part of the trilogy (*Fellowship of the Ring*). [79] It was also the biggest five and three day box office ever ($61.5m) for a December movie—helping push the film industry to the $9 billion in grosses mark for the first time in film history (The spectacular DVD "Fellowship" collection released prior to the opening of the second film installment also helped to spur the larger audience interest and hence, opening attendance numbers). LOTR's popularity continues into the millennium. Peter Jackson's first installment of the franchise, *The Hobbit: An Unexpected Journey*, opened strong on December 14, 2012 and by March 5, 2013 surpassed the $1 billion mark worldwide. On December 11, 2013, the second installment, *The Hobbit: The Desolation of Smaug*, fared equally as well and quickly became the fourth highest-grossing film of the year with a worldwide total of $953,066,855.00, just shy of the billion dollar mark. It is expected the third and final film, *The Hobbit: The Battle of the Five Armies* (2014) in the *Hobbit* trilogy will fare equally as well at the box office, or better.

Both the first, second and final installment of the *LOTR* trilogy received positive reviews by critics and audience members alike. It swept both the 2004 Golden Globes and the Academy Awards winning 10 Oscars, including Best Picture and Director.

But back in 1975, Lucas's vision had no parallel. In addition to missing references in the *Star Wars* script to Jung, Campbell or Tolkien, most executives could not find references or the homage to Akira Kurasawa's, *The Seven Samurai* (the Hollywood version made in 1960, *The Magnificent Seven*), or *The Hidden Fortress*. Even more perplexing, *Star Wars* was not a "normal" type of science fiction film manufactured by the current Hollywood—it was not *2001: A Space Odyssey*, *Planet of the Apes*, or anything similar. There were no lofty sentiments, no modernist social satire, and no gut-wrenching lesson to be learned. *Star Wars* was antithetical to what was being served on a daily basis to audiences and studio execs alike.

Lucas and his agent, Jeff Berg, debated where to send the treatment. Universal never formally declined, but had no interest in epics, especially from a director who recently finished a film they all believed was an un-releasable disaster. While Ned Tanen was still debating the fate of *American Graffiti*, Lucas and Berg smuggled a print to Alan Ladd, Jr., or "Laddie" as he was called at Twentieth Century-Fox, where he had just taken over as head of production. Ladd was interested in talking to Lucas, but before Lucas could talk *Star Wars* to Ladd he needed to have both United Artists and Universal decline their first rights of refusal options on the treatment. United Artists couldn't make heads or tails of the treatment and courteously declined. Universal took a bit more time, but even with a positive review of the treatment by an in-house reader, Ned Tanen did not have enough faith in Lucas' abilities as a director to give it a go-ahead—and in doing so cost Universal the most popular (and lucrative) film series in the history of cinema. Lucas was relieved and quickly pitched the story to Alan Ladd, Jr. who was just as enthusiastic in making the film as Lucas. Both shared a love of old movies and Ladd recalled, "when he [Lucas] said this sequence is going to be like *The Sea Hawk*, or *Captain Blood*, or *Flash Gordon*, I knew exactly what he was saying. That gave me confidence that he was going to pull it off."[80]

The "High Concept" Blockbuster 115

The deal for "The Star Wars" (as it was first called having gone through a myriad of drafts) was made on the first of May and only promised Lucas money to develop the script. Then *American Graffiti* came out in August. Suddenly, it was a whole different playing field. By October, everyone knew *American Graffiti* was a huge success. Now, Michael Pye and Lynda Myles state, "*Star Wars* was not some obscure science fiction project. It was the next film from the man who brought you the mega-hit, the super-film, the most profitable film ever to cost less than $1 million to make."[81]

LUCAS THEMES AND SIGNATURES: MYTH AND THE JOURNEY OF THE HERO

From the start Lucas wanted to make a movie that would engage a mass audience on a large scale. Like any competent corporation, Lucas did his homework and spent time on market research. He steeped himself in myth, fairytales, old movies and serials and emerged with an appealing space opera fantasy pastiche that gave the audience "A New Hope" in a hopeless world. He tried to find what had been "lost" in the recent past and gift wrap it all up in a "quest." Lucas reminisces:

> I research kids' movies and how they work and how myths work; and I looked very carefully at the elements of films within that fairy tale genre which made them successful.... I found that myth took place over the hill, in some exotic far-off land. For the Greeks it was Ulysses going off into the unknown. For Victorian England it was India or North Africa or treasure islands. For America it was out West. There had to be strange savages and bizarre things in an exotic land. Now the last of that mythology died out in the mid-1950s, with the last of the men who knew the old West. The last place left "over the hill" is space.[82]

Lucas was firm that the general public should not be encouraged to see the film as esoteric science fiction, but as something more tangible and audience friendly, something they could relate to, a folk tale breathlessly paced like a cliff-hanging Saturday serial—"space fantasy" fit the bill perfectly (and began the trend toward genre-pastiche).

In the character Luke Skywalker, Lucas single-handedly brought back the traditional American hero that had been out of vogue for a number of years. Luke Skywalker like Buck Rogers before him (and after ironically) was just an average Joe who kept his wits about him. The idea of *Star Wars* was simply to make a real "gee-whiz" movie—a high adventure film for kids, a pleasure film that would be the end result of Coppola's coaxing and direction. The audience gorged itself on the new movie fare, over and over again (helping the box office rise higher and higher).

Repeat viewing really began with *Star Wars*. One reason for this may be that *Star Wars* presents a wonderful coming of age story and follows the journey of the hero well. It brought back the old myths that had been lying dormant for a number of tumultuous years. Lucas took these myths and reworked them as the basis for *Star Wars*. Lucas admits,

> *Star Wars* came out of my desire to make a modern fairytale. In college I became fascinated by how culture is transmitted through fairy tales and myths. Fairy tales are how people learn about good and evil, about how to conduct themselves in society. Darth Vader is the bad father; Ben Kenobi is the good father. The good and bad mothers are still to come. I was influenced by the dragon-slayer genre of fairy tale—the damsel in distress, the evil brothers, the young knight who through his virtue slays the dragon.[83]

Lucas further elaborated,

> The struggle between good and evil within us has been around since the beginning of time. All mythology and all religions address it, and it's the most intimate struggle that we cope with—trying to do the right thing and what's expected of us by society, by our peers, and in our hearts. The issues of falling from grace and being redeemed, and the strength of the family and love—they're all very primary issues.[84]

From the very beginning, Lucas knew he did not want to make *2001*. He wanted to make a space fantasy that was more in the genre of

Edgar Rice Burroughs that pre-dated its more recent incarnations.[85] In other words, Lucas was nostalgic for the grand narratives that had been lost in the ever-increasing post-modern shuffle, and longed to recreate a lost past that a weakening of history only partially recovered by nostalgic narratives, could reclaim. As such,

> the mythic process is a learning device in which the unintelligible—randomness—is reduced to intelligibility—a pattern: *Myth may be more universal than history.*[86]

To find such a universal, Lucas steeped himself in primary and secondary books on fairytales, mythology, and even social psychology. An anthropologist at heart, Lucas was determined to "create a new myth" for a de-mythologized Western society that since the 1960s, had lost a sense of cohesive community that was part and parcel of mythic storytelling. Although he acknowledged the importance of science fiction in the 1950s, and the fears of the atomic bomb that manifested in the monsters that came from outer space, he firmly believed that our society was in dire need of fairytales, fantasy stories, and the *real* heroes portrayed in myth. During his research, as mentioned earlier, Lucas discovered Joseph Campbell's seminal 1949 text, *The Hero with a Thousand Faces*, based on Jungian psychological archetypes, that detailed both the universal and the sub-universal local myths that permeate our society and lives. Campbell explained about Lucas' interest in his book,

> I was invited by George Lucas to his place in San Rafael to see all his films. He told me that it's my books, particularly *The Hero With A Thousand Faces* . . . that lie behind his *Star Wars* films. I see Lucas continuing a major concern of modern life and shifting from the world of literate minds to the popular masses who seem to me to be running the world.[87]

From Campbell's book, Lucas took as *Star Wars'* foundation the most fundamental myth of all—the myth of the hero in which the hero confronts issues of separation, initiation and return. Anyone who has ever seen the *Star Wars* trilogy can for the most part see how closely the trilogy parallels the hero archetype structure outlined by Campbell. This use of such a fundamental myth can perhaps account for *Star Wars'* universal appeal. Good story, interesting characters, exciting special effects, and clever marketing would account for the rest.

In 1997, the "Star Wars: The Magic of Myth" exhibition debuted at the Smithsonian's National Air and Space Museum and toured internationally for many years thereafter. The exhibit drew heavily on the Hero's Journey by foregrounding archetypes and mythic themes outlined in Campbell's paradigm, including: a young hero who has faithful companions, a meeting with a wise guide or mentor, training with magical weapons, the rescue of an endangered princess, a series of superhuman tests and trials, an atonement with the Father, and heroic sacrifice and resurrection, to name a few. A book put out by Lucas Books in 1999, further reinforced the connection between *Star Wars* and Campbell's work and was likewise titled, *Star Wars: The Power of Myth* (an obvious nod to Joseph Campbell's book, *The Power of Myth,* published in 1988 based on his collaboration with Bill Moyers in the PBS series of the same name),. [88] Lucas takes what Campbell has written and uses the "Journey of the Hero" paradigm to explain how myth functions in the *Star Wars* epic. The introduction of the book makes the correlation between the classic myths and *Star Wars* clear, explaining:

> Every civilization on Earth has told mythic stories to express its aspirations, achievements, and the deeper meaning of life. From the earliest times, myths have excited and inspired us because they serve to describe the human experience. Myths show us what we are capable of as individuals. The *Star Wars* classic trilogy has come to represent one of the great mythic stories of our time. Luke Skywalker's adventure, starting from his farm boy beginnings and ending with the fulfillment of his spiritual quest to become

a Jedi knight, is a hero's journey that speaks to the modern age. George Lucas, *Star Wars'* creator, has dramatized the saga of an epic struggle between good and evil in a universe complete with its own cultures, languages, landscapes and heroes. Contemporary characters enact a mythic drama. Swords, sorcery and chivalry combine with hyperspace travel, blaster weaponry, and droids. Now, with the release of The *Phantom Menace*, the first episode in the *Star Wars* saga, we can discover more of the mythical dynamics of the *Star Wars* universe." [89]

While illustrating correlations between *Star Wars* and other myths, the publication of this book also insures inclusion of *Star Wars* into the mythic canon itself. Luke Skywalker is positioned via photo and, or, script on every page right next to the likes of King Arthur, Sigfried, and other classic western mythic heroes.

The utilization of such a myth immediately plugs it into the collective unconscious, if you will, and begins the individual spectator's journey toward epiphany and illumination. This universal tapping in to the general human condition is what separates *Star Wars* from what some might consider the "senseless escapism" of which Lucas is accused. Lucas is not just dealing in mindless, new age drivel—rather he has found a way to crack away at the very mystery and meaning of life. Lucas just does not hold up a mirror to society, he asks it to look beyond its own image (in an age of images) to its very core—to its very origins. This process is what separates *Star Wars* from other pedestrian science fiction films bereft of the transformational effects of myth (most just stay at a localized level and never go beyond the mundane). Of course, Lucas is not the first to do such a thing and will not be the last.

Everywhere, in every culture, all over the world, mythologies abound with the tales of heroic journeys and quests that feature a hero who ventures forth from the world of common day into a region of supernatural wonder, where (s)he encounters fabulous forces over which a decisive victory is won at great peril. Unscathed or wounded, the hero comes back from the mysterious adventure with the power to bestow boons on his fellow man.[90] By successfully completing his wondrous journey of transfiguration, the hero shows us the marvelous gift of life ever renewed. Viewed in this way, the heroic myth becomes a dynamic narrative process through which all sorts of meaning can be derived. It also becomes a viable metaphor for the stage of life and rites of passage, which human beings undergo in their own lives. The mythic hero is a personification of society and a symbol of the archetypal individual. His or her story is constantly being told and retold in many cultures and operates at both a universal and local level (especially in oral traditions, rituals, fan cultures, etc.).

Campbell explains that the hero myth at the center of *Star Wars* deals with issues of self-individuation and spiritual growth. This "hero" narrative always contains three main elements, these being: (1) a hero, the protagonist with whom we may identify or sympathize, (2) an environment in which the hero acts, and (3) a narrative, which describes that interaction between the hero and his fictional environment. Two things may be said about his narrative of the hero myth: (1) The hero undergoes a rite of passage, often a rite of initiation, which ultimately, but not always, leads to a change in status for the hero; and (2) during the hero's rite of passage, the hero encounters various archetypal images, beings, symbols and situations which test the hero's courage and stamina and which can affect the hero's spiritual, intellectual, social and psychological development. A "happily ever after," though never guaranteed, can be read as a transcendence of the universal tragedy of man. The objective world remains what it was, but because of a shift of emphasis within the subject, is beheld as though transformed. The way of illumination is never easy (just ask Yoda or any Jedi knight).

While "universals" are important and are the "stuff" of myth, they must be regarded in relation to cultural sub-universals that are attached through the mechanizations of each society's culture. (Likewise, *Star Wars* must be viewed within the context of American culture.) As a rule, cultural narratives deal with every day life "stories" that are both basic and fantastic and run the gamut from making love and making war, raising a family to watching TV. In all these varied situations, myth attempts to answer questions people would rarely think, or dare to think, of asking. (Myth, by its very nature, tries to name the un-nameable.) In making that attempt, one of myths primary functions is to pose—through spoken narrative and the visual imagery of movies—alternative or virtual worlds in which experience departs radically from the everyday. Myth, at both a universal and localized level, always tries to grasp the fundamental problems of human existence framing them in understandable stories. No one lives in Luke Skywalker's world, just as no one lived in those of Oedipus or Prometheus, but the Greek myths, as well as the Ur-hero myths or those based upon it (*Star Wars*), still find an audience. The reason for this mass mobilization is clear—myths provide distillations of experiences which define humanity and which, because the virtual world of experience is forever changing, provide a glimpse into possible futures, into alternative realities unstably contained in everyday life and awaiting birth as flesh and blood constructions. Campbell states,

> Mythology...conducts individuals through the ineluctable psychophysiological stages of transformation of a human lifetime—birth, childhood and adolescence, age, old age, and the release of death—in unbroken accord simultaneously with the requirements of this world and the rapture of participation in a manner of being beyond time.[91]

It is in the small breakthroughs of the local and/or mundane into a universal transcendence, Campbell suggests, especially through the mediation of art that we are able to recognize through metaphors an epiphany beyond words (beyond time). Once reserved exclusively for religion, the Holy Land has become secularized (along with religion) and is in no special place. It is every place that has ever been recognized and mythologized by any people as home (inner or outer worlds, movie theatres, etc.). God has passed into the realm of metaphor where he is known by the transcendent epiphanies that occur everyday. God is the ultimate metaphor—the unknowable and un-nameable.

Star Wars: A "Force" in Merchandising

> George Lucas created *Star Wars* with the toy by-products in mind. He was making much more than a movie.
>
> Mark Pepvers, Fox Executive, cited in Justin Wyatt, *High Concept*, 152

Lucas has explained in countless interviews that he wrote the film for toys—meaning that he had merchandizing in mind including all the paraphernalia and sideshow "goodies" that go with a successful film—the T-shirts, records, models, kits, and dolls (they weren't action figures, yet).[92] James Surowiekie of *Slate* magazine states, "It's safe to say that *Star Wars* single-handedly created the film merchandising business . . . . . It is a classic example of a company creating a market rather than responding to an existing one. No one knew how much kids wanted action figures until they were offered them."[93] In his book, *Star Wars: From Concept to Screen to Collectible*, Stephen Sansweet states,

> In 1978, the first full year that Kenner offered *Star Wars*, it sold 42,322,500 of them for a total of more than $100 million, making it the most successful movie-related toy line up. Far and away the best sellers were the mini-action figures, which came in twelve varieties; Kenner sold 26,106,500. (Considering the quality, and the original price of $1.96 each, it is amazing that collectors are now paying up to $100 a piece for some of the first figures mint on their cards.) The next-fastest movers were the boxed jigsaw puzzles (2,462,400). Since the smallest had 140 pieces, that meant more than one billion *Star Wars* puzzle pieces. The smallest sellers were two large figures that were exclusive to the J.C. Penny Christmas catalog that year, but were sold widely in 1979. In a popularity contest, the large R2-D2 figure narrowly beat out C-3PO, 14,000 to 13, 400. [94]

Besides toys, and even before an audience had seen a single frame of the film, Lucas made sure that his first priority—to take the control away from the studio executives—would occur. In one of the best deals of all time in film history, Lucas refused $500,000 in lieu of control of all merchandising, publishing, music and sequel rights (including a small fee). Fox considered themselves lucky (what was there to merchandise anyway and who cared about a sequel?), operating in an "old" Hollywood mode, agreed to Lucas's deal and gave him $9 million to film the project (final cost of $11.5 million), but still maintained rights to the final cut. Lucas *almost* got everything he wanted.[95] But toward the end of the shooting, amid delays brought about by on-set illness, sandstorms destroying standing sets in Tunisia and other unforeseen production difficulties, Lucas needed more time and more money to film the now famous cantina scene as well as other pick-ups.

Soon after concluding his original deal with Fox for *Star Wars*, Lucas formed Lucasfilm, Ltd., Industrial Light and Magic, and Skywalker Sound —both seeded with money eventually earned from *American Graffiti* to help with the research and development of new technologies needed for the many special effects that would power the film. The kind of special effects Lucas wanted did not exist, so they were created "as needed" along with the film. Lucas knew what he was doing and should be fully credited with making these films a reality. The special effects R & D at ILM (a subsidiary of Lucasfilm set up in 1975 in Van Nuys), although worth it, had eaten heavily into the film's production schedule and budget. John Dykstra perfected a computerized motion-control system for traveling matte photography that made the process cost-effective, if inexpensive, enabling Lucas to create hundreds of complicated stop-motion miniature sequences for *Star Wars* at a fraction of their cost in earlier films ($2.5 million was spent on traveling matte effects for *Star Wars* compared to $6.5 million spent for fewer mattes for *2001: A Space Odyssey*).[96] Fox threatened to pull the plug due to rising costs, but at the eleventh hour Alan Ladd stalled these decisions at the studio. Lucas vowed that, henceforth, he would take control on all other projects and control "the means of production." Lucas learned that it did not matter if you wrote the script, you had to own all rights in order to maintain control. Copyright meant nothing if you did not retain ownership. And Lucas realized how much the studios had profited from his copyrights. To play ball with the executives and producers, Lucas had to become one, so he made the decision to build Skywalker Ranch in Northern California.

While ILM focused on ways to make space travel and new worlds more "real," Skywalker Sound (financed like ILM from *American Graffiti* profits) worked toward making the film-going experience more thrilling and developed technologies for use in theatres (Dolby and THX). *Star Wars* became the first film both recorded and released in six-track Dolby stereo (and Dolby was awarded the technical Academy Award the following year for its work on *Star Wars*). Both ILM and THX changed the movie going experience forever. The quick pace of *Star Wars* and the layering of special effects, which had never been seen before, completely changed the way people experienced movies. The same people went back to see the film again and again, not just because they were hungry for the "message," but for the visceral experience, both visual and aural. In order to see and hear all the special effects, an average movie-goer had to see the movie at least three or four times. From that point forward, audiences got their tickets to "take a ride." It was pinball on a cosmic scale.

Lucas's rights to *Star Wars* merchandising allowed him to turn a nice profit. Not until *Star Wars* did the full potential for blockbuster profits from a movie beyond its box office returns really become evident. Before now, the actual film was the single commodity. Stars had pitched products on the side for years (like makeup, etc.), but these products were not directly tied into the film's profits (product placement, yes; profits, no). No one had ever thought of exploiting ancillary rights to this magnitude before Lucas. Systems of production and distribution weren't in place at any of the studios. It is no secret that Lucas made most of his millions and billions not from the film itself, but from his sizable take for *Star Wars* related toys and other related tie-ins. Lucas says, "In a way this film (*Star Wars*) was designed around toys. I actually make toys. I'm not making much from directing this movie. If I make money it will be from the toys."[97] Since the film has been licensed to over fifty companies, with Kenner Toys producing seventy *Star Wars* products alone, total sales figures are not readily available, but within the first year, merchandising had accounted for at least $300 million for *Star Wars*.

Part of the films' amazing success as a licensing property has been its diverse set of interesting characters. And although Lucas had designed the film with an eye toward merchandizing tie-ins and retained licensing control through Lucasfilm, Ltd., he could never have foreseen the bonanza of sales in books, toys, cereal boxes, records, posters, and all things *Star Wars* that made him a millionaire many times over and turned Lucasfilm, Ltd., into a $30 million dollar corporation. (By 1997 that figure would grow. Lucas's net worth was estimated at $2 billion and Lucasfilm, Ltd. corporate holdings at $5 billion, and by 2011 his personal net worth had grown to $3.2 billion, selling the company in October 2012 for $4.05 billion.) It is interesting to note that *Star Wars* related merchandise ultimately has earned more than the film itself, more than $1 billion retail, and $4 billion by 1999). Prior to the release of Star Wars in 1977, consumers worldwide would spend less than $5 billion a year for licensed merchandise. By 1990, that figure rose to $66 billion.[98]

When all was said and done, *Star Wars* made almost $3 million the first week of its limited release on May 25, 1977. Fox had decided against opening wide and had only placed the film in forty-two theatres in twenty-eight cities, with 70mm and Dolby stereo for major markets, together with a carefully marketed campaign that was targeted especially to twelve to twenty-four-year-olds first and secondly to those in the twenty-five to thirty-five-year-old bracket. It was not the greatest start date since school was not out, but it would be perfectly situated to go head-to-head with Columbia's *The Deep*. Everyone (including Lucas) was stunned. By the end of August 1977, it had made over $100 million. People could not get enough of seeing the film and most went on to become multiple viewers. Post-release telephone surveys for *Star Wars* showed that 40 percent of its audience had seen the film three or four times by the end of August 1977; most of those who saw the film again were teenagers and some of them had even seen the film between thirty and thirty-five times or more. These multiple viewings came about for a variety of reasons, but one that is often overlooked, can be attributed to the new practice of "clearing" out the theatre after each film showing. In the past, theatre-goers were able to sit through the next screening without consequence. Not so beginning with *Star Wars*. This in turn, created "lines"—which became a badge of honor for those participating in the phenomenon and created more press for the "event." Fans could talk to other fans standing in line with similar interests ("I saw this film twenty times") and could compare notes on the film, further establishing a *Star Wars* community.

The film ran throughout 1977 and then was re-released in 1978 and 1979—earning $262 million in rentals worldwide. (Re-released again in 1997 with a new set of special effects laid down alongside and on top of additional footage, the *Star Wars Special Edition* trilogy has grossed several hundreds of millions of dollars more by itself.)

Lucas had his hit. More like a home run. More like a home run and touch down at the same time. To top it off, the film was nominated for ten Academy Awards and received seven in all, including: art direction, sound, original score, film editing, costume design, and visual effects. A win, however, for direction was noticeably absent. It also won two Los Angeles Critics Awards and captured three Grammies for its score. By the end of the 1970s *Star Wars* had become the all time highest grossing film and had set a standard for the new breed of filmmakers and a new way of filmmaking. *Star Wars* led the entire decade in profitability, a record that would not be broken until January 1983 with the arrival of Steven Spielberg's *E. T.: The Extra-Terrestrial*.

The corporations that owned the studios looked to their ancillary rights and the best, most profitable way to exploit them throughout their existing subsidiaries—for many this was uncharted territory. While Lucas and his producer Gary Kurtz were heavily involved in the merchandising of the film from the start, most of the work fell to Charles Lippencott, one of a few of the Lucasfilm employees who was hired to generate publicity for the film. His business card read: Vice President for advertising, publicity, promotion, and merchandising. Lippencott was a USC film school buddy of Lucas's and after graduation was hired by MGM as a film publicist. He bumped into Kurtz in 1975 and it was then Lippencott learned of Lucas's "space fantasy" and was intrigued and signed on with Lucasfilm a few months later. Not long after, Tom Pollock (Lucas's attorney who would later become Chief of Universal Pictures) struck the first merchandising deal—Ballantine Books was to publish the *Star Wars* novelization, the script, and a book about the "making of the film" (one of the many "making of" films/books to be developed during the decade).[99]

The novelization of *Star Wars* by Lucas came out December 1976 and sold out its first printing of 125,000 in less than three months. Instead of going for another printing, Ballantine decided to wait until the film came out to reprint to see if it would be worthwhile. It was. More than 5 million paperbacks were printed world-wide by 1992, in a variety of translations. December also brought the first theatrical trailer of the film to theatres—an unusual ploy for a film opening six months later. Even more unusual was that two trailers had been made, one by Fox and another by a TV commercial producer picked up by Lucasfilm. Between the two, Alan Ladd decided to use the trailer developed at Lucasfilm. This trailer was accompanied by a full-sized theatrical poster, an expensive, black and silver Mylar sheet that announced in big, bold letters, "Coming to Your Galaxy This Summer."[100]

At about this point in the marketing campaign, prior to the films actual release in May 1977, Pevers (at Fox) and Lippencott in marketing sent out hundreds of letters to manufacturers telling them about the terrific potential *Star Wars* had as a licensing vehicle, especially as it related to toys. The response of the manufacturers was negligible, not a strange reaction considering the new trails *Star Wars* was blazing in merchandising and licensing. Bernard Loomis, president of Kenner, a visionary like Lucas who had seen publicity about the film in the *Hollywood Reporter* and was intrigued by the prospects of *Star Wars* toys from the start, took the risk and it wasn't long before that risk paid off—hundreds of times over.[101] Probably the only *Star Wars* spin-off that didn't do well throughout the years was the ill-conceived 1978 *Star Wars Holiday TV Special, everything else turned to gold.*[102] *Star Wars* was a certifiable film industry phenomenon and those in charge sat up and took notice. Anticipated future profits in ancillary markets pushed many corporations to acquire more and more companies that might distribute and manufacture potential wares they could spin off from the films produced at the studio. In this way, the corporate strategies after the merchandising successes of Star Wars in the late 1970s prefigure the synergy of the 1990 conglomerates. Even Fox and Columbia, two studios that had staunchly held out in the late 1970s against corporate takeover had to pay attention to what Lucas was doing. All studios from this time forward began to diversify their business interests across platforms to enhance cash flow and minimize risk.

Notes

1. *Los Angeles Times*, 17 March 1971, p. 1: "If the country as a whole is in a recession, the motion picture business is in an out and out depression. More than half the 30,000 local film union members are out of work. In some crafts joblessness is said to be running 85-90 percent." Also see David A. Cook. "Formative Industry Trends: 1970-1979," *Lost Illusions*, 9-11.
2. *George Lucas: Creating an Empire: Biography*, DVD, produced by A & E Television Networks. (New York: A & E Home Video, 2002).
3. Judy Klemsrud, "Graffiti is the Story of His Life," *New York Times 123 (7 October 1973)*, sec 2, 1.
4. Ibid., sec 2, 13.
5. Dana White, *George Lucas*. Minneapolis: Learner Publications Company, 53.
6. Steven Farber. "George Lucas: The Stinky Kid Hits the Big Time," *Film Quarterly*, Spring, 1974, 8.
7. Ibid., 9.
8. Jameson, "Postmodernism and Consumer Society,"115-116.
9. Jameson, *Postmodernism, or the Cultural Logic of Late Capitalism*, 68.
10. Anne Friedberg, *Window Shopping: Cinema and the Postmodern* (Berkeley: University of California Press, 1993), 168.
11. Jameson, *Postmodernism*, 296.
12. Ibid., 21.
13. Fredric Jameson, "Nostalgia for the Present," *South Atlantic Quarterly* 88, no. 3, Autumn 1991, 303-323.
14. Friedberg, *Window Shopping*, 188.
15. Ibid..
16. *Mad Men*, "The Wheel." Prod. Matthew Weiner. American Movie Classics (AMC), New York. 18 Oct. 2007. Television.
17. Larry Sturhahn, "The Filming of American Graffiti," *Filmmakers Newsletter*, 7, no.5, March 1974, 22.
18. Marc Le Seur, "Theory Number Five: Anatomy of Nostalgia Films: Heritage and Methods," *Journal of Popular Film*, 6, no. 2, 1977, 193.
19. John Baxter, *Mythmaker*, 120.
20. Peter Biskind, *Easy Riders, Raging Bulls: How the Sex-Drugs-Rock'n'Roll Generation Saved Hollywood* (New York: Touchstone, 1998), 244. For a

similar version of the *American Graffiti* screening for the executives, see Michael Pye and Lynda Myles. *The Movie Brats: How The Film Generation Took Over Hollywood* (New York: Holt, Rinehart and Winston, 1979), 128; John Baxter. *Mythmaker: The Life and Work of George Lucas* (New York, Avon Books, 1999), 136.
21. David A. Cook, "The Film Generation," *The New American Cinema*, Jon Lewis, ed. (Durham, NC: Duke University Press, 1998), 20.
22. Michael Pye and Lynda Myles. *The Movie Brats: How The Film Generation Took Over Hollywood* (New York: Holt, Rinehart and Winston, 1979), 128.
23. John Baxter, *Mythmaker: The Life and Work of George Lucas* (New York: Avon Books, 1999), 141.
24. Earl C. Gottschalk, Jr., "The Spectaculars," *The Wall Street Journal*, 10 August 1974, 1.
25. David Cook, *Lost Illusions: American Cinema in the Shadow of Watergate and Vietnam, 1970-1979* (Berkeley: California University Press, 2000), 43.
26. Ibid., 43-44. As mentioned in earlier chapters of this book, with the collapse of the studio system after the Paramount Decree in 1948, the majors were forced to return to their original structure in which production, exhibition and distribution were all separated, yet financing and marketing remained concentrated in the major studios. Using *Jaws* as an example, one can see that much of its success can be attributed to Universal's savvy distribution and marketing strategies from which independent exhibitors reaped ticket sales of monumental and historic proportions.
27. Stephen Farber, "Hollywood's New Sensationalism: The Power and the Gory," *The New York Times*, 7 July 1974, sec. E., 1.
28. David Cook, *Lost Illusions, American Cinema in the Shadow of Watergate and Vietnam*, 26.
29. James P. Forkan, "Paramount Exec is Adman of Year," *Advertising Age*, January 8, 1979:S2, 1, and Gary Edgerton. "High Concept, Small Screen," *Journal of Popular Film and Television*, 1991 Fall: 114-127.
30. Justin Wyatt, *High Concept: Movies and Marketing in Hollywood* (Austin: University of Texas Press, 1994), 8. Also see Claudia Eller, "Katzenberg Memo: Rivals' Reactions Range from Accord to Scorn," *Variety*, 31 January 1991: 1.
31. J. Hoberman, "1975-1985: Ten Years That Shook the World," *American Film* (1985 June), 36.
32. Richard Schickel, *Irreconcilable Differences*, Time, 8 October 1984, 82.
33. Justin Wyatt, *High Concept: Movies and Marketing in Hollywood*, 8-11.

34. Will Tusher, "Schwarzenegger as the Tooth Fairy?" *Daily Variety*, 29 August 1991, 3.
35. Justin Wyatt, *High Concept: Movies and Marketing in Hollywood*, 8-11.
36. Ibid., 16.
37. Justin Wyatt and R. L. Rutsky, "High Concept: Abstracting the Postmodern," *Wide Angle* 10, no.4 (1988), 42.
38. It is interesting that this type of blockbuster thinking became especially rampant after the Yankelovich Report, commissioned by the MPAA in 1967, was published on industry marketing practices. This report concluded that without a tie-in with a familiar book or play, pre-release publicity did not help create public awareness. So conglomerates that owned a publishing house and a studio (or other means of communication) made the most of it. Good examples of this early use of "synergy" can be seen in the dealings of Paramount with Simon & Schuster through Gulf & Western; Universal with G.P. Putnam's Sons through MCA; Warner Bros. with Warner Books through Warner Communications, to name a few.
39. Alexander Doty, "Music Sells Movies: (Re) New (ed) Conservatism in Film Marketing," *Wide Angle* 10, no. 2 (1988): 72. Doty states, "Perhaps Hollywood's growing awareness of a large and wealthy 'youth market' finally led industry publicists to fully recognize the potential for music-and-movie exploitation implicit in the conglomerate entertainment networks."
40. Barbara Klinger. "Digressions at the Cinema: Reception and Mass Culture," *Cinema Journal 28*, no. 4 (1989): 14. Klinger argues, "Promotional categories will often tend to diversify the text by addressing several of its elements, including subject matter, stars, and style. But this particular type of inter-textual zone cannot be settled within the textual system; rather, it raids the text for features that can be accentuated and extended within its social appropriation." Klinger's raiding of the text is illustrated at the point when the fictional world of the high concept film reaches beyond the film itself and into the realm of the promotional music video, etc.
41. Justin Wyatt, *High Concept*, 46.
42. David Cook, *Lost Illusions: American Cinema in the Shadow of Watergate and Vietnam, 1970-1979*, 40.
43. Thomas Schatz, "The New Hollywood," Jim Collins et. al., eds., *Film Theory Goes to the Movies* (New York: Routledge, 1993), 17.

44. Stuart Byron, "First Annual Grosses Gloss," *Film Comment* 12, no. 2 (March-April 1976): 30.
45. Carl Gottlieb, *The Jaws Log*. New York: Dell, 1975, 15-19. This highly illustrated book takes a detailed look at the production of the film. The book was rushed into publication and print in 1975 as part of the *Jaws* extensive marketing campaign.
46. Stuart Byron, "First Annual Grosses Gloss," *Film Comment* 12, no. 2 (March-April 1976): 30.
47. Joseph McBride, *Steven Spielberg: A Biography* (New York: Simon & Schuster, 1997): 258.
48. A. D. Murphy, "1975 Record Film B.O. Nears $1.9-Bil: Variety Key City Grosses Up More Than 90 Percent," *Variety*, January 14, 1976, 1, 86; A.D. Murphy. "Universal Pics Make Film History: 1975 World Rentals at All-time High of $289-Mil," *Variety*, January 21, 1976, 1; and A.D. Murphy. "Universal's Whale of Pix Biz Share: Jaws Makes U No. 1 with 25 Percent Domestic Gross," *Variety*, February 11, 1976, 1. See also: David A. Cook, *Lost Illusions*, 43.
49. Thomas Schatz. "The New Hollywood," *Film Theory Goes to the Movies*, 16-17.
50. David Cook, *Lost Illusions: American Cinema in the Shadow of Watergate and Vietnam, 1970-1979*, 42-43.
51. Michael Pye, and Lynda Myles, *The Movie Brats: How the Film Generation Took Over Hollywood* (New York: Holt, Rinehart and Winston, 1979), 237.
52. David Cook, *Lost Illusions*, 43.
53. Peter Biskind, "The Young Lions: Raging Days, Boogie Nights," *Vanity Fair* (March 1998): 56.
54. Stuart Byron, "*The Searchers*: Cult Movie of the New Hollywood," *New York*, 5 March, 1979, 45.
55. Peter Biskind, "The Young Lions: Raging Days, Boogie Nights," *Vanity Fair*, 250.
56. Ibid., 252.
57. Ibid.
58. Coppola's last work as a "true" auteur was the legendary *Apocolypse Now* (1979).
59. Timothy Corrigan, "Auteurs and the New Hollywood," *The New American Cinema*, Jon Lewis, ed., 43.
60. Ibid., 44.
61. Peter Biskind, "The Young Lions: Raging Days, Boogie Nights," *Vanity Fair* (March 1998): 256.

62. Peter Biskind, "The Young Lions," *Vanity Fair*, 256.
63. David A. Cook, *Lost Illusions*, 64.
64. J. Hoberman, "1975-1985: Ten Years that Shook the World, *American Film*, Vol. X, no. 8 (June 1985): 42.
65. *Time*, 30 May 1977, 57-58.
66. Pye and Myles, *The Movie Brats*, 137.
67. Jane Feurer, "Reading Dynasty: Television and Reception Theory," *South Atlantic Quarterly*," 88, no. 2, Spring 1989, 446.
68. James Monaco. *American Film Now*. New York: Oxford University Press, 1979, 169.
69. Pye and Myles, *The Movie Brats*, 136.
70. George Morris, "George Lucas' *Star Wars*," *Take One*, July-August 1977, 9-10.
71. Terry Curtis Fox, "Star Drek," *Film Comment*, July-August 1977, 9.
72. Kenneth Von Gunden. *Postmodern Auteurs* (London: McFarland & Company, Inc., 1991), 76.
73. Stephen Schiff. "The Repeatable Experience," *Film Comment*, 18, no. 2, March-April 1982, 36.
74. Fredric Jameson, "Politics of Theory," *New German Critique* 33, Fall 1984, 54.
75. Interview with Michael Blake, child actor, makeup artist, biographer of Lon Chaney, December 10, 2002.
76. J. R. R. Tolkien. *Lord of the Rings*, collector's edition (New York: Houghton Mifflin, Co., 1974).
77. Joseph Campbell, *A Hero With A Thousand Faces* (New York: MJF Books, 1949), 181.
78. Ibid.
79. *Daily News*, "Towers" Break December Box Office Records," December 23, 2002, 1, 6.
80. John Baxter, *Mythmaker*, 146-147.
81. Michael Pye, and Lynda Myles, *The Movie Brats: How the Film Generation Took Over Hollywood*, 131.
82. Ibid., 133.
83. Aljean Harmetz, "Burden of Dreams: George Lucas," *George Lucas: Interviews* (Jackson: University Press of Mississippi, 1999), 143.
84. Ann Thompson, "George Lucas," *Premiere* 12, no. 9 (May 1999): 68.
85. Ibid.
86. J. Bruckner, "Joseph Campbell: 70 Years of Making Connections," *New York Times Book Reviews*, 18 December 1983, 27.

87. Ibid.
88. Joseph Campbell. *The Power of Myth*, with Bill Moyers, Betty Sue Flowers, ed. (New York: Doubleday, 1988).
89. David John, ed. *Star Wars: The Power of Myth*, New York: DK Publishing Limited, 1999, 5, 10-25.
90. Joseph Campbell, *A Hero with a Thousand Faces* (New York: MJF Books, 1949), 30.
91. Joseph Campbell, *Inner and Outer Reaches of Space: Metaphor as Myth and as Religion*, (New York: New World Library, 2002), 20.
92. Justin Wyatt, *High Concept*, 152.
93. James Surowiekie, "*Star Wars* Toy Story: A *Star Wars* Tale for Your Galaxy Enjoyment," *Slate*, 25 December 1989.
94. Stephen Sansweet, *Star Wars: From Concept to Screen to Collectible* (Chronicle Books: San Francisco,1992), 71.
95. John Baxter, *Mythmaker*, 178. Also see Garry Jenkins. *Empire Building: The Remarkable Real Life Story of Star Wars* (New York: Simon & Schuster, 1997).
96. Ibid., 181-182. For more on ILM's history see Mark Cotta Vaz and Patricia Rose Duignan. *Industrial Light + Magic: Into the Digital Realm* (New York: Ballantine, 1996).
97. Ibid., 174.
98. Stephen Sansweet, *Star Wars: From Concept to Screen to Collectible*, 14.
99. Stephen Sansweet, *Star Wars: From Concept to Screen to Collectible*, 56-57. Also see John Baxter, *Mythmaker*, 173-179.
100. Ibid., 57-58.
101. Ibid., 52-57.
102. John Baxter, Mythmaker, 264-265. The *Star Wars Holiday Special* TV show featured Chewy's family waiting for Chewie's arrival "home for the holidays." As Han and Chewy dodge Imperial Stormtroopers throughout the galaxy in the Millennium Falcon, Chewy's wife and his son, as well as his father check by video-phone (which oddly is in English, while the Wookies are clearly grunting in their own language) with Leia, Luke, and others, for news of his progress. The "special" is an odd mish-mash of 'comic' vignettes and strange additions that don't appear to have anything to do with the general program (For example, in one vignette Chewy's father gets a present, an odd mechanical hat looking thing that he places on his head, and in a few moments has a sexual fantasy/interlude about Diahann Carroll—very strange and a bit inappropriate for the intended audience). On the surface one won-

ders what motivated Lucas to give his stamp of authorial and corporate approval to this gaffe, especially in light of how protective he has been about *Star Wars* product. John Baxter is the first to broach the topic and explains that a TV production company, Smith-Hemion, approached Lucas with the suggestion for a *Star Wars* holiday special to air during the Thanksgiving weekend. Although Lucas was extremely busy with *Raiders of the Lost Ark*, he agreed to suggest a story, asked the stars from *Star Wars* to participate, attended some production meetings and produced script notes (to either add or delete scenes, dialogue, story, etc.). When Lucas saw the final product, he is said to have been horrified, but it was too late to stop the broadcast—though he did remove his name as screenwriter. When the program aired on November 17, 1978 reaction ranged from incredulous to appalled. It is reputed that Kenner killed their new line of Wookie figures and CBS never aired the special again. No history or filmography authorized by Lucas ever mentions it and Lucas won't permit the specials to be issued on video. Lucas has said, per John Baxter, if he had a hammer and enough time, he would smash everyone of the copies—and one could hardly blame him. Currently, it can only be had by buying a bootleg VHS copy off the internet. Wookies do not speak in any recognizable language, rather they express themselves in a series of grunts and groans. Keeping with the traditions of the original *Star Wars* this was what occurs through most of the two-hour program. How Harrison Ford, Carrie Fisher, Mark Hamill, including guest stars, Bea Arthur, Harvey Corman, Art Carney, Diahann Carroll, and Jefferson Starship, valiantly went through the paces required of them is a wonder.

Chapter 4

Building the Empire

From Auteur to Entrepreneur

Luke Skywalker: Master, moving stones around is one thing (raising an X-Wing Fighter from a swamp) is totally different.

Yoda: No! No different! Only different in your mind. You must unlearn what you have learned.

Luke: All right, I'll give it a try.

Yoda: No! Try not. Do. Or Do not. There is no try.
— The Empire Strikes Back

The entertainment business is impacting so many other parts of our economy today: It's driving traffic in fast food chains, it's selling toys, it's selling cars, it's selling sneakers. Consumers are making choices on everything from French fries to pajamas based on entertainment properties.
Michael Wolf, the Offices of Booz, Allen and Hamilton

It's all tied to one purpose: creating a stream of rights that may start off in motion picture theatres, then move to cable, network, off-network, and foreign; or might start in the legitimate theatre, or may go directly to cable. It doesn't matter where it ends up.

> The point is that we will own the software every one of those media needs.
> Michael Eisner (on Paramount's strategy for the 1980s)

> I'm beginning to impress even myself—and I don't like that.
> George Lucas, 1985

Probably the most significant phenomenon of *Star Wars* was its creation of the first true film franchise and with it the New Hollywood we experience today. Before *Star Wars,* studios were apt to give away merchandising rights in trade for free publicity and, even if they did become involved in licensing for profit, as was the case with *Jaws* and product tie-ins like T-shirts, etc., the products had little life or value apart from the film. Once the film was over, so followed the tie-ins. But after *Star Wars*—the "holy grail" of licensing—things changed and the merchandising of the film became an industry unto itself. Ironically, tie-ins and product marketing in the early 1980s, started to drive the concept and selling of the film rather than the opposite. Movies like *The Care Bears* (1985) and *My Little Pony* (1986), David Cook explains, were just a few of the many movies used to launch product lines—a practice that continues today (Barbie's *Rapunzel,* 2002, or the re-establishment of the 1980s Strawberry Shortcake franchise in 2003, and toy spin-offs, *Transformers* in 2007, and *Smurfs* in 2011, are perfect present day examples of a feature film made to sell toys; other toy manufacturers such as Lego, Play Doh and Hot Wheels are following suit).[1]

Other film series such as the *Star Wars* trilogy (1977-1983), *Star Trek* (1979-to present) and *Batman* (1989-present), *Indiana Jones* (1981-present), including the latest additions; eight *Harry Potter* installments (2001-2011), *Lord of the Rings* trilogy (2001, 2002, 2003), as well as *The Hobbit series* (2012, 2013, 2014), and *Spiderman* (2002-present), including all Marvel Comic hero films (*The Avengers, Thor, Iron Man,* X-Men, etc.), are huge product franchises whose branded merchandise is worth many billions of dollars in excess of box office sales. The perfect franchise, *Star Wars* reached $1.3 billion in box office sales by 1997, while video sales and rentals accounted for $500 million, CD-ROM and video games sales accounted for $300 million, clothes and accessories for another $300 million, books and comics for an additional $300 million and toys and playing cards accounted for another $1.21 billion.[2] James Sterngold suggests that, "franchises have life cycles that must be carefully tended and shrewdly planned."[3] Disney, in particular, was one studio that heeded that advice.

While all the rage during the late 1970s to mid-1980s, the *Star Wars* franchise began to lose momentum from a lack of novelty and nurturing, but it took off again with a vengeance by 1991 when Timothy Zahn's next-generation best-seller, *Heirs to the Empire*, introduced the franchise to a whole new generation that had never seen the original trilogy in the theaters. The book generated multiple best-selling sequels and kept fan interest alive until 1997 when the digitally changed "*Star Wars Special Edition*" trilogy hit the theatres and sparked excitement over the franchise once again. This "Special Edition" also paved the way for the launching of the all new *Star Wars* trilogy at the millennium, beginning with *The Phantom Menace* (1999), then *The Attack of the Clones* (2002), soon followed by *Revenge of the Sith* (2005). Both the "Special Edition" and the *Phantom Menace* made millions while being lauded by the *New York Times* who viewed this licensing strategy as, "one of the most impressive and tautly engineered pieces of marketing prowess ever conceived, as well as an example of what the movie industry has become: art in service of a huge commercial superstructure that needs constant feeding."[4] (Lucas recognized that the small screen is no less important than the big and likewise could use some feeding. *The Clone Wars*, one of TV's most highly-ranked and watched animated TV series, further refreshed the *Star Wars* franchise in 2008, and followed suit.)

By the time the above quote was written by the *Times* in 1997, it had become clear that throughout the 1980s merchandising had risen from the category of ancillary income to become an important, if not necessary, studio revenue stream, and that all the major studios operated huge consumer-product divisions.[5] Over the past twenty or so years, two studios in particular profited from this franchise mentality—Disney and Warner Bros. And while the *Star Wars* films have all been distributed by Twentieth Century Fox, Fox has not traditionally been known for exploiting a film franchise whereas both Disney and Warner Bros. have. (Perhaps this is due to the fact that Lucas owns most, if not all the rights to the franchise, and Fox has never found another film product to exploit in this same way.) For this reason, it is worth the short digression to take a look at the success of these studios to examine how their fortunes have progressed in the post-*Star Wars* environment via the blockbuster-scale film and the resultant media franchise.

The trademark Disney franchise is, hands down, the animated feature. Oddly enough, this was not the case during the mid-eighties when "Team Disney" took over the helm (Wells, Katzenburg, Eisner et al.). While Disney was cranking out a few successful live action films (*Down and Out in Beverly Hills*, 1986; *The Color of Money*, 1986; and *Ruthless People*, 1986), there had been no animated hit in years. Katzenburg was on a mission to reestablish the animated feature as Disney's signature product and establish these "signatures" as successful and revenue-producing franchises. In just a few years, by 1988, the animation department at Disney had grown from 150 to over 700 employees, had produced the seminal animation/live action feature, *Who Framed Roger Rabbit?*, a fully animated feature, *The Fox and the Hound*, and released a successful reissue of the classic *Bambi* (1942). Disney's first real animated hit came with *The Little Mermaid* (1989) and from that point forward reveled in blockbuster hit after hit with both its new animated features and classic reissues: *The Jungle Book* (reissue 1990), *Beauty and the Beast* (1991), *Aladdin* (1992), *Snow White and the Seven Dwarfs* (reissue 1993), *The Lion King* (1994), *Pocahontas* (1995), *Toy Story* (1995), *The Hunchback of Notre Dame* (1996), etc. These signature pieces continued well into the early 2000s, but after Katzenburg left the fold to establish Dreamworks, the animated feature at Disney has experienced less monumental successes.

Building the Empire 141

As an example, one of the first releases from Disney after Katzenburg's departure, *Treasure Planet* (2002), bombed terribly at the box office (cost $140 million to make and only returned $34.7 gross domestic between November 2002 and January 2003—a huge disappointment) and forced Disney to show a year end loss—a loss that clearly was felt all along the synergy food chain. The bomb also cost the president of Disney's animation feature film division to lose his job and be relocated within the Disney machine, (since that time the Disney animated feature experienced a comeback), but during the 1980s and 1990s, these animated features helped create a Disney sensation.[6] *Variety* states in 1993:

> While filmed entertainment accounts for approximately thirty-five percent of Disney's total operating income, Chairman Michael Eisner readily acknowledges that the animation division drives the entire company—providing rides for theme parks, products for the merchandizing division, even inspiration for the logo for Disney's new hockey team, the *Mighty Ducks*.[7] [although the *Mighty Ducks* was a live action film].

Along these same lines, Disney used another interesting franchise strategy in 1996 by producing a live-action version of its 1961 animated hit, *101 Dalmatians*—winning both huge box office dollars and a profitable product line that produced over 17,000 related *Dalmatian* items.

Warner Bros. on the other hand, specialized in the lone-hero, action adventure formula—most notably Clint Eastwood and Mel Gibson vehicles, whose enduring association with that particular studio almost makes them a New Hollywood equivalent to the contract stars of the old system.[8] Both have headed up familiar Warner film series—Eastwood with the *Dirty Harry* films and Westerns, Gibson with the *Lethal Weapon* films (considered franchises unto themselves). Although vital to Warner's success, these stars and their film series do not come close to the importance of its signature franchises—*Batman* (1990s), *Harry Potter* (2001-present), or *Lord of the Rings* (2001, 2002, 2003).[9] Corie Brown noted in *Premiere*:

> Warners is the studio that *Batman* built. Not only did the $250 million grosser create the billion dollar *Batman* industry, it inspired Semel and Daly to create the worldwide chain of Warner retail stores, as well as give a boost to the long-dormant animation division. Semel states in the article, "The first picture that blew us out was *Batman* . . . It was the first time we utilized the whole machine of the company. The marketing, the tie-ins, the merchandising, the international." [10]

The success of the *Batman* franchise, during this time, like that of *Star Wars*, is almost incalculable, considering the amazing range of related products generated since the 1989 series resurrection. The film brought in $250 million domestically, $160 million internationally, $180 million in videocassette sales and generated over a half-billion dollars in worldwide merchandising. Not bad for a day's work. The sequel, *Batman Returns*, was a box office hit, but a merchandising disappointment. Its poor ancillary afterlife was attributed to a variety of factors: a darker story, lack of identification or interest in the unsympathetic Penguin antagonist, and Michael Keaton's grim portrayal of *Batman*. Based on the low merchandising numbers, Warner Bros. decided to "lighten up" the next series/franchise installment, *Batman Forever*, and replaced the director, the hero, and centered the story and merchandising campaign on Jim Carrey's Riddler—what many considered a more upbeat type of nemesis. Clearly a move based on merchandising possibilities rather than solid filmmaking. Fortunately or not, the *Batman* series redesign was a success. *Batman Forever* grossed $185 million domestic and $150 million international, and was a merchandising bonanza. According to the head of Warner Bros. consumer products division, Dan Romanelli, *Batman Forever* generated over $1 billion in licensing and tie-ins. In 1996, the *New York Times* reported that Batman merchandise had earned over $4 billion.[11] A current refresh of the Batman franchise beginning in 2005 with *Batman Begins* starring Christian Bale (*The Dark Knight*, 2008; *The Dark Knight Rises*, 2012) has also struck gold and returned a big profit to the studio. Since 2001, The *Harry Potter* franchise has proved just as lucrative, if not more so, for Warner Bros.

The 1996 revenue figure for *Batman* did not include the Batman-related theme-park rides—another tie-in. A good example of this "synergy" happened in May 1992, when Six Flags (half-owned at the time by Time-Warner) unveiled "Batman—The Ride" to coincide with the opening of *Batman Returns*. Six Flags then introduced another ride, "The Joker's Revenge," in 1996 to coincide with the next in the series, *Batman Forever*.

Home video and the success of *Batman* in that format further illustrates the market penetration of the franchise and the importance of the film "library" (so cavalierly given away for nothing just twenty to thirty years before). Both Disney and Warner Bros. have dominated the field but have done so utilizing very different strategies. Thomas Schatz, states:

> While *Batman* set an industry standard as a "sell-through" (versus rental) videotape with just over ten million units sold, it was actually an exception for Warner's, which has preferred rental over sell-through—thus maintaining the value of its own library rather than the 'home libraries' of consumers. Disney pioneered the sell-through strategy, retailing its animated franchise hits on cassette via its Buena Vista Home Video arm, with both reissues and new titles breaking one sales record after another. In 1993, for instance, *Aladdin* sold 10.6 million copies in only its first three days, en-route to a record total of twenty-four million; and in 1994 *Snow White and the Seven Dwarfs* surpassed that total, generating over $300 million in home-video revenues.[12]

As impressive as the *Batman* franchise has been, *Harry Potter* as franchise has gone above and beyond culminating in the opening of Universal/Warner Bros. Orlando's theme-park, *The Wizarding World of Harry Potter, Hogsmeade* on July 18, 2010 and then, Diagon Alley on July 8, 2014 (replete with full scale replicas of Hogwarts, Hogsmeade, Diagon Alley, The Forbidden Forest, and other HP fare), which only whetted the appetite for the release of the final Harry Potter film installments in 2010 (*Harry Potter and the Deathly Hallows, Part I*) and 2011 *(Harry*

Potter and the Deathly Hallows, Part 2). Throughout it all, Time-Warner has continued to concentrate on beefing up its own library, with the TBS merger in 1996 adding over 3,500 new feature film titles to the Warner Bros. title holdings of roughly 1,100—pushing total titles in their library far beyond those held by other majors and mini-majors.

As an aside, in 1996, Turner led the field in number of library titles (3,522), followed by Universal (3,101), Sony (2,327), Fox (2,077), Orion (1,986), MGM/UA (1,523), Warner Bros. (1,102), Paramount (908) and Disney (548). Of the 1,100+ titles that Warner Bros. does hold in its own right are vintage *Looney Tunes* shorts (Bugs Bunny, Daffy Duck, Road Runner, Elmer Fudd, etc.) which have, through the years, enjoyed amazing success in syndication—their shelf life may even make them some of the most valuable of the Warner Bros. franchises (despite the demise a few years back of the Warner Bros. merchandising stores featuring these characters). In 1996, for example, total revenues of merchandise related to Warner Bros.' *Looney Tunes* reached over $3.5 billion.[13]

All these revenue figures just underscore the importance of merchandising and product licensing as a function of the healthy franchise—which may be the single most significant development in the New Hollywood brought about by the business-savvy Lucas and the success of *Star Wars*. By the mid-1990s, worldwide retail sales of all licensed products surpassed $100 billion for the first time ever; roughly 70 percent of that business was done in the USA. Sales of only the entertainment-related merchandise in 1995 was estimated to near $28 billion, or one-third of all sales worldwide.[14]

But the benefit to the media conglomerates does not end here. Besides producing these enormous revenues, merchandising and product licensing helped to forge brand-name identity, product differentiation and awareness, with hundreds of thousands of licensed products branding not only the film, but the studio as well. Tie-ins usually can be counted on to ignite more rapid and efficient expansion into foreign markets and can lead to highly-visible joint ventures with high-profile corporations—from fast food giants to toy and video game manufacturers. When dealing with the fast food kings, promotional and financial benefits are substantial and worth noting. Burger King's deal with Disney for *Toy Story* in 1995 was worth an estimated $45 million in ads and other promos.

The success Disney has enjoyed in licensing and merchandising encouraged Michael Eisner to develop the Disney-owned chain of retail stores—playing shrewdly another aspect of the consumer products division. The move was not a real stretch for Eisner, not very surprising considering both the synergy-related and economic benefits of the studios selling their own entertainment-related products. The first such retail store opened in 1987 in Glendale, California. It was a huge success and in four years Disney expanded the chain to 50 retail outlets—outwardly competing with its licensees for what *Business Week* touted as a "$2 billion U. S. market for Disney knick-knacks."[15] Throughout the rest of the 1990s and to the present day, Disney has continued to expand its global reach and number of retail chain stores with a lucrative return. Building on this entertainment-related product theme, in 2001, Downtown Disney "shoppertainment centers" were added outside each Disney park in California and Florida where people could, without paying for an entry ticket, shop, dine or enjoy a variety of Disney sanctioned entertainments. In 2013, Downtown Disney Florida began an extensive remodel from "downtown" to "small town,"—completing the shopping-entertainment--reality evolution that morphs the "shopping store" into a "fabricated downtown," then expands the "fabricated downtown" even more into an "idealized small town" where one can "live" and find gratification, entertainment, even love, not via human relationships with other people, but rather, by the purchase of the product of your choice.

The amazing importance of the studios' retail chains and consumer products division cannot be stressed enough, the ultimate objective being the ability to blur the boundaries and distinction between shopping (consuming) and entertainment and create, in *Variety's* own words, "theme–park-style gift shops."[16] Whatever the studio's product inventory, the inventory must be kept in perpetual renewal requiring more and more blockbuster hits to fuel the franchise machine. With the spiraling costs of production, this requires that more and more money be spent on production and marketing costs, driving the "risk-reward" quotient steadily higher. In 1990, the average film cost roughly $28.8 million to produce (an average cost of 169 major studio productions) with an additional $11.6 million needed for marketing (prints and ads), by 1995 the average cost rose to $36.4 million (average of 212 productions), with $17.7 million for marketing, pushing the total cost per feature over $50 million.[17] (Today's figures are much higher, closer to $80-$100 million or more.)

The ability to exploit a variety of media outlets has helped insulate the studios against potential box office disappointments. The higher the production costs, including skyrocketing above-the-line fees for talent, etc., the higher the need to recoup spent revenues. Many argue that because conglomerates are so diversified and so much money can be made in a variety of markets under the parent company umbrella, that it is difficult to consider that any film can actually lose money these days. While in many cases, this is true, and a well played hand in diversified ancillary markets can stave off the creditors (as was the case with the disastrous *Waterworld* in 1995 or *Last Action Hero* in 1993), allowing flops to earn out their investments when studios take advantage of first-money revenues and licensing fees, etc. (such as in selling of TV, foreign and video rights, etc), it nevertheless causes a very noticeable hiccup (if not a strong shudder) along the synergy chain. While diversification can be seen as a tool to hedge a bet, it can also help to hurt the parent company as well. For instance, *Treasure Planet* (2002), was the first animated film by Disney to really do poorly at the box office in years. Because the film cost over $100 million to make and brought in a fraction of that at the box office, Disney was forced to post a year-end loss since they were faced with a deficit in projected revenues—not only at home—but across *all* ancillary markets.

The highly successful *Lilo & Stitch* (2002) helped pay many of the debts and loss of revenues incurred by *Treasure Planet*, but even that was not been enough to recoup the lost ancillary revenues or cost of, and lack of interest, in what has been dubbed Eisner's folly, *Disney's California Adventure*. All indicators suggest that Disney needs the "boost." Disney had been under fire for diluting the programming of ABC and making poor decisions that helped push the network toward the brink of bankruptcy. In 2003, Disney was under scrutiny for an internal memo sent to ABC executives ordering that all products must come from Disney, period. All independent producers were let go that were not Disney affiliated, further insuring a blander programming diet. Both the dictates of the memo and lack of independent talent are a case of synergy gone awry. At the same time, Disney was also reportedly ordered to pay over $20 million for tax fraud and evasion, which clearly called into question Eisner's position as CEO at the "House of Mouse" helm.[18]

Probably one of the best examples of synergy that did not work (or an example of a business trying to create synergies that were never there), according to Stephen Prince in his book, *A New Pot of Hollywood Gold: Hollywood Under the Electronic Rainbow: 1980-1989*, occurred when Coca-Cola purchased Columbia pictures for $692 million in June 1982.[19] The link between movies and sodas was weak at best. By contrast, synergies between publishing, recorded music, broadcast and cable television that are part and parcel of Time-Warner or that between News Corp. and Fox are certainly stronger. These types of mergers in the late 1970s and early 1980s and beyond connected groups of information and entertainment media that could be used to easily cross-promote one another's products (e.g., *Batman* as film, book, record and soundtrack, T-shirt, music video, graphic novel, and comic strip, etc.). Soda pop, on the other hand, is not a recognized form of media. Any way you look at it, it would prove difficult to establish any type of synergies between Coke's soft drink operations and its newly acquired entertainment business sector (owners suggested synergy to stockholders via metaphor, not market—"We believe that the thirst we quench is no greater than the thirst for entertainment.").

Throughout the 1980s, Columbia never attained a leading market share position and stumbled greatly in poor project (*Ishtar*) and management choices (David Puttnam). By the end of the decade, Coke sold Columbia to Sony Corp. (where synergy was better realized) having decided to focus on global soft drink leadership—something it understood best.[20]

Ad-buys in the 1980s accounted for $1.94 billion—an astounding increase of 107 percent over a five-year period and have only increased in the ensuing years. Disney more than any other capitalized on ad-buys, and was highly criticized for spending so much. But studio head, Joe Roth, dismissed such thinking as narrow minded, "You can't think of advertising in terms of domestic theatrical films alone," he said, "A major studio spends to stimulate all of the revenue streams, from merchandising to video to theme parks . . . . To not see the strategy of release dates and ways to create event advertising as weapons sometimes equal to the movie idea is missing the point."[21]

FROM CORPORATIONS TO CONGLOMERATES: SYNERGY, SOFTWARE AND THE "SURE THING"

> I took the money I'd made from *Star Wars* and popped it into *The Empire Strikes Back*, and the money from *Empire* into *Return of the Jedi*. Each film has paid for the next.
>
> George Lucas

Stephen Prince points out that the movie business made a radical shift by the end of the 1970s and its product underwent a substantial, and far-reaching transformation whose implications were still being worked out decades later. As a result, Hollywood ceased operating as a film industry and film stopped being its primary product. Instead of making movies, the industry shifted to the production of "filmed entertainment" –an enterprise that encompassed production and the distribution of filmed entertainment in a variety of different markets and media. "Film both became and still was not a film in the sense that the audience might go

Building the Empire

and see *Raiders of the Lost Ark* which was a film, but might also play a "Raiders" video game or go on the ride at Disneyland, which was not."[22]

Until the 1980s, the question brought up by Stephen Prince in his book and posed by film critic and theorist, Andre Bazin, "What is cinema?" and a second question, " Where is cinema?" could both be answered in relatively simple terms. Bazin celebrated cinema for its ability to exactly reproduce the world on the screen. He believed that a film's specificity resides completely in its ability to catch the light rays bouncing off the world into the camera lens and freeze time. The photograph becomes and is the physical trace of the actual object represented.[23] Ergo, for many, cinema could be defined as something that was screened, viewed by an audience, and reflected the world in which we lived. Before the 1980s, this definition held true. Cinema could be described as something someone saw in a theatre or on television. Cinema was celluloid and movies were consumed in a specific and restricted set of locales. Hollywood was in the movie business and produced readily identifiable products. Typically then, an individual could study the industry by examining the film product and the companies and the studios, generally, that produced it. This type of study generally required no conceptual ambiguity regarding the parameters that defined the object and the study. In the 1980s, the game rules changed. Not only did the home video market (which became a virtual sell-through gold mine) and the licensing operations change the playing field, but also the proliferation of non-theatrical markets and their effect on the industry and its operations. Home video, a small burgeoning market in the 1970s, exploded during the 1980s, and cable TV, pay cable, and pay-per-view joined it in broadening the venues and formats for entertainment production and distribution. Actual celluloid "film" became confined to use in theatrical venues, and in all other markets, vanished. Video soon replaced the use of film (or became combined with the use of film) in all phases of filmmaking production—especially in areas of post-production (e.g., editing, pan and scan, telecine, etc.). Ironically, film studios soon found themselves in the position of making films for ever-expanding video markets.

As the business of film changed so did the filmmaking art. The movement from film to video and the markets where video proliferated (the small screen), also impacted the aesthetics of the medium and films that were shot in 1:85 ratio for the big screen soon found themselves subject to panning and scanning with adaptation to the smaller screen and aspect ratio (1:33), in many ways, brutalizing the carefully constructed colored and timed image. Some filmmakers embraced the smaller ratio and soon took up setting up shots that would eventually play best on the small screen (e.g., heavy use of close-ups, rapid MTV montage, etc); overall film stylistically seemed to be moving in that direction anyway (perhaps due again to the increase of television viewing). Home viewers quickly traded the aesthetically enriching film viewing experience at a theater for the ease of watching films on video at home—helping with the boom in the home video market. Film became degraded as something "special" and was soon identified by the viewing public as video itself ("Let's go pick up a film"). Film became video.

According to Stephen Prince, the 1980s stand as a seminal decade. Prince suggests that,

> The scale and legacy of the industry's changes make this decade comparable in significance to the other two transforming events in the history of American film, the coming of sound in the late 1920 and the industry's loss of its theatres in the late 1940s. Each of these earlier events defined a before and an after for the film industry... The eighties branded the industry in a comparable fashion, taking it away from film and toward filmed entertainment, changing the corporate structure and affiliations of the companies producing filmed entertainment, and setting the industry on a course toward globalization and a new oligarchy of planetary media titans.[24]

Prior to the 1980s, the studios had affiliated with large parent corporations, but overall many of these companies tended to operate a diverse set of business segments that were for the most part unrelated. Gulf and Western Industries who owned Paramount was a perfect example of this type of old-school conglomerate—having business segments in such

Building the Empire

unrelated areas as sugar harvesting, oil, automobile replacement parts and movies. While the studios remained under the umbrella of parent companies and conglomerates in the 1980s amid a wave of mergers and acquisitions, the structure of the conglomerates underwent a radical sea change in order to survive. Film studios ended up in the hands of global media and communication giants where synergy was the name of the game.

These changes in the consolidation of media and communications conglomerates in the industry have been far-reaching, and have bled into the 1990s and beyond with a series of large mergers that wed media programmers (a more apt word for "film studios" today) with strong distribution venues. For instance, in the mid-1990s Viacom purchased Paramount Communications for $10 billion and then bought up Blockbuster Entertainment, a national video rental chain of approximately 3,000 stores. The reason for such strategic merger maneuvers has been to control and exploit the many hybrid markets for entertainment programming. Viacom is now in a position to use a particular property and get the most mileage out of it that it can possibly get. Viacom can take a popular film character and generate a tremendous amount of revenue by marketing the product as a movie (Paramount), a cable presentation (*Showtime, The Movie Channel*), a book (*Simon and Schuster*), or a comic book/graphic novel, a video rental (*Blockbuster*), a Broadway musical, a theme park ride (*Paramount*), a T-shirt, or a video game.

The next year, 1995, Walt Disney Company bought ABC/Capital Cities for $18.5 billion—wedding a content provider to a national television network, an acquisition that gave Disney/ABC an amazing distribution system for programming. This acquisition gave Disney access to 80 percent of the sports network ESPN, twenty radio stations, eight television stations, a radio network, foreign television operations, seven daily newspapers, thirty-four weekly newspapers, and a wide assortment of special-interest publications (only lacking a partridge in a pear tree, which would come almost 20 years later with the acquisition of Marvel

Comics and Lucasfilm, Ltd.). The same year Time-Warner and Turner Broadcasting agreed to merge their combined operations, putting Time-Warner in charge of an even larger media empire, including: Warner Bros., HBO (film and TV production), and Turner's Castle Rock Entertainment, New Line Cinema and Cable News Network, CNN International, Headline News, TNT, WTBS and Turner Classic Movies (and one wonders how television news has become big entertainment). Jon Lewis notes "To understand how the companies themselves view this new Hollywood, consider...[company] references to 'profound political and economic changes,' ostensibly referring to Reaganomics and deregulation... and the conspicuous omission—the conspicuous irrelevance—of such outmoded 'old Hollywood' notions as divestiture and free trade." [25] The excerpt below from the 1989 Annual Report of (newly formed) conglomerate Time-Warner supports Lewis's keen observational claim:

> In the 1980s, we [Time, Inc. and Warner Communications, Inc.] witnessed the most profound political and economic changes since the end of the Second World War. As these changes unfolded, Time, Inc., and Warner Communications, Inc., came independently to the same fundamental conclusion: globalization was rapidly evolving from a prophecy to a fact of life. No serious competitor could hope for any long-term success unless, building on a secure home base, it achieved a major presence in all of the world's important markets. With this goal in mind, Time and Warner began discussions on joint ventures. The more we talked—the more we learned about each other—the more obvious it became that the most significant and exciting possibility was a synthesis that would lift us to a position neither could achieve alone. In a season of history when technology has combined with political and social change to open vast new markets, we are a company equipped to reap the greatest benefits.[26]

"The merger of Time and Warner," Lewis continues, "took shape at the moment of record prosperity in Hollywood; the entertainment business had become an increasingly well-integrated, federal regulation (FCC, FTC and Justice Department interference) had been all but eliminated, and everyone who could afford to make a product was making money. It is important to look at the Time Warner merger neither as an isolated event, nor as a landmark deal later aped by other companies. Instead, the merger should be viewed in light of the larger picture of this newest of New Hollywood's, one in which Time Warner was a logical consequence."[27]

Likewise, Rupert Murdock's Fox News Corp. continued to grow into a huge film, television and publishing giant. In 1996, with its acquisition of New World Communications, the media giant owned and operated twenty-two stations in the top 10 markets, making it the biggest and most competitive TV station owner in the entire nation.

Lucas began to do a little entrepreneurial work of his own and founded no less than eight companies after the successes of *Star Wars* under the Lucasfilm, Ltd. banner. These included: ILM, Skywalker Sound, THX, Lucasfilm Licensing, Lucas Digital, and LucasArts Entertainment Company, Lucas Games and LucasLearning (which specialize in interactive games, special effects, merchandising and licensing, educational multi-media, new digital technologies, creative sound design, just to name a few). Even Steven Spielberg refers to himself as an independent moviemaker working within the Hollywood establishment. After the success of *E. T.*, Spielberg was quick to found his own production company, Amblin, and strike a deal with Universal for space on the lot, a few years later, while retaining his hold on the production company. Spielberg also co-developed (with some of Hollywood's biggest power brokers), DreamWorks, SKG—Hollywood's newest mini-major (later purchased by Paramount Studios for $1.6 billion in 2005). Both the careers of these mini-moguls in and of themselves indicate just how much the movie industry had changed by the beginning of the 1980s.

During the decade, not all mergers produced a series of synergy winners. As mentioned earlier, Coca-Cola should have stuck to soft drinks and stayed away from movies. Likewise, Matsushita (who could not get a handle on what was happening in the New Hollywood) caused more problems than provided solutions with its acquisition of MCA/

Universal. Uninterested in media expansion and acquisitions, MCA/Universal's parent company put a quick end to discussions centered on purchasing CBS in partnership with ITT. Ergo, when Matsushita sold the MCA/Universal to Seagram's the same year (1995), the studio did not have a national television distribution system in place—putting the studio at a complete disadvantage in comparison to other more savvy content providers that controlled a multitude of distribution systems. The purchase of MCA/Universal by Seagram's was equally disastrous. [28] All these developments are part and parcel of the transformational processes that began in the 1980s, so that now the question of "What is cinema?" as well as "Where is cinema?" is much harder to define since Lucas appeared on the filmmaking scene. Theatres where cinema was primarily viewed are but a small part of a variety of interlocking markets. Film is the software that feeds these markets and rationalizes their existence.[29]

Nothing takes place in a vacuum, so it should come as no surprise that the "merger-mania" that redefined the studios was a subset of larger structural changes

in the U. S. economy. Prince is quick to point out that what was happening in Hollywood was an economic trend affecting a large range of American businesses nationwide. In the 1980s, the U. S. economy witnessed the longest sustained period of merger-acquisitions activity in history—hitting a grand total of 31,105 transactions carrying a dollar value of $1.34 trillion.[30] Merger-acquisitions was nothing new to the U. S. business landscape. What was new was a corporate willingness to use that type of business activity strategically, and implement long-range business plans, instead of as a tool for use in exceptional circumstances.

Mergers and acquisitions would no longer be handled as a hit or miss or temporary phenomenon brought about by short-run economic and financial influences that over time did not pan out. Rewards were too lucrative, the advantages too compelling, the techniques too strategically viable for the modern wheeler-dealer to drop the ball. To support this business atmosphere, a new infrastructure appeared consisting of law

Building the Empire 155

firms, investment bankers, financial analysts, accountants, strategic planners, etc., whose time and full resources were spent on merger and acquisition operations. Buyers understood that big revenues lay in booming entertainment markets and that the newest and most lucrative growth sectors would be in the information industries.

In all of this, media industries stood out and became the third most active industry segment from 1980 to 1989 and the second most attractive industry for foreign buyers (an attraction that highly impacted the Hollywood studios). Rupert Murdoch described the interest and strategic shift from businesses geared toward extraction of raw materials to those that created and processed information:

> We are witnessing the beginning of the transition from the industrial society, in which wealth was created by processing raw materials, to an information society, in which wealth creation will depend on the processing of information...a golden age will come to those countries which turn this wealth of information into knowledge effectively .... Movies are global media ... I am sure that the global top league will basically consist of five or six very large media companies.[31]

Because the flow of this type of information is global, the planet became the new market. By the end of the 1980s, foreign markets accounted for more than 50 percent of all sales, News Corp., Ltd., Time, Inc., Sony and Matsushita, became the media giants that gobbled up whole film studios and coupled film production and distribution with their other information-based operations, helping to transform the industry forever and create the boom in theatrical exhibition that accompanied it.[32]

Although already discussed briefly on an aesthetic level, the home video market, on a different level—that of exhibition—impacted the industry the most. Of all the various ancillary markets that blossomed during the 1980s, including cable television, pay-per-view, pay cable and home video, home video grew to be the most instrumental in changing the general public's viewing habits and its relationship with film as well as the revenue streams which were returned to the studios and, thereafter, the parent companies.

Home video was the last place the studios expected a windfall. If anything they were concerned about piracy and the public's interest in purchasing a tape that would be placed in a video library for repeated viewings. (But who would want to do that, the studios thought, especially at the price originally offered, around $80 a video?) Studio heads wrestled with the prospect of home viewers making copies of their films at no additional charge. As it stood, rental viewers could see the film as many times as they would like before returning it or paying additional rental fees. Economics and logistics just did not seem right to generate revenue in the home video market. Once a tape was sold to a national (or international) wholesaler and they in turn sold it to retailers, the studios did not see a dime from the rental of that tape to home viewers.

The studios, disgruntled with the rental market, took a different tack and took the plunge into the "sell-though" market where they controlled direct sales of videos to consumers. Not until 1982 did this become a viable market. With the cost of videos hovering around $80-$90 per title, there were not many buyers. Only when Paramount discounted the price to $39.99 for *Star Trek II* did the videos start to sell—generating sales of over 100,000 tapes. Paramount led the field in this area, discounted prices even more, and in just a few years were selling hundreds of thousands of videos in the sell-through market. *Raiders of the Lost Ark* (1981), for instance, in the fall of 1983, posted initial unit sales of 420,000, which translated into a high retail gross of $30 million dollars. It was not long that sell through videos which were gobbled up by consumers were used in other ways to generate revenue. *Top Gun* (1986) was the first of many blockbusters to carry commercial sponsorship (Diet Pepsi). The commercial was shot using characters of the film and retained *Top Gun's* aesthetic style, helping sell both commodities. Commercials and film became indistinguishable from one another—an interesting point in fact. By the end of the decade, although troublesome as a rental, home video in its sell-through capacity easily emerged as the most important of ancillary markets.[33] Pay cable was a major source of revenue, pay-per-view (the expected gold mine) less so, but home video was hands-down the biggest revenue generator of them all by the end of the decade. Pay television (all licensing of films for pay-cable presentation) and sell-through home video outpaced film revenues taken from theatrical exhibition alone.

Interestingly enough, the wave of mergers and acquisitions during this time also led to a de-conglomeration of many of the companies who were too diversified and needed to divest themselves with unrelated market segments (or business areas) to better concentrate on related areas of production and further mergers and acquisitions. Wall Street supported this move toward divestiture and production concentration and synergy by penalizing the stock prices of firms that it believed were over diversified. Financial analysts were quick to denounce a company that had too many financial operations underneath its umbrella that were considered incompatible with the company's primary business orientation. The de-conglomeration of Gulf & Western Industries into Paramount Communications, Inc. in the late 1980s is a perfect example. G & W changed its name to PCI, Inc. and was restructured into a more rational and focused enterprise with a clearer sense of mission, direction and purpose.

The Rise of the Talent Agency

While all the mergers and acquisitions, divestitures and economic as well as cultural changes in the U. S. were going on in the 1980s, something else was happening to change the face of the film industry and impact it for years to come. Since the late 1950s and 1960s, with the demise of the contract system, Hollywood lost command of its in-house talent—from leading ladies to writers and grips. By 1980, no studio had on contract such a wide array of talent and craftsmen. The studios, as discussed in earlier chapters, now functioned as distributors, producers and financiers of films who were forced to find talent "for hire." But to get to the talent, the studios were required to work with talent agencies that had, over the years, grown tremendously in power and status. The biggest and most powerful of these agencies were by far Creative Artists Agency (CAA), the William Morris Agency and International Creative Management (ICM). These big three agencies comprised a virtual cartel. Sue Mengers, one of the most powerful agents during the 1970s, was coaxed out of retirement in the 1980s to take advantage of the new climate in Hollywood in order to head up William Morris. She put it most succinctly, saying, "Right now agents have more power than the studios. Studios need the agents because the agents are the major suppliers of talent and material . . . . What used to drive us crazy is that we would work very hard to help put a picture together and then the picture would be finished, there would be a preview, and we would be told that no agents were allowed."[34]

During the 1980s, you could be sure that agents, now taken seriously as important industry players, were one of the first to be invited to any party, preview or early film development discussion. By controlling talent, agents soon came close to controlling the business. Studios were no longer the center of film production they once were—a notion completely antithetical to the studio's efforts to consolidate and control the power of filmmaking through mergers and acquisitions. As deal making became a fundamental part of the filmmaking process and the amount of people who were making deals increased, so did the decentralization of the industry.

The clearest indication that the respect and awe given agents and managers was real was in the corporation's willingness to hand over coveted top studio executive posts to many of them. The studios valued people who knew talent and could acquire talent and had the ability to package and market it. These skills were part and parcel of the business of filmmaking and the move of agents to the executive studio suites was a natural. Ergo, the paradox of the 1980s, Stephen Prince explains,

> ...the agents got films made, and the majors attempted to recoup this ability by hiring agents to help [fill] top executive positions.

Building the Empire 159

> But from the standpoint of talent, the majors were on the outside and were forced to compete for the services they needed in order to get product to fund their distribution arms.... And the top stars, directors, and writers found that their greatest profit potential came from NOT aligning themselves with the majors."[35]

Indeed, talent during this decade forward profited nicely and so did their agents. The power shift that had been going on since the anti-trust suits had been filed in the late 1940s came full circle in the 1980s. Even while inflation ran rampant during this decade, salaries of talent increased at an alarming rate (stars could guarantee box office). Stars who had commanded fees of less than a million dollars just a few years prior, with the help of their agents who also profited at 10 percent, were soon getting often up to twenty times that amount. George Lucas in the late 1970s pointed out,

> We are the pigs ... We are the ones who sniff out the truffles. You can put us on a leash, keep us under control. But we are the guys who dig out the gold. The man in the executive tower cannot do that. The studios are corporations now, the men who run them are bureaucrats. They know as much about making movies as a banker does. They know about making deals like a real estate agent. They obey corporate law; each man asks himself how any decision will affect his job. They go to parties and they hire people who know people. But the power lies with us—the ones who actually know how to make movies.[36]

Studio executives cowed by the need for talent, the power held by the agencies and the belief that blockbuster films required to be made for high-costs in order to return high revenues, took the bait and bit—hook, line and sinker. The executives knew that a good "package" (star, director and writer), especially a well-known international star, helped pre-sell the film product and helped to guarantee its successes at both the domestic and foreign box office (including all other ancillary markets). So in many cases, although spiraling talent fees certainly contributed greatly to an upward pressure on the costs of doing business, it was considered a good way of hedging your bet and an acceptable form of business practice in the industry.

Although the biggest changes in the 1980s occurred within the business structure of the industry, other changes also took place in the political area, in the films that were produced, and the ways they were produced as well as the filmmakers who actually made them.

The Lucas-Spielberg Phenomenon/Syndrome

> *Star Wars* swept all the chips off the table.
> William Friedkin cited by John Baxter, *Mythmaker*

> I don't know if I'd put the blame on us [for creating a blockbuster mentality], but I'd put the blame on us for developing the super-high-charged movie. One of the things we tapped into—not just Steven and I, but our whole 1960s generation—is that we didn't come from an intellectual generation. We came from a visceral generation. We enjoyed the emotional highs we got from movies and realized that you could crank up the adrenaline to a level way beyond what people were doing when they treated film as a more literary medium.
> George Lucas, cited by Goldstein, *LA Times Magazine*, "The Force Never Left Him," 2 February 1997

> The victory of the Reagan agenda changed everything in America and by as early as 1982 had also changed the very nature of Hollywood films.
> William Palmer, The Films of the Eighties

Lucas and Spielberg have been both glorified and demonized (sometimes by the same people) for their part in helping make Hollywood what it is today. Glorified, because in many ways, they single-handedly revitalized the industry and breathed life into a Hollywood that had fallen on hard times. Vilified, because while revitalizing the industry, they also helped—many believe—push the industry toward the commercial to the detriment of the aesthetic. Admittedly, filmmaking has always walked a fine line between art and commerce. Although "art" is what the business produces, it is difficult to get away from the fact that filmmaking is, and always has been, a business. Big budgets, blockbuster box office numbers, and the movement from studio to conglomerate coupled with the materialistic, big business, laissez-faire era of Reaganism can take the lion's share of blame (or credit, depending upon what side of the artistic/money ledger you are on) for this corporate movement toward fascination with a "bottom line" and big revenue numbers. The conglomeration of Hollywood, as discussed previously, is to "blame," if indeed, any blame is to be given. Lucas and Spielberg just happened to make what the corporations wanted—money, and the blockbuster promised the biggest payday. It is interesting that the artists have been demonized while the corporations go unscathed. Perhaps it is easier to point a finger at a person than a corporation. Lucas and Spielberg never forced the populace to buy one ticket. They only made the type of films that the public wanted. Nothing happens in a vacuum, so to say Lucas and Spielberg are to "blame" for this trend is to ignore culture, history, and American business practices.

By the time the 1980s came to a close and blockbusters were firmly entrenched in the system, it was clear that power had moved from director to producer (manager/agent) as supervision of film production tightened. Filmmakers who could put on a "suit" and function as both director and "creative" producer more easily navigated the New Hollywood waters.

When Reagan came into office in the 1980s, he ushered in an era of conservatism that emphasized reassurance and "sure bets," an environment of low risk with all the promise he would make us "feel good about being an American." This turn from the raging liberalism of the 1960s in the United States to a more conservative set of ideological and moral belief systems had been going on for some time and was easily personified in the Reagan presidency. Hollywood, being the societal compass that it is, gradually took the more conservative approach to filmmaking.

From the delivery of *Jaws* forward—during a time when conglomerates and businessmen took control of Hollywood, the commercially viable movie naturally took precedence over the creative film. A more materialistic emphasis, stimulated by Reaganomics, seemed to, in many cases, overshadow older standards of critical taste and social consciousness. Not surprisingly, the producer versus the director, in many cases, took over the media spotlight. The 1980s, more than any other decade, was a seminal film decade of commercial performance, a "yuppie" decade, where status was judged almost exclusively in materialistic terms. Whereas the generation of the 1960s can be classified as "shapers," the generation of the 1980s are better classified as "shoppers." The most prominent icon in the films of the 1980s is probably the shopping mall.

However, a growing cynicism toward government and politicians that appeared to operate with a wink and a nod ("Just don't get caught"), was eventually mirrored by a cynicism that began to appear in American films. This cynicism took shape, interestingly enough, on a national fixation with materialism exemplified in the "yuppie" phenomenon. This fixation with materialism could also be seen in Hollywood's approach to film. As one critic put it in 1984, "In Hollywood, truth is measured in box-office receipts."[37] Film critics and movie executives alike became more and more enchanted by box-office numbers (as were the "yuppified" American materialistically driven audience). Industry players used these numbers as marketing tools to generate business and exploited them for all they were worth—and they were worth a lot. According to *The Economist* "between 1984 and 1988 the average cost of making a film soared from $14.5 million to $20.7 million. By 1989, the blockbuster *Batman* cost over $75 million to make and eventually grossed ten times that much."[38] By 1989, Hollywood was a $5 billion industry (and by December 2002, that figure radically rose to $9 billion, and by December 2010, to $10.68 billion, with no sign of diminishing anytime soon). [39]

During most of the 1980s and into the 1990s, a basic conservative political agenda was the status quo, reinforced by the Gulf War. Many critics during this period remarked on how the Reagan administration and the blockbuster films of Lucas and Spielberg played off of one another. (The escapism of Lucas and Spielberg equated to wanting to see "feel good films" and the Reaganomic political escapism of the day translated to "It feels good to be an American.") While this may be true in some sense, it is certainly not true in others. While many critics and supporters would like to give Lucas and Spielberg, et al. the credit (or blame) in helping to support the Reagan presidential agenda, it would be just as silly to suggest Reagan be blamed (take credit), or is solely responsible for the move toward blockbuster films. Films released during this time period, such as *First Blood* (1982) or its sequel, *Rambo: First Blood Part II* (1985), rather than either those of Lucas or Spielberg, would appear to more readily support the Reagan administration's political interests. Other "conservative" films like *Top Gun* (1986) were created, not for any political reasons, but in response to the studio's desire for high-concept blockbuster product and software.

Even though the film industry reflected a more conservative mood during the 1980s, and looked for marketable projects based on presold reputations, there was still a dearth of diverse and thought-provoking films made by a cadre of exciting new directing talent that did not so easily fit this conservative bill *(e.g.,* the "slasher" films, controversial films like *Cruising* and *Last Temptation of Christ*, or independent fare such as *Mishima*). New ancillary markets, the home video market in particular, helped sell films that might otherwise be considered box office flops, lessening the pressure on some filmmakers to produce blockbusters, allowing less costly and spectacular films to play a role in the overall market. The proliferation of ancillary markets most certainly allowed new directors, such as Oliver Stone et al., to gain notice making "small" films (read: small budget, small audience, small concept, etc.) that a decade earlier might never have been produced and seen the light of day. This group of new directors included, the Cohen brothers, Paul Schrader, Jim Jarmusch, David Lynch, Tim Burton, John Sayles, Paul Schrader and others. Smaller, artistic and controversial films, which dealt with politically hot issues, were also getting made as well.

William Palmer in his book, *The Films of the Eighties* points out that, "The films of the eighties portrayed a post-Vietnam War world attempting to disengage from its recent troubled past while at the same time attempting to overcome its own cynicism and find some hope for the future." [40] During this time other major threats, including the looming possibility of nuclear war and rampant global terrorism, were also strongly felt as part of the 80s experience. While American films consistently explored these various international issues, "they also were quick to focus the lens on local social issues, such as the farm crisis, racism, the society's expanding gender consciousness, and the rise of the yuppie materialistic ethic." [41] Films which embodied these concerns, suggest Palmer, included: "*Ragtime* (1981), *A Soldier's Story* (1984), *A Passage to India* (1984), *Betrayed* (1988), *Alien Nation* (1988), *Mississippi Burning* (1989), *Who Framed Roger Rabbit?* (1989), *Do the Right Thing* (1989)--racism—or apartheid—as in *Cry Freedom* (1987), *A Dry White Season* (1989), and even *Lethal Weapon II* (1989)—or the corruption and violence beneath the surface of small-town American life—as in *Body Heat* (1981), *Gremlins* (1984), *Blood Simple* (1984), *Witness* (1985), *At Close Range* (1986), *Blue Velvet* (1986), *Betrayed* (1988)—were also examined in clusters of eighties films." [42]

The auteurs, however, that had established their careers in the previous decade, Francis Ford Coppola included, did not fare as well as the newer (artistic) directors who found a niche in the New Hollywood system. Viewed with some trepidation since the failure of *Heaven's Gate* and the studio that made it (UA), auteurs were persona non grata in the industry. They were generally scorned or brought on-board with some concern. (As an aside, John Sayles' picture, *The Return of The Secaucus Seven* in 1980 made for $125,000, $60,000 of it Sayles' own money, was held up as an outstanding example of independent and artistic thriftiness. The distributor, Specialty Films and Libra Films, marketed this film as the antithesis of *Heaven's Gate* whose bloated, auteur driven budget had killed a studio and showcased "auteurism run amok.") Most struggled throughout the decade to find financing and many of the 1970s auteurs found their careers had stalled in the upbeat, concept-based, blockbuster, bottom-line driven New Hollywood of the 1980s. These included Robert Altman, Peter Bogdanovich, Brian De Palma, and Martin Scorsese.

A bleak, cynical film like John Carpenter's *The Thing* that laid bare the social milieu of the times, did not have a chance against Spielberg's *E. T.* which opened the same weekend. Coppola, the last of the true auteurs, fared no better.[43] *Apocalypse Now* (1979), budgeted at $12 million, was what might be considered a cursed production. Crewmembers fell ill, natural disasters and a multitude of other far-reaching and expense problems, eventually tripled the film's cost. Probably one of the greatest war (and anti-war) films ever produced, its brilliance was countered by a myriad of flaws. It did not matter that the film was nominated for eight Academy Awards and received two, or that it shared the Palme d'Or at Cannes, *Apocalypse* was considered by many as an outstanding example of auteuristic hubris and folly. The film damaged Coppola's standing in the New Hollywood community and helped push the economic dominos in a direction (e.g., demise of American Zoetrope, box office flop of *One From the Heart*, etc.) that ended in Coppola becoming just one more Hollywood director for hire. Like many other 1970s auteurs who hit upon hard times in the 1980s, Coppola (like Altman, for instance, with *The Player* (1992)), found redemption in the 1990s. His stylized *Bram Stoker's Dracula* (1992), which came in on time and under budget, grossed a whopping $200 million and brought Coppola back into favor. Coppola's artistic and creative ability was able to shine through the film triumphantly even with the "constraints" of the blockbuster system. Coppola's talent as auteur was never more evident. Of all the early auteurs, only Woody Allen, continued to be somewhat successful (likely due to choice of material, audience appeal and choice of small, low-budget films).

For the most part, though, genres and "sequels" filled the bill and masked the turmoil bubbling just below the filmmaking surface brought about by so many mergers and acquisitions. Studios would rather see a good idea go stale, than try to come up with another surprise hit out of nowhere. Sequels were the perfect, low-risk project for the studios, which were now owned by large conglomerates—the result being an increased pressure to produce a profitable film slate. Sequels—the tried and true models of filmmaking—also brought a sense of stability to the free-floating chaos that permeated the decade, therefore, genre and sequel production out-paced and out-sold all other films during the 1980s. Sequels made up a large part of the decade. If it worked once, then it would work twice ... maybe even three times or more (a mantra Lucas would strategically follow—particularly in the 1990s and into the 2000s with first his "New Edition" release of the original newly digitized version of the *Star Wars Trilogy* and his "Prequels"). Lucas was ready for the onslaught of sequels, having negotiated all sequel rights away from Fox at the *Star Wars* contract table and put up his own money (from *Star Wars*) along with bank financing, for the production of *Return of the Jedi* (1983) as well as *The Empire Strikes Back* a few years later. Both were huge successes, and with the money made from *Jedi*, Lucas financed Skywalker Ranch—one of the largest post-production facilities in the world. Other noteworthy blockbuster sequels of the decade included, *Superman II, III* (1981, 1983), *For Your Eyes Only* (1981), *Rocky III, IV* (1982, 1985), *Star Trek II, III, IV* (1982, 1984, 1986), *Staying Alive* (1983), *Indiana Jones and the Temple of Doom* (1984), *Indiana Jones and the Last Crusade* (1989), *Rambo: First Blood II* (1985), *Police Academy 2* (1985), *Karate Kid II* (1986), *Aliens* (1986), *Beverly Hills Cop II* (1987), *Crocodile Dundee II* (1988), *Lethal Weapon 2* (1989), *Back to the Future, Pt II* (1989), *Ghostbusters II* (1989). The trend in sequels has not diminished, in fact it may have increased due to a need for large conglomerates during recent decades, like AOL Time Warner, Viacom, ABC/Disney, and Vivendi, to produce profitable film slates. [44]

For example, in 2002 "sequel-mania" titles read like this: *Return to Neverland* (2/15/02), *The Scorpion King* (4/19/02), *Jason X* (4/26/02), *Star Wars: Episode II—Attack of the Clones* (5/16/02), *The Sum of All Fears* (5/31/02), *Men in Black II* (7/03/02), *Halloween: Resurrection* (7/19/02), *Stuart Little 2* (7/19/02), *Austin Powers in Goldmember* (7/26/02), *Spy Kids 2: Island of Lost Dreams* (8/07/02), *Santa Claus 2* (11/1/02), *Harry Potter and the Chamber of Secrets* (11/15/02), *Die Another Day* (11/22/02), *The Friday After Next* (11/27/02), *Analyze That* (12/06/02), *Lord of the Rings: Two Towers* (12/18/02), *Star Trek: Nemesis* (4th quarter '02). The *Cinema Editor's* Fall 2002 issue has emblazoned across its front cover, "Year of the Sequel: More Money Was Spent on Sequels in 2002 Than Ever Before in Movie History: What's the Story Behind Hollywood's Love Affair With Second Acts?"[45] The *LA Daily News* touts the 2003 film 'line up' along these lines, "studios have stacked 2003 release schedules with so many sequels, remakes and films based on well-known characters that at least matching last years record $9.4 billion box office take is a strong possibility . . . . This years coming schedule is very much like 2002's . . . . The sequels are easier to market and looking at what we know is out there, we should at least pass the $9 billion mark again." Sequels continued to thrive in 2003 and into the decade, and included such titles as, *X-Men 2, Charlie's Angels: Full Throttle, Bad Boys 2, Fast and the Furious 2, American Wedding, T3: Rise of the Machines, Matrix Reloaded, Legally Blonde 2: Red, White and Blonde, Jeeper Creepers 2, Spy Kids 3, Lara Croft: Tomb Raider: The Cradle of Life,* and *Fellowship of the King.* [46]

The most popular genre during the 1980s, and no surprise here, was fantasy/science fiction. To date, the 1980s were the most high-tech of decades and its films, especially in the area of fantasy and science fiction, embrace the 1980's love affair with machines and with it an increased interest in machines over people. The genre was dominated by the highly technical, mega-blockbusters of George Lucas and Steven Spielberg, including *The Empire Strikes Back* (1980), *E. T.: The Extraterrestrial* (1982), *Return of the Jedi* (1983), all of which spawned many other lesser films that featured video game styles, emphasized space battles, featured new to the screen "cool" special effects, used fast-paced narratives and comic book and movie serial type of characters. In all, these films and this genre in particular, helped herald a new wave of films which could showcase the early applications of computer animation, sound and overall digital effects which are certainly evident today.

Sound especially came into its own during the decade, and Lucas was at the forefront of this technological improvement.[47] With the birth of the THX sound system pioneered by Lucas, which provided exhibitors with the ultimate theatre sound system (especially when wedded to Dolby Stereo), theatre owners learned that they could use the upgrade for marketing, guaranteeing a nice revenue return on their initial investments. Appropriately, Lucas rolled out the system with the release of *Return of the Jedi* (1983) heightening the credibility and physicality of the visual effects, thereby giving audiences a "bigger bang for their buck" and a much more enjoyable film "ride." As such, Lucas is one of the only filmmakers in film history to specifically create and pioneer technology specially tailored to enhance the narrative of his own movie (sound and visual effects), and thus, the viewing and cinematic experience. Action-Adventure films likewise benefited from the new technology and were also some of the highest revenue generators during the 1980s. The joint efforts of Lucas-Spielberg on the *Indiana Jones* trilogy, serves as one particularly good example.

Dystopic science fiction also led the pack and worked in stark contrast to the Lucas-Spielberg "feel good" fantasies. Taking the policies of Reaganomics to a pessimistic end result, these dark portrayals of the future helped to balance the overt optimism of the fantasy blockbusters and challenged the viewer to hold up the mirror to see what, without much effort, we could become. These films included the seminal *Blade Runner* (1982), *Alien* (1979), *The Terminator* (1984), *Robocop* (1987) and *Total Recall* (1990). Dominant symbolic motifs of this period portrayed a society or a family under imminent threat, and nowhere does this motif ring more true than in these dystopic commentaries (recall Sandra Connor in *Terminator II* looking at the playground, dressed as the archetypal mother ala 1950s, unable to protect the children who are melted by the impact of a nuclear bomb as she stands by—helpless in her attempt to do anything). Palmer suggests,

> If in the films of the seventies nothing was ever what it seemed to be, in the films of the eighties everything is simply out of control, and the world is fiercely struggling to stave off chaos. If in the seventies, political thrillers were most worried about corruption and cover-up within America's domestic government and corporate institutions, in the 1980s those films are most worried about the chaos of the wide world from which America had always held itself aloof intruding upon our previously safe domestic life.[48]

Other genres were present during the decade, but did not fare as well. Gangster films were one of these. Westerns had lost their mythic allure (and were relegated to the small screen in abundance where they prospered) except when placed in outer space as was *Star Wars*. (As noted previously, many elements of Ford's *The Searchers* can be found in *Star Wars*—such as a kidnapped girl {Leia}, two men who search for her, one experienced, the other naïve {Han and Luke}, a fearsome tribe with a vicious leader who raids and kills {the Empire and Darth Vader}, and a pair of comical characters who help find the girl {C3PO and R2D2})[49]

In relation to the films of Spielberg and Lucas, the rest of the playing field was filled with a wide array of films that focused on current issues and hot 1980s topics (e.g., the farm crisis, Vietnam war, cold war, yuppieism and growing materialism, gender issues and concerns, etc.), including issues relevant to the international stage that dealt with problems centering on worldwide terrorism exported from Iran, Libya, South America, even Russia, which threatened to violate the safe boundaries of the continental U. S., thereby helping to further plant seeds of paranoia in American society. Independents were seen in abundance and provided filmgoers with a choice at the theatres and at home, the direct opposite of what many critics have previously written of the era.

Many of these independents and more mainstream films provided a moral battleground over issues of film censorship (regarding sex, violence, etc.). The struggles over film censorship were fierce—a virtual tug of war between the conservatives, the New Right and the liberal Left—fracturing American culture into divided, hostile groups, clearly evident even today. Stephen Prince points out, "Thus, New Right political activity during the 1980s expressed anxieties over the state of American culture and society, anxieties rooted in the perception of a growing adversarial culture whose constituents—radical students, women's rights, gays, bohemian artists and intellectuals—were seen as threats to their own values and preferred norms of social authority."[50] Indeed, the greatest threat to film censorship may continue to resurface in the forms of censorship from outside the industry.

It has been observed that Hollywood often appears to be in the business of "an endless exploration of the dreams, wishes and growing pains" of teenage children."[51] Some critics at the time implied that Spielberg and Lucas were in the same business. Reagan even observed that modern day secularism was throwing away the tried and time-tested values upon which American civilization was based (i.e,, small business, small government and local communities organized around a sense of family and church). In line with this thinking, films that were made during this time that did not portray America and Americans in this more conservative light often came under fire.[52] Not always running blatantly counter to this vision, Lucas and Spielberg's films and those of other noted blockbuster filmmakers did, however, carry a subtle criticism in a parody and irony of the prevailing culture via themes, characters, or plots.

Through it all, Spielberg and Lucas solidified a foothold in American culture and business and personally profited in the meantime. They also, for right or wrong, acted as catalysts for change not only in the business practices of the industry (e.g., high concept, blockbuster syndrome, merchandizing, proliferation of ancillary markets, strengthening of conglomerates through streamlining de-conglomeration to handle synergy opportunities, etc.), but filmmaking, in general.

Many critics discuss the impact of Lucas and Spielberg as a product of the Reagan era which stressed reassurance and the status quo. And while that kind of alliance does hold true in some cases, the train had already left the station in others (As mentioned a few pages back, Reagan cannot, to reiterate the obvious, nor can Lucas/Spielberg take all the credit or blame for every or all filmmaking choices that have fallen into practice over the past twenty or so years—many perhaps, but certainly not all.) Rather than set up a "bad guy" antagonist in this drama, what we need to do is look at how filmmaking changed during this period and to what effect.

Reassurance, inarguably, is a keynote of the period as well as a return to sequels and recognizable genres—which to a large extent, were reworked to reflect the mood of the audience. On one level, one could argue that this need for reassurance organically came from the corporate need for "software" that could guarantee a synergistic return of revenue. On the other, if the audience were not looking for such reassurance, they would not buy the tickets. Both pressures were working in the system. Lucas and Spielberg were savvy enough to tap the needs of the film-going audience (and those of the conglomerates) and produce product both needed and wanted. Lucas was quick to notice that films of the 1960s-1970s (bleak, pessimistic, "real") had not only stripped filmmaking of any "sure thing" (e.g., a recognizable genre that is easy to sell), but also had helped to intensify the effects of Vietnam, Watergate, etc., further promoting a sense of malaise, angst, and anxiety throughout the American culture.

Harkening back to the old myths, Lucas borrowed heavily from them and wrapped them in a recognizable genre for easy public consumption. And with some revolutionary special effects thrown in for good measure, *Star Wars* became a real ride away from the past and a hyperspace jump into the future (both real and imaginary). The films had everything people were looking for: (1) definable and likeable heroes; (2) recognizable genres (albeit pastiche); (3) magic and spectacle; (4) special effects that transformed the world, allowed a new way of seeing things; and a coming of age story replete with all the mythic characters and trials and tribulations that confirmed its existence—and ours. People were given a reason, a hope and a path to pursue that allowed good to triumph over evil; black and white values in a very gray world. Many, if not most, during the late 1970s and throughout the 1980s, and into 2000, responded to such a tale.

Reassurance and "believing it will make it so" type of magical thinking may have been at the root of many audience members repeat viewings, but the reasons vary. Some did like the reassurance repetition brought, but others were entranced by the special effects (another form of primitive magic), spectacle and a new way of seeing things. The rapid montage, although edited as such by Lucas to admittedly cover up a few flawed special effects, allowed the viewers to see and feel things differently on a visual/visceral level. In the past, you might have watched *Flash Gordon* in his space ship and imagined experiencing the flight, but until *Star Wars* you had never actually experienced on a visual and auditory level what it might have felt like to be in the seat, the driving force behind the ship. Lucas expanded, compressed and recombined components of space and time to suit his needs—jarring the audience into experiencing a film differently. The close-up and slicing and dicing of space and time also forces the view, and specifically forces the viewer to see what they are allowed to see (the cliff-hanger narrative likewise forces attention). Nowhere is there time to reflect or breathe. Lucas's new THX sound system served to amplify the experience. Along with space and time, *Star Wars* introduced, or reinforced, the mixing of genre and the building of pastiche and bricolage—all symptoms of the postmodern experience. First one narrative/genre is referenced, then another, then another still —each combination and recombination of the old creating something new, always changing, never stagnant, an endless recyclable return— an endless shell game—furthering the tension on the screen and in the viewer. Interestingly enough, this became the predominate style from the 1980s forward, predating MTV's use of the quick montage, close up, and slicing and dicing of time and space. David Bordwell points out,

> During the 1970s and 1980s, norms of faster cutting and more fluid, close up camera movement made complex staging within the shot a rare choice. In a sense, the mug-shot solution reinforced that tendency, reducing staging to an even more simplified lateral arrangement than was seen in the early wide-screen films.[53]

Recently, with the introduction of the *Lord of the Rings* trilogy, have we seen a change in style so that now viewers are allowed wide shots of sweeping vistas and spectacular depth of field view (more reminiscent of the John Ford westerns of the 1950s and 1960s). The viewer is allowed to take it all in and appreciate the far-reaching expanse and vastness of the Tolkien world (and impact of the characters involved in it), a rare treat these days where all the films look the same—a video game played on a big screen. (Use of wider angles and composition within the frame versus a fragmented, illusory reality of timely close-ups and chopped up body parts point more to an original or referent rather than a constructed reality, and presupposes both the absence and presence of what is, was or could be. It gives the viewer more of a sense of history and identity.)

One must keep in mind, though, that not only did Lucas "slice and dice," but while touching on the original un-distilled myths, Lucas also borrowed bits and pieces from reworked fairy tales, old cliff-hangers, serials, and the like. This postmodern practice of borrowing bits and pieces from the past and reconstituting or "frankensteining" them into something else may have helped to start the trend toward derivativeness that continues today. Currently, films are copying a film derived from *Star Wars* that was derived from *Buck Rogers* that may have been derived from Grimm that may have been derived from Homer, which may have been derived from a more primitive original myth. In all these copies and translations which have been glued together with references from other stories, the original gradually gets lost and can be replaced with something seemingly "less than," or in some cases, like *Star Wars*, create something completely new, fresh and original. Perhaps, and more than one person has said it, repeat viewing of a film is due to the viewers need to find some "thing" that is not there, or something they feel they have "lost" in their own lives. Viewers play out an endless return to find the "lost object" (call it a what you will, a search for origins, the breast, the *object petit a*, *The Holy Grail*, etc.), but in all the copies cannot hope to ever find it—yet continue to search nonetheless since all the indicators point toward finally finding "it." Like Twinkies, the search brings pleasure, but does not fill you up or give you what you need. It does not truly satisfy, only promises.

Then, of course, there is the two more practical explanations mentioned before: Effects were layered so heavily that it required three or four viewings to see everything that was happening on the screen. But probably the most practical reason for repeat viewing points to a new exhibition practice of "clearing out the theatre" after each screening. Prior to *Star Wars,* folks could stay and watch a film as many times as they wanted. No longer. Now you had to pay every time you wanted to see the film. The original "lines" which then and now signaled an "event," (lines which are reenacted today by fans, incidentally) were in many cases, just people who wanted to see the film again but were required to pay again to view it. After one paid a few times, once could chat with co-liner-uppers and talk *Star Wars* and brag about how many times they had seen the film ("I've seen it 10 times".... "Oh, yeah?! Well, I've seen it 12 times!"—and so on.). Soon a sense of *Star Wars* community was built (similar to the Trekkers, the Tolkien fans in the 1960s and1970s, then again in 1990s and 2000s along side thousands of Harry Potter fans), which in turn, boosted sales of tickets and all forms of merchandising.

Besides, the *Star Wars* trilogy and other films of the 1980s were fun to see. Period. Because they were fun to see, some thought they were childish and not worthy of critical examination. One could argue both, "yes" and "no." There is no denying *Star Wars* is escapist and pleasurable entertainment and this pleasure is probably one of the strongest components of the Lucas/Spielberg Phenomenon/Syndrome. It was made in reaction to other "heavier" films that focused on social issues and hot topics of the day. A viewer can only see so many "heavy" films filled with un-likeable characters (e.g., drunk, violent, angry, depressed, confused, abusive people) until they become weary of such a weighty diet. Cinema has always been a place of escapism, a place where one can get away from the dreary constraints of everyday living and pretend to be something other than what you are and take on the guise of another, imagine a "once upon a time-ness"—out of place, out of time, out of self. Escapism can be liberating and allow us to dream of something better in ourselves and in our world. Rather than running "from" it may in fact be you are running "toward" self-reflection and identification (as in any mythic quest). The journey on the screen may parallel a journey of the self. It may only be a problem of semantics. Exchange the negative escapism with 'creative play' and our critical understanding of the film changes.

But by whatever name, not all view these type of films favorably. Robin Wood is not the first to suggest (nor the last to argue) that films that construct one like a child are inherently disturbing. Wood states,

> The category of children's films has of course always existed. The 1980s variant is the curious and disturbing phenomenon of children's films conceived and marketed largely for adults—films that construct the adult spectator as a child, or, more precisely, as a childish adult, an adult who would like to be a child. The child loses him/herself in the fantasy, accepting the illusion; the childish adult both does and does not, simultaneously. The characteristic response to *E. T.* (heard, with variants over and over again) was "Wasn't it wonderful?" followed instantly by a nervous apologetic. "But of course it's pure fantasy"...That the apology (after all, the merest statement of the obvious) has to be made at all testifies to the completeness of the surrender on another level of indulgence.

Wood goes on to say,

> certain problems arise in discussing (and attacking) the films. It is, in fact, particularly difficult to discuss them seriously. The films themselves set up a deliberate resistance: they are so insistently not serious, so knowing about their own escapist fantasy/pure entertainment nature, and they consistently invite the audience's complicity in this. To raise serious objections to them is to run the risk of looking a fool (they're "just entertainment," after all) or, worse, a spoilsport (they're "such fun").[54]

Wood is aware here of the film's use of parody, yet is not fully appreciative of its many other elements. During this period, the critical reception given Lucas, Spielberg and other "fun" films of the 1980s runs completely counter to public sentiment. It could be that these critics were still steeped in a more formalist approach (like Wood). It is as if the more popular the film, the more distrustful and dismissive the critics became and have continued to be. True, these films do evoke an uncomplicated range of emotions and sentiments and do synthesize the classical/modern/postmodern elements, while endorsing old-Hollywood virtues that stress a delight in an economical, easy to follow kind of storytelling. There is emotional immediacy followed by irony and a joy of filmmaking that is both enthusiastic and upbeat.

It is a present day fairytale set "a long time ago, in a galaxy far, far away" that promises the happily ever after. It has all the neat gizmos and gimmicks of the future along with all the conventions of the cinema's past (sinister nobles, outlaw saloons, brave knights, narrow escapes and dashing flyboys). It makes us feel a longing for the unnamable thing that is always being lost, but promises that, as we push toward our future, we will be able to figure out a way to get it back. Again, the audience responded enthusiastically on every count, and, yet again, this response by the popular audience provoked just the opposite response in critics who unapologetically overlooked the many merits of the films (and not just overlooked, as with a lack of nominations by the Academy, but outwardly denounced). So why does the pleasure of Lucas/Spielberg films cause such a divide and provoke such unrest?

Agreed, the pleasure these films give do seem to reconstruct the viewer as a child and with their familiar narrative patterns and classical invisible editing do seem to lead one by the hand through a world fraught with fears and terrors ("Will s/he make it?), promising to see you home safely to a familiar place, where you are happy, loved and rewarded. These films may even reinforce the "good ol' values" of our capitalistic society, warts and all, but it also reinforces the belief that you can make it in a hostile world—good will triumph over evil, wrongs will be set right and ultimately punished. Perhaps we need to be reconstructed as a child from time-to-time in order to remember what it is like to believe in one's self as a parent does a child—to trust in ourselves. This reconstruction while perhaps reinforcing a patronizing patriarchy that suggests, "Daddy will take care of you" also presupposes an adult who believes in you, supports your actions, and wants you to succeed.

Star Wars, like many of the other films of the 1980s, has this internal conflict that balances the social impact of the 1950s–1970s and undercuts the authority of the reigning patriarchy (Evil Empire) with the promise of a more tolerant and accepting "father law" (the New Republic). This set up and tension (reinforcing the status quo while exposing its dark underbelly) does not allow the viewer to complacently go into that dark night where regression to the womb is complete.

On the downside, this "false" narrative which is fed directly to the viewer in many other films (outside of the *Star Wars* canon), may cover the fact that there really is nothing to say—merely do—covering up a lack of true story and narrative—where daring-do or blow 'em up takes the place of meaningful dialogue or personal interaction. This perceived lack of imagination, replaced by faculty of invention, can be used to cover up originality (of plot, etc.) that reinforces the "old patriarchal" rule and ideologies. The construction as a child coupled with a strong genre in some of the 1980s films (most notably in the films of Steven Spielberg) may be credited with helping to overcome the fear or helplessness or chaos that many grappled with during the decade brought about by the cold war, free-floating nuclear anxiety, and the social upheavals of the previous twenty years. Wood argues this "Don't worry, you can't do anything anyway" hopelessness versus reassurance syndrome helped lull society into a false sense of security and ultimately acts as a deterrent to any useful action (e.g., the antagonist of *Raiders*, a more sophisticated, older father type, keeps stealing Indy's "toy." Indy eventually prevails, but it takes a powerful artifact—the Ark of the Covenant--to help him do it. The viewers of this "good/bad" struggle who are not super-human heroes therefore conclude, "If Indy has such a tough time .... What can I possibly do to make a change?"). And Lucas has argued these many positive points, as I have done here, against any type of negative criticism. But what both Lucas and Wood as well as many others at the time had neglected to consider is how history and a sense of self is structured through an understanding and relationship with time and space. When time and space are changed—sliced and diced/expanded and compressed —for example, the viewer's understanding of the world cannot but be changed as well. But these stylistic changes were occurring culturally years and years before Lucas thought of *Star Wars*.

Certainly, there is nothing inherently wrong with pleasure for pleasure's sake and cinema certainly helps fill the bill. The problem occurs when it is taken to extremes on the screen, or in society. Robin Wood sums up the *Star Wars* "project" as something that "puts us back in our place, reconstructs us as dependent children, and reassures us that it will all come out right in the end; Trust Father."[55] And the controversy rages on and on and on.

LUCAS AND SPIELBERG: A MOVE TOWARD DIGITAL

Lucas and Spielberg capitalized on their box office hits in the 1980s and 1990s as did other influential directors (and director/producer teams), including: Don Simpson and Jerry Bruckheimer, John Hughes, John Landis, Jon Peters and Peter Guber and Robert Zemeckis.

Steven Spielberg, the most prolific during the period, directed no less than seven films, including: *Raiders of the Lost Ark* (1981), *E. T.: The Extra-Terrestrial* (1983), *Indiana Jones and the Temple of Doom* (1984), a segment of *Twilight Zone: The Movie* (1983), *The Color Purple* (1987), *Empire of the Sun* (1987), *Always* (1989), *Indiana Jones and the Last Crusade* (1989). As a producer he was just as prolific with 17 films to his credit, giving boosts to the careers of Joe Dante, Lawrence Kasdan and Robert Zemeckis. Films included: *Used Cars* (1980), *Continental Divide* (1981), *Poltergeist* (1982), *Twilight Zone: The Movie* (1983), *Gremlins* (1984), *Young Sherlock Holmes* (1985), *The Goonies* (1985), *Back to the Future* (1985), the television series, "Amazing Stories"(1985), *An American Tail* (1986), *The Money Pit* (1986), *Batteries Not Included* (1987), *Innerspace* (1987), *The Land Before Time* (1988), *Who Framed Roger Rabbit?* (1988), *Dad* (1989), and *Back to the Future, Part II* (1989).

As a director, Spielberg was responsible for some of the top blockbusters of the decade, including *E. T.*, which powerfully touched the audience in ways to which other films could only aspire. Although nominated for an Oscar (as were other films in the Spielberg oeuvre), *E. T.* did not win, but in 1985, Spielberg was awarded the Irving B. Thalburg Award for Lifetime Achievement. It is interesting to note during his speech at that time that he called to arms filmmakers to create a more literate cinema—where ennobling ideas and themes could be explored. Although Spielberg's films had been nominated for Oscars, he was never a winner. True to his word though, Spielberg's work took on a different flavor and he devoted his time to projects like *The Color Purple* and *Empire of the Sun*, adaptations which, indeed, took on decisively more "adult" themes and issues—a tone he carried into the 1990s first with *Schindler's List* (1993), *Amistad* (1997) and then with *Saving Private Ryan* (1998) and the even bleaker *A. I.* and *Minority Report* (2002). Stephen Prince points out that,

Spielberg's work was a major influence on the blockbuster turn in contemporary cinema, but his ambitions as filmmaker clearly transcended this category of production. The 1980s were a transitional decade for him, taking his work from the seminal popularity of pictures like *E. T.*, and his seventies hits, and toward the ambitious and complex issues of human evil and moral redemption that he regularly examined in the nineties.[56]

Based on a story by Lucas who also co-produced, *Raiders of the Lost Ark* (1981)—the second highest grossing trilogy after *Star Wars*—opened the decade and forever teamed Lucas and Spielberg together, and on the heels of *E. T.* and *Star Wars* certified them both as blockbuster filmmakers extraordinaire. It was an immense success and reinforced the desire (of both the filmgoers and studio executives) for big, spectacular, blockbuster fare. The deal Lucas made with Paramount for *Raiders* was even better than the one he made with Fox for *Star Wars*. As producer, Lucas kept all rights to the negative and all ancillary markets (even Spielberg has not made such sweet deals—he takes a percentage and a fee, but retains no rights). Paramount just took a fee for distribution. By the end of the 1980s, Lucas and Spielberg accounted for 10 of the all-time biggest hits in movie history, all surpassing $100 million in rentals. Only in recent years has *Titanic* (and another James Cameron film, *Avatar*, as well as many others) blown all these records away, topping the scale at over $471 domestically to date.

During the latter half of the decade, Lucas, like Spielberg, kept busy. Other than his involvement with the *Star Wars* trilogy, Lucas produced and co-produced a large body of work and, like Spielberg, was responsible for boosting the careers of many new directors like Lawrence Kasden, re-teamed with his mentor, friend and struggling auteur, Francis Ford Coppola, who with Lucas's help introduced the talents of Akira Kurasawa to the West. Produced projects during this time include: *Kagemusha* (1980), *Body Heat* (1981), *Raiders of the Ark* (1981), *Twice Upon a Time* (1983), the television movie, *The Ewok Adventure* (1984), *Indiana Jones* and the Temple of Doom (1984), TV movie, *Ewoks: The Battle for Endor* (1985), a television series, "Ewoks" (1985), *Latino* (1985), *Howard the Duck* (1986), *Labyrinth* (1986), *The Land Before Time* (1988), *Tucker: The Man and His Dream* (1988), *Willow* (1988), and *Indiana Jones and the Last Crusade* (1989). In addition to his television and film work, Lucas helped design two Disneyland attractions—one directed by Coppola, shot by academy-award winning cinematographer, Vittorio Storaro, and starring Michael Jackson was a 3-D film "experience" called *Captain Eo* on September 12, 1986. The film was a Star Wars-esque "space opera" themed short which pitted Michael Jackson against an evil spider woman that enslaves the populace, who after watching him dance and hearing him sing about the need to "get along," transforms into an earth mother type played by Angelica Huston. It ends with everyone singing and dancing in the streets, in an utopian happily ever after—the tag line on all promo materials promising, "We Are Here To Change The World." This short film was retired in 1998 and replaced by another 3-D showpiece, *Honey I Shrunk the Audience*, based on the similarly named film. Recently however, on the heels of Michael Jackson's tragic death on June 25, 2009, *Captain Eo* was brought back to replace "Honey" for an encore "tribute" screening (February 23, 2010-present). The other Disneyland *Star Wars* attraction was an effects-laden "ride" (really a film within a ride) called "Star Tours" (1987) which allows participants to fly through the Death Star (by use of an automated screening room), and defeat the Empire, while evading Empire capture. Recent improvements have been added to this ride opening May 20, 2011, including new digital 3-D, characters and destinations.

During the 1980s, Lucas begins to perfect his use of synergy to promote his film productions. Whether promoting his film *Willow (1988)*, or overseeing the promotion and production of the original *Star Wars* narrative, Lucas is careful to include and exploit every possible ancillary market-—each part of the Lucas empire working like an enmeshed synergistic gear, perfectly created to serve and promote the other. As a prime example, this use of synergy can best be seen in Lucas' involvement with the *Star Wars* story—one of the most carefully watched and controlled secular stories on earth. Lucas's *Star Wars* is a singular story (unlike *Star Trek* which is purely episodic) that takes place in a finite, expanding universe. Everyone working on the story has in their possession "The Bible" which is a chronology of all events that have ever occurred in the *Star Wars* universe—all the films, the books, the related stories, comics, CD-ROMs, Nintendo games, role-playing grids, etc.; and each medium is coordinated painstakingly with all the others as every new story produced is sold simultaneously in several media. If you see a moon in the background of a particular video game, you can be sure it has a name, a culture, a history, and a people that might appear later in another game, or has/will be featured in a new book.

Throughout all this, Lucas kept his nose to the grindstone developing Skywalker Ranch (which was set up as a one-stop-shop for directors interested in writing, editing, and mixing their films) and the capabilities of Industrial Light and Magic (ILM) in San Rafael which, through extensive R & D, created the next generation of filmmaking production tools vital to the industry. In the downtime between the production of Lucas's *Star Wars* films, ILM opened its doors to outside vendors, soon establishing itself as "the" special effects house in the industry, racking up fourteen Academy Awards and nominations by the 1990s.

These ILM film projects include: *Dragonslayer* (1981), *The Dark Crystal* (1982), *Star Trek II: The Wrath of Khan* (1982), *E. T.* (1982), *Starman* (1984), *Star Trek III: The Search For Spock* (1984), *Indiana Jones and the Temple of Doom* (1984), *Out of Africa (1985), Mishima* (1985), *The Goonies* (1985), *Back to the Future* (1985), *Cocoon* (1985), *The Golden Child* (1986), *Star Trek IV: The Voyage Home* (1986), *The Money Pit* (1986), *Empire of the Sun* (1987), *Star Trek: The Next Generation* (1987), **Batteries Not Included* (1987), *Innerspace* (1987), *Harry and the Hendersons* (1987), *The Witches of Eastwick* (1987), *The Last Temptation of Christ* (1988), *Cocoon II* (1988), *The Accidental Tourist* (1988), *Who Framed Roger Rabbit?* (1988), *Always* (1989), *Back to the Future, Part II* (1989), *The Abyss* (1989), *Ghostbusters II*

(1989), *Indiana Jones and the Last Crusade* (1989), *Star Trek V: The Final Frontier* (1989), and *Field of Dreams* (1989). Taking all these films into consideration, it comes as no surprise that ILM became synonymous with cutting-edge special effects and put its mark on a decade's worth of filmmaking.

At the same time Lucas was researching and developing digital effects and technology (including EditDroid and SoundDroid), he also turned his attention to sound. Lucas set up what he called "The Technical Building" at Skywalker Ranch which eventually allowed Lucasfilm to lead the industry in high-end sound design for filmmakers while at the same time functioning as a professional recording stage for many well-known musicians and vocalists.

By the end of the decade and into the 1990s, ILM helped to single-handedly push the industry toward more extensive use of computer generated filmmaking which Lucas wholeheartedly supported as a tool to give filmmakers not only greater creative freedom, but more importantly for Lucas, more creative control (filming and post-production processes will all be digitally based and be controlled by the flip of a switch and turn of a knob by those under the direction of the filmmaker/producer of the film).[57]

Lucas has been noted as saying, "Before, once you photographed something, you were pretty much stuck with it. Now ... you can have complete control over it just like an artist does, and that to me is the way it should be ... you can make shots conform to your idea after the fact, rather than trying to conform the world to what your idea is."[58] It is interesting that this quote should come out of the *American Cinematographer*. In speaking with many cinematographers, it appears many are concerned that the manipulation of the digital image has creative limitations. Allen Daviau, ASC, a distinguished cinematographer who worked with Spielberg on *E. T.* and was involved in recent restoration, revisions and DVD development, agrees that the use of the digital camera does allow for freedom of movement, but not so much creative freedom.

He explains that while a digital camera would be great to take up in a plane for a dog-fight scene in *Top Gun*, say, (since you don't need to keep reloading a digital camera like you do a film camera), it doesn't have the range, "forgiveness" or pliability of film. When going back into the vault where a negative of *E. T.* had been well preserved for many years, the print struck off the negative looked just as clean and crisp as it did twenty years before. Spielberg exclaimed at the screening of the new print, "It looks as beautiful as it did in 1983!" All the technical data/cards which accompanied the negative were there and relayed all the information about timing, color, etc., that was necessary to re-strike the print to the exact specifications of the original. Digital has no such records of information to work from and does not allow for this archiving of information so vital to the preservation of the original artwork in the form in which it was intended to be created. With digital—what you see on the computer screen is what you get (and even then when you print it off the computer, it does not always look the same, and adjustments must be made . . . not to mention the lack of standardized exhibition facilities).

And twenty-five years down the road, as digital evolves and changes (there is currently no industry standard), it is highly unlikely that the original work created by the artists will easily survive the transition from one digital set up and platform to the next. In only the past few years, film and video technology has evolved rapidly. Since the 1990s many movie cameras have been broken and are irreplaceable. What happens to all the video tapes that now exist, but cannot play in currently used cameras or on other viewing platforms (and vis a vis)? They will exist, but many images will be lost and never seen again. What of the more evolved camera hard drive systems? The original would effectively be destroyed at its creation—only copies would remain, if that. The question remains, "How does one navigate this need to store and save endless platforms (thousands of old cameras, VHS and BETA players, memory sticks, card readers, DVD players, etc.) to view or screen old film data?" The Smithsonian has been trying to doing just this, but the task is daunting. Daviau states, "I guess they could write down which knob to turn when [on every machine], but the knobs will have gone through radical changes in twenty-five years ... it will be difficult if not impossible to capture the original information as well as is done currently with a film negative."[59] Further, film has a decidedly wider range and has the capacity to be manipulated as easily as digital (Kodak has just come out with a new stock which mimics digital) on a multitude of levels. Credit must be given to Steven Spielberg for his restoration of *E. T.* He laid down the original as shown in 1983 right next to the reworked version of twenty years later, giving viewers both the original experience and the director's version/vision so they could see all the changes for themselves and come to their own critical conclusions (Lucas did the same with his originally released Star Wars trilogy spanning 1977, 1980, 1983, and his 25th Anniversary *Special Edition*). It is not surprising that ILM was also instrumental in helping make Spielberg's vision of *E. T.* fly again.

At any rate, Lucas stands as one of a handful of filmmakers who can say they have created the UR-epic-myth of modern cinema that has "the force" to transcend the medium and become one of its inescapable artifacts. Along with everything else, Lucas's influence on American film is readily felt in his creation, development and avid support of digital production methods and effects technology. His commitment to digital is tremendous, not only on screen, but in the classroom. In 2006, Lucas pledged $175 million to remodel and endow the University of Southern California School of Cinema-Television. Today, the newly named USC School of Cinematic Arts, resembling more a studio lot than schoolroom, stands as testament to his digital commitment. In the 1990s at USC, students stopped cutting frames of film on a flatbed or moviola and moved to cutting digitally on Avid . The current USC mandate to "go digital" will be complete in May 2012 when the last class to touch a camera using actual film stock will graduate from the film school. After 2012 all film students at USC will cut digitally and be taught with digital cameras—period.

Lucas should be congratulated for his work in many arenas, as well as his many entrepreneurial skills that were put to keen use developing, creating and maintaining some of the most profitable businesses in the world (yes, I said, world) today—a true fete and tour de force—while maintaining complete control. It is odd that this aspect of Lucas's career is not remarked upon and studied more. When looked at squarely, Lucas, the self-made businessman, is quite an amazing story in itself. Prince states, "ILM was the engine driving the effects and digital revolutions in modern film and Lucas became the industry's technological visionary, fixed on the digital future of film and transforming it away from its photomechanical phase."[60] Visionary, to be sure. The man who changed filmmaking, but destroyed the use of using "film" itself? Maybe, maybe not. The ending to the story has yet to be written.

The 1990s: Budget as Aesthetic: Profit and the Bottom Line

> In today's media world—to paraphrase E. M. Forster—everything connects. A feature film, a theme park, a toy store, and a computer game have a lot in common: they feed off each other as they play off each other. When one considers that *The Lion King* (1994) took $80 million at the box office, but made $220 million as a videocassette, one can understand why commentators have argued that a film today is merely a bill-board stretched out in time, designed to showcase tomorrow's classics in the video stores and the television re-runs.
>
> Thomas Elsaesser, The End of Cinema As We Know It

As we move from the 1980s into the 1990s and the early 2000s, one cannot deny that there were some rather dramatic changes in the exhibition and distribution of Hollywood films and other entertainment products. The introduction of new technologies was certainly responsible for some of these changes, but the political-economic context in which these innovations were introduced played a vital part as well. Overall, through the early 1990s, Hollywood continued along the somewhat volatile course charted through the 1980s. Companies merged, partnered and collaborated as never before to tap and dominate the world markets.

Deregulation and globalization tendencies set the stage for Hollywood in this era as much as technological development and after examination it seems clear that these factors can scarcely be separated.

It is also true that audiences of the mid-1980s and 1990s experience mass-media culture differently from previous generations. VCRs made viewing more flexible and convenient, cable has provided a wide range of programming choices (many with special interest channels that cater to smaller audiences), additionally folks were able to participate in media production themselves with the introduction of inexpensive video equipment. Technologies introduced by the corporations of the 1970s and 1980s provided the film industry with more varied distribution outlets making home video and cable a revenue bonanza for the studios—which has allowed for less reliance on theatrical exhibition overall. An individual could actually buy, for a reasonable price, a copy of their favorite film and take it home and screen it on television. People no longer had to wait to watch an annual screening on television of a particular film (e.g., *Wizard of Oz*), or wait for a re-release of the film in the theatres. Cable stations also allowed for more frequent film viewing. Video sales and rentals alone topped $17 billion in 1992 and ticket sales broke all records the following year.

But do more markets mean less risk? With the ballooning cost of blockbusters to feed the conglomerate machine, spreading the risks across a variety of diversified markets certainly has helped hedge one's bet. It also helped provide "legs" to films which did not do well at the box office. Yet, even so, the risk to studios are still tremendous and many, by decade's end, began to follow new trends in film financing, including, but not limited to, pre-buying or pre-licensing deals, up-front foreign sales, public offerings (e.g., Disney raised production funding through public offerings such as Silver Screen Partners), or limited partnership funds (e.g., Twentieth Century Fox raised $63 million through limited partnership funds called American Entertainment Partners),[61] or partnering with other studios (e.g., *Fox* partnered with Paramount on *Titanic* to share $200 million in direct costs and an eventual $400+ million profit).

Overall, filmmaking in the 1980s and early 1990s was an industry that "brought home the bacon" both at home and abroad. Over and over, the U. S. film industry received praise for its success in foreign markets, representing one of the strongest net exports in the country. And as more and more global markets opened up, Hollywood capitalized on the revenue these new markets provided.

In the 1990s, film more than ever, became inextricably tied to corporate matters. If it takes $80 to $120 million dollars to make a movie in 1990, then it better make money (compare that with the $2 million it took to make a film only twenty years earlier). Elsaesser uneasily jokes,

> At this level, the Hollywood story has much to do with the arms race. What Hollywood has done is to have continually raised the stakes: by making filmmaking ever more costly and extravagant, it has made sure that the number of competitors has become smaller and smaller . . . the high cost of moviemaking is rather like the membership fees to country clubs and golf courses: it is designed to keep out the undesirables, the upstarts. It is designed to keep most of the world's countries from being able to afford a film industry. And it keeps most of the world's independent filmmakers from getting their films into the cinemas.[62]

In the end, the ultimate product of the motion picture business was profit and motion pictures were but a means to that end. It did not really matter whether the conglomerates produced and sold cars, or movies, Cokes or silicon chips, television programs, computer software or stars, junk food, sound or images—the basic business practices remained the same. When a filmgoer purchases a ticket, Thomas Elsaesser suggests, they are really taking out a contract, "which in exchange for our money, we are guaranteed (temporary access to) a normative, quality-controlled product." In this way, cinema has evolved into both a product and a service and presupposes the simultaneous coexistence of two systems. Elsaesser continues,

> One ... is concerned with turning an experience into a commodity: the film lives in the collective mind as an event. The other is concerned with providing a service: the theatre, the comfortable seats, the ice cream and soft drinks, as they provide the pleasant atmosphere of simulated luxury for time out with friend or lover ... cinema is both industry and culture ... two systems sitting on top of each other.[63]

But this is precisely the objective of studios and their parent companies, to steadily eradicate the distinctions between film culture and consumer culture; it is an understandable objective to a culture industry which often times subordinates craft to commerce. Indeed, Thomas Schatz explains,

> The imminent convergence of movie theater, theme park, and retail store is the New Hollywood equivalent of the studio-owned movie palace of old—i.e., the site at which "the whole machine of the company," in all its integrated glory, can be most efficiently and profitably exploited.[64]

You would also think that new market outlets would produce more feature films. The statistics for total domestic theatrical releases paint a different picture. From 1986 (472 titles released) to 1991 (424), the trend is downward. Distributors point to the mega-salaries of stars and higher distribution costs for prints and ads, which continue to escalate, along with inflated costs associated with the major studios operations (read: blockbuster mentality).

Accordingly, an uneven distribution of the wealth likewise did not change much. The wealthier in the industry became increasingly wealthier. A 1984 survey by the *LA Times* stated, "that more than 100 stars, directors, producers, writers, agents, and studio executives have built fortunes of $50 million or more in the last few years."[65] A good example of this, Steven J. Ross (Time Warner) hit the top of Forbe's list of best-paid chief executives, receiving combined compensation of $302 million in 1990. Paramount's Martin S. Davis and Disney's Michael Eisner made the list the following year. At the same time, ironically, Hollywood unions (comprised of the folks actually making the movies) were losing strength and members to a proliferation of non-union films (which in many cases were "fronts" for studio pictures, e.g., *American History X* was first ran under the title *Two Brothers* while in pre-production and early production in order to fly under union radar and keep costs down . . . not an unusual studio ploy, especially in regards to the common studio practice of negative pick-up financing, and the like) and more and more run-away productions, forcing them to make concessions demanded by profit-seeking studios. The proliferation of "runaways" reaches epidemic heights during this time, (continuing even today), threatening "home-grown" production and fracturing and fragmenting the talented crew base/pool. Tax incentives are being worked out to the satisfaction of some of the studios (not all), but for many too little came too late to help with the problem of local Hollywood economies. Not since the 1950s and 1960s has the run-away situation been so bleak.

The current situation echoes previous Hollywood crises. During the 1950s, as mentioned in earlier chapters, the arrival of television both challenged Hollywood's entertainment hegemony and forced filmmakers to lower costs, television's rapid arrival—the number of TV sets grew from 160,000 in 1947 to seven million in three years—cut employment in the Hollywood trades by nearly half. By 1956, movie theater attendance had dropped 50 percent from a peak in 1946. New York reasserted itself as the entertainment capital of the U. S. [66]

Emerging digital technologies present a similar challenge today. New media, computer-generated imaging, computer games, and broadband transmissions—have all opened up opportunities for potential rivals to LA's cultural dominance. Lucas's Skywalker Ranch and Letterman Digital Arts Center (now owned by Disney, October 2012) are primary examples in the San Francisco Bay area in Northern California where the development of new technologies have helped in the creation of such firms as ILM, Pixar and Pacific Delta Images. Other filmmaking centers include Seattle, Dallas, Florida and New York. All these competitive pressures, along with escalating production costs in the 1990s and into the next century, started a shift of TV and filmmaking to lower-cost areas. In the past, during the 1950s, this shift helped to create a whole new industry of low-budget films shot in Italy, Spain and other southern European countries—epitomized by the Spaghetti Western and other classically themed movies (*Jason and the Argonauts*, etc). But today, the search for lower costs are sending both TV and film production to Canada, Australia and New Zealand. For example, the entire *Lord of the Rings* and *The Hobbit* films continue to be shot in New Zealand where production costs are cheaper. Today, skilled crews abound around the globe. The only difference in shooting international is the cost. There are no substantial boundaries anymore. Subsidies offered by foreign countries are proving too attractive to filmmakers to resist. Australia, for example, implemented a 12.5 percent tax rebate in July 2002, for all big budget and television productions. Parts II and III of *The Matrix* franchise are among the blockbusters that have been, and will be filming in Australia. Among recent big budget films being shot in Canada are: Disney's *Open Range* with Kevin Costner, Robert Duvall and Annette Benning; Twentieth Century Fox's *X Men 2* and the Paramount thriller *Timeline, to name a few.* When governor of California, Arnold Schwarzenegger seemed determined to keep production local and could not be swayed from his decision to have *Terminator 3* (T3) filmed in Los Angeles.[67] And although Schwarzenegger kept T3 in town, he was unable to do much else during his role of governor to support tax incentive programs for local productions overall.

The migration of production to Canada has attracted most of the attention, particularly from the industry's powerful craft unions. In 1999, local guilds reported a cost to the U. S. economy of $10.3 billion in lost taxes, wages, and spending according to a joint SAG-DGA report. The report documents a 185 percent increase in runaway productions shot abroad from 1990-1998. Of 716 U. S. projects produced in 1990, 100 were shot abroad; by 1998, the 1,075 U. S. film and TV productions included 285 shot abroad. It is estimated by the Center for Entertainment Industry Data and Research that the U.S. economy has lost approximately $4.1 billion in economic benefits—equating to about 25,000 jobs per year since Canada began offering tax subsidies to film production companies in 1998.[68] Estimates of the resulting job losses by the Directors Guild of American and the Screen Actors Guild reach over 52,500. Most affected are thousands of blue-collar film workers: boom operators, gaffers, set dressers, drivers and grips who make Los Angeles their home. Many of these workers used to spend much of their time on locations in other states. But when production moves to Canada, work goes to local crews, hired under that country's highly protective labor laws. The UCLA Anderson Forecast estimates jobs in the Hollywood motion picture production business fell 11.8 percent to 133,600 in February 2002 from 151,400 in March 2001. Along these lines, the UCLA economists believe many of the eliminated jobs will not be filled again due to the continued move of many feature productions to lower-cost locales.[69]

The move to Canada during this time seems in large part due to the decline of the Canadian dollar, or the "loonie." At the same time, both the Canadian federal government and several provinces have instituted financial incentives to lure production. But even if California and City Hall counter with incentive packages of their own—which they have, offering wage-based tax credits on small to midsized productions (10 percent credit on $5 million or less films), and an increase on reimbursement caps for films that are shot on public premises—the long-term ability of LA's film industry to compete for lower-end production work may be limited (especially considering a lack of incentive for big budget films to stay local). It seems a blatant case of too little, too late. Canada offers producers $435 back from each $1,000 they spend, plus benefits of an exchange rate favorable to the U. S. dollar. The constant search for cheap locations, sound stage spaces, and crews extend beyond Canada and Australia to closer locales like Mexico. Tax breaks and other incentives will help stop the runaways, but a concerted and coordinated regional effort to maintain superior levels of craftsmanship, improved cooperation between suppliers and producers to keep an eye on regulatory costs will all help as well. But this approach will require cooperation among government, labor and the studios.[70]

The challenge here is not so much based on a lack of cooperation, but the real lack of loyalty the corporations that own the studios feel toward the work force, place, and craft that is crucial to such a concerted strategy. The insertion of Wall Street and other "out-of-towners" has increased the studios' worries about any risk. Rather than looking at the long-term solution and investing in their business, most studios seem content to be little more than passive distributors and financial partners—taking the attitude, "let the next guy in charge deal with it." Others, like Warner Bros. are eager to unload their studio facilities and sound stages to independents.

Many industry executives based in New York, Los Angeles and the Bay Area, are contemptuous of a Hollywood where the financial bottom line has become increasingly more important now that the major studios are owned by larger conglomerates like Viacom, AOL Time Warner and Vivendi. Barry Diller more than once spoke out on the terrible way LA is organized and continues to try to supplant Hollywood production with many smaller, locally based studios that are scattered around the country. Few Los Angeles-based executives really express a strong commitment to maintaining the region's entertainment complex. Disney tops this list. As a global giant, Disney must invest in other countries and regions. Yet, as the company has drastically cut both its own film budgets and development staff at home, it has also given up much of its core creative franchise to people outside Disney and the region. Even at "home," Disney consistently supports efforts outside LA and farms out work to outside vendors, both Miramax (a New York-based company) and Pixar (farms out R & D to outside companies) are good examples. Similar scenarios are being played out all over town—at Fox and Universal—

where outsiders are increasingly gaining creative control and production steadily shifts overseas. If not actively restrained, these practices will lead to a "hollowing out" of Hollywood that may leave it facing the same fate of local aerospace industries in the 1990s.[71]

And while discussions around new technologies often centers on "new potentials" and "new growth" or "television of abundance," etc., the range of programming has not been enhanced particularly with the introduction of new distribution outlets. More does not always mean better or different. It can also mean that there is just more of the same distributed in a variety of ways. Diversity, one may say in this case, is not multiplicity. Interestingly enough, our collective cultural synergy seems to have developed alongside the synergy of the corporations who produce and distribute cultural products. Actually, it is not that surprising considering that once a story or character is created and developed it is moved into a variety of different formats via vertical and horizontal integration. The original cultural artifact, such as a film or film character, is copied and shared among corporate and cultural stakeholders (from businesses to fans). For example, films are made into TV programs since the same companies that often produce and distribute feature films also create prime-time programming. *Hercules* the movie, becomes *Hercules* the video, *Hercules* the children's TV show, *Hercules* the merchandise, etc., resulting in less diversity from conduit to conduit (or distribution outlet to outlet) than one would originally think. Elsaesser uses an exceptionally good analogy of the pinball machine to describe how the conglomerates make money through integration/synergy. It is worth the time to repeat here:

> the new integration/synergy model can be seen as a sort of pinball machine...The media entertainment business is such a pinball machine: the challenge is to "own" not only the steel ball, but also as many of the contacts as possible because the same "ball" gets you even higher scores, that is, profits. The contact points are the cinema screens and video stores, theme parks and toy shops, restaurant chains and video arcades, bookstores and CD record

shops. By contrast, the independent producer only has his little steel ball, and if he is not careful, he has to stand by and watch as all the others owning contact points make money off his/her film.[72]

To even further reduce the possibilities of diversity in programming, many of the cable stations, etc., recycle the same programming over and over. Rather than evolving, our culture seems to be recycling (a postmodern condition, to be sure). Not only recycling, but also watering down. The prevalent political correctness of the 1990s to present holds any controversial content at bay (or wrapped it up so well that no one but the savvy picked up on the political nuances). Not only was this a political strategy taken by many of the studios, but more importantly for them, a money issue. Find a film that will appeal to the greatest common denominator and watch your revenues increase. Inoffensive and non-controversial films can be marketed to the largest possible audience. You can hear the sound of a cash register go off every time such a film is conceived.[73]

Despite the technological developments during the 1980s and early 1990s, the social relations of corporate Hollywood remained the same and were poised to move into the next decade. They were ready, for the most part, to capitalize on change and diversify activities as profits dictated. The studios (and the conglomerates that owned them) demonstrated this flexibility by expanding beyond movies in theatres and on television. Time Warner, Paramount Communications and Viacom, Disney Corp. and Capital Cities/ABC and then Time Warner and Turner Broadcasting (along with America Online) continued the move toward conglomeration and horizontal and vertical integration. Ironically, in the 1990s, these big Five controlled the market more completely than did the "old" Big Five in the Old Hollywood system some fifty years before ever did. This further conglomeration happened in tandem with a growth in globalization (or internationalization) and an interest by foreign corporations during the decade which speculated in the "film studio market" (during the 1990s, a variety of foreign companies took control of many of the film studios) and tried to take advantage of merchandizing possibilities, ancillary markets and formats, and the variety of delivery and exhibition systems. And while many studios maintained corporate offices in Hollywood, the financing, distribution, production, and exhibition of American films become complexly global in scope where national boundaries no longer seem relevant. Spielberg has said, commenting on the global success of *Jurassic Park*,

> Once upon a time it was a small gathering of people around a fire listening to the storyteller with his tales of magic and fantasy. And now it's the whole world . . . that's what has thrilled me most about the "Jurassic Park" phenomenon. It's not 'domination' by American cinema. It's just the magic of story-telling, and it unites the world.[74]

As described, *Jurassic Park* may be a little light in plot and character development (stronger in cautionary theme: consumerism, entertainment, and science run amok—a Disney theme park nightmare), but it is one heck of a "gee-whiz" well-crafted theme-park ride, full of dazzling digital effects—the epitome of a franchise triumph in 1990s terms. "To survive the 1990s," wrote Peter Bart, "a company must mobilize a vast array of global brands to command both content and distribution. Indeed, such an enterprise must be more than a company—it must be a virtual nation-state."[75] The willingness of the FCC and Congress in the 1990s to deregulate the media industry (e.g., the revised Communications Act), enables the Big Five (Viacom, Disney, Time Warner et al.) to compete more easily in the high-stakes global market with very few constraints, a prospect that boded well for the conglomerates, but perhaps not so well for the aesthetics of cinema or the enlightenment of the audience. Schatz worries that,

> the continued growth and ever expanding power of these media giants will test...whether these communication empires and the moguls who control them have any real sense of moral, political,

and cultural responsibility to the global community which their companies are both creating and exploiting.[76]

Along these lines, the principles of filmmaking remained for the most part the same, and filmmakers and films were considered a success based on box office dollars. And the audience lined up for tickets to the big movie—the big event, the blockbuster—in droves. The blockbuster today, as in the past, can be defined as a movie with a "big" subject and bigger budget (a "big" subject such as a disaster, world war, the end of life as we know it, a monster from the deep or space, a death battle in the galaxy, etc.), and foregrounds a young, handsome male hero who uses lots of fire power, has secret knowledge, or must complete a hopelessly difficult mission. The story is usually based on a traditional story, usually a combination of sci-fi and fantasy, sometimes happens against the background of quasi-historical events (usually idealized), with a slew of Western archetypal heroes rounding out the stage—in short an extension of fairytales with guaranteed happy-ever-after endings as evidenced via many of the successful franchises seen today.

Sometimes quality special effects, use of available technology and blockbuster come together, as in *The Matrix* (1999). Pat Mellencamp in her essay, "The Zen of Masculinity: Rituals of Heroism in *The Matrix*," unabashedly enjoyed the film in all its postmodern punk and techno-grunge aesthetic splendor and recognized its contribution to current blockbuster fare, supporting the claims of the editor and visual effects supervisor of the film who state,

> "*The Matrix* is the first film of the millennium, monumental, groundbreaking, with a new visual style that will be remembered."[77]

Stylistically, without a doubt, *The Matrix* made an impact. Many of the teasers seen currently mimic the use of black/blue green mise-en-scene of the *Matrix* "real world" which is sucked dry of any red—life here is monochromatic and green-toned, and is played out against a tattered, grainy, electric space where reality is dark, gothic and mythic in tone. A perfect example of the postmodern film style, it blends Asian and American film genres, live action, animation, and other media well. Genres are sliced up and served a multitude of ways. It seamlessly blends CGI, live action and digital effects so that it is almost impossible to tell the difference between what has been staged or computer-generated, blending real and computer generated bodies at will. Mellencamp states,

> This synthesis between live action and CGI, between film and TV, like the theme of a film itself, joins ...the film is a hybrid, a mutable object ... [a] dimensional film [where] special effects are not primarily used for 'razzle dazzle'. On the contrary, they move the narrative and tell the story, which is rare. The special effects are critical to the movie .... it celebrates the paradox of so many science fiction films—criticizing technology in the narrative while using it to entertain us in the movie theatre .... Popular culture is in flux; the forms are changing into multimedia, and with this will come altered subjectivity. *The Matrix*, *Being John Malkovich*, and *Run Lola Run* are reconfiguring narrative, and refiguring difference differently. They are all vanguard films, cultural signposts of change. They are also terrifically entertaining.[78]

But unlike *The Matrix*, the quality of many blockbusters did not fulfill these kind of viewing expectations—unless they were for simply bigger, louder, but not better, films (e.g., *Waterworld*). Jon Lewis suggests,

> Film production resembled nothing so much as a high-stakes poker game, a game in which all the players bet heavy on the audience's continued desire to see and hear bigger and louder movies. During the 1990s...a film was made primarily in order to exploit the new image and sound capabilities of the newly equipped digital and Dolby theatres (e.g., *The Matrix*, 1999). It was a strategy that carried with it the promise of astronomical profits and paydays .... Only players with enough money to safely play in such a high-stakes game had any chance of walking away from the table a winner.

Lewis further suggests that, "so long as there is so much money at stake and at risk, we can all relax. Even if films will soon no longer exactly be films, even if cinema is once and for all (in some specific, narrow way) really dead, it's not like there will be nothing for us to pay for and watch in the future." [79] It's hard to believe that the large studios like Disney would sit back and allow that to happen. "Catch them young and keep them forever," used as a Disney motto and Lucas/Spielberg formula takes into consideration this tenet that if you get children used to something early, they'll stay with it all their lives (when my two-year-old discovered Disney, this writer's house looked like a Disney Mall store, as a case in point).

Many of the films during this period were stylistically excessive and more "bang" was considered a better sell for the buck instead of "smart." Case in point—while I was working at Rastar Productions on the Sony Pictures lot during the latter half of the 1990s, it was commonly understood that the studios were looking for heavily laden special effects movies—MIB, Bad Boys—lots of bang and holler—nothing soft or "small." At one pitch meeting at Columbia Pictures where I worked as Head of Development for producer Ray Stark, I can remember giving them a script that I thought was smart, funny, witty and extremely well written. They would not bite. I pushed, I pleaded, I begged my producer and the studio to make the film. "Ah, honey, who wants to see Shakespeare these days ... forget about it." In the end, Columbia did not make the film. It was fortunate Miramax was in the market for a "smaller" film and more intellectual fare. The film was *Shakespeare in Love,* and subsequently, went on to win Best Picture in 1998.

Wheeler Winston Dixon hits the studio's search for "bigger bang" on the head, and reflects on the " a scattershot explosion of images" which he considers a tipping point in film viewing, citing the introduction of rapid cutting with the introduction of MTV. Viewers weaned on the rapid cutting of images, the quick transitions from black and white to color and different stocks and grains, and the seemingly meaningless manipulation of film speed over-laced by special effects have produced a generation, Dixon laments, that seeks the instant and constant bombardment of the image over the slow development of a complex narrative. New filmmakers, in their effort to keep this new audience entertained, are quickly abandoning the classic shot structure which required "courage to hold on to a close up of an actor's face, the patience to build up to a mood through a lengthy establishing sequence," for this more visceral, yet less satisfying, or meaningful style of storytelling. [80] This explanation certainly echoes Robin Wood's assertion that the blockbusters of today foster escapism. Dixon further goes on to say:

> Plots are reduced to the simplest...: here's the good guy, here's the bad guy, here's the conflict, the good guy wins...Contemporary audiences don't want complexity, they want hand-holding simplicity, in which every step of the narrative construction is heavily foreshadowed and plays out in a non-disruptive manner. Because of the wide variety of new and competing media, more has become less. Escape is everything, delivered in small doses, never leaving the viewer truly satisfied. Of course, there are examples which contradict such a treatise, but these films are the growing exception and not the general rule. [81]

The 1990s were touted as part of an independent film revolution. But were they really? Katzenberg in his now legendary internal "memo" to Eisner et al., in 1991, lamented "the tidal wave of runaway costs and mindless competition" and "the blockbuster mentality that has gripped our industry." Successful, good films are based "on two elements—a good story, well executed" where the bottom line was not commercial, but conceptual. "We must not be distracted from one fundamental concept: the idea is king." The memo, though motivated at the time by cost overruns and the weak box office of *Dick Tracy* (with direct costs of $46 million to make and $55 million to market and release), but also the success of *Pretty Woman*, along with *Ghost* and *Home Alone*, relatively "small" films that out-grossed such blockbusters as *Total Recall, Die Hard, Hunt For Red October, Back to the Future III, Another 48 Hours* and *Days of Thunder*, advocated a return to "the kind of modest, story-driven movie we tended to make in our salad days."[82] In 1991, six of the summer's top 10 films were low budget productions. This trend was an aberration. The industry slumped in 1991, but by 1993 Hollywood was enjoying a robust recovery and blockbusters with big budgets came back with a vengeance. The DreamWorks SKG merger accomplished by Spielberg, Katzenburg and Geffen in the fall of 1994 only seemed to some to reinforce the "blockbuster mentality" Katzenburg so woefully lamented a few years before.

Independent distributors, producers and directors were quickly appropriated by the mainstream and bought up by conglomerate machines. (A perfect example of this was Miramax's purchase by Disney for $60 million, which included their library, and New Line/Fine Line's movement toward main stream, blockbuster fare and mutation from independent to mini-major with the help and purchase by Turner/Time Warner to the tune of $600 million.) Many independents joined forces with the studios in order to compete in the more commercial marketplace (pay higher salaries for stars or properties, e.g., New Line's production of *Lord Of The Rings* {LOTR}, have the ready cash to purchase distribution rights to already produced films at Cannes, or find rescue for box office flops in the home video market, etc.), but while many were able to develop strategies to maintain market presence (franchises, aggressive marketing and publicity), their mergers with larger companies have created, Justin Wyatt contends, "a curious hybrid, the 'major independent'" continuing,

> The major independents have fragmented the market place for independent film further and further—through producing films parallel to the majors and stressing art house acquisitions, which have the potential to cross over to a wider market...The net effect is a contraction in the market for independent film, bolstering the status of the majors and major independents, and creating an increasingly competitive market for those smaller companies. This movement towards the major independent as a market force

constitutes a key shift in the industrial parameters of independent film, studio moviemaking and the New Hollywood.[83]

During the 1990s, some companies tried a different tack, one that harkened back to the 1960s and 1970s. But it did not work. Savoy Pictures that touted itself as a haven for "auteurs" closed shop in 1996 after just a few short and agonizing years in business. Their misjudgment of both film and the privileging of directors over strong producers (or an affiliation with a conglomerate/studio) led Savoy to one expensive flop after another (i.e., Andrew Davis's *Steal Little, Steal Big*—cost: $35 million with a box office return of only $1.3 million). And while it is important to have a stable of smaller films that can make some big money for the media kings via the like of New Line or Miramax, such as *The Full Monty* or *My Big Fat Greek Wedding*, Hollywood remains a high-octane business.

Auteurism during the 1990s, while used as a brand name to sell product, did not play out in New Wave terms except, perhaps, as put forward by Dana Polan, as a political act (or as a Lucas/Spielberg type auteur-entrepreneur). Polan suggests,

> In an age seemingly geared to standardization, one way to stand out is by cultivating one's image as a special creative figure, as an artist. There is even a complementariness of liberalism and auteurism. Both structure the world according to a binary opposition in which, opposed to crush the systems of authority and governance, there stand solitary figures who by their force of will try to stand up for personal identity and self-worth . . . . Liberalism and auteurism both start with the personal, with the potential for the individual to fight to make a difference . . . . it is particularly tempting to see here an allegory of filmmaking: the artist struggles to complete his project as the men in power worry about cost and eventually remove him from the scene.[84]

Auteurism has never been paired with liberalism in this way before—not quite so succinctly. Taking this point of view into consideration, it is no real wonder then, that auteurism blossomed in Europe and across

America when it did in the 1960s. Civil rights and unrest, protests around the world and at home, fueled in part by the war in Vietnam, etc., all contributed to the American individual's belief that not only had "the man got them down," but lied to boot (disillusionment as after World War I). Likewise this basic distrust and attitude also made itself known by the younger crowd entering the crumbling studios whose executives hailed from the "old" school of thinking and filmmaking.

The liberal 1960s mantra "don't trust anyone over thirty" was no more apparent than during the struggle between the old studio regime and the infusion of new talent (e.g., Coppola, Lucas, and the wave of other newly minted film school auteurs) into the system. It is also no wonder that the notion of auteur after the 1960s and 1970s began to diminish in the climate of a Republican regime. Auteurs were appropriated into the political machine and used for profitability (and those who did not play along, did not get to play at all, e.g., Robert Altman). People also came to appreciate the work of the many hundreds involved in the filmmaking process that enabled the auteuristic "vision" to live on the screen—a final vision that was based on the vision of hundreds over a period of many years (a film takes a long time to make and during that time goes through a series of drafts and changes). The art is a collaborative one, perhaps even more so with all the technological changes that require additional expertise and craftsmanship. Auteurism—if you really look at it—has always been the reigning American theme in film, the arts and life in general—even more so in the last couple of decades. It is the Horatio Alger myth, a bit of the American Dream and all the stuff of American heroes ("I'm the ONE" . . . "I gotta be me!"). It is an adolescent coming of age story where the hero to be makes a choice to go up against Goliath—and ultimately wins the prize (riches, the princess, adoration of many, etc.). Pat Mellancamp in her "Matrix" essay hits upon this theme: "The overriding message of the film is that our belief in our self remains steadfast, there is nothing we cannot accomplish or become. Our thoughts, which we learn to focus and discipline, create and determine our world . . . . Each obstacle we surmount will make us stronger and will give us the awareness we need to move forward."[85] This is a perfect definition of the American auteur, the hero of American myth and liberal ideology.

Notes

1. David Cook, *Lost Illusions: American Cinema in the Shadow of Watergate and Vietnam*, 51.
2. James Sterngold, "The Return of the Merchandiser," *The New York Times*, January 30, 1997, sec. C-1.
3. Ibid., sec. C-6.
4. Ibid., sec. C-1.
5. Tiiu Lunk, *Movie Marketing: Opening the Picture and Giving it Legs* (Los Angeles: Silman-James Press, 1997), 254-255.Greg Hernandez, "Disney Juggles After Failure," *Daily News*, Business, 4 January 2003, 1, 3.
6. Greg Hernandez. "Disney Juggles After Failure," *Daily News*, Business 4, January 2003, 1, 3. See also "Profit Dip at Disney," Guy Hernandez, *Daily News*, 31 January 2003, Business, 1-3
7. "Animated Features Spur Rising Surge," *Variety*, 18 October 93, 1.
8. *Hollywood Reporter*, January 5, 1995, 1.
9. Alex Billington, *"It's Official-New Line Cinema is Dead!"*FirstShowing.Net, 28 Feb 2008. http://www.firstshowing.net/2008/its-official-new-line-cinema-is-dead/ (accessed July 18, 2011). *The Lord of the Rings* is a Warner Bros. franchise. In 1993, Ted Turner's Turner Broadcasting purchased New Line Cinema and soon thereafter, in 1996, purchased Time-Warner. During these periods of acquisitions and mergers, New Line Cinema functioned as a separate studio entity yet technically was a wholly owned subsidiary of Time-Warner. On February 28, 2008, after the receipts had been counted for the New Line Cinema bomb, *The Golden Compass*, all that changed. Time Warner announced that New Line Cinema would from this moment become a fully functioning unit of Warner Bros.. and no longer produce, market, or distribute films outside the Warner Bros.. purview.
10. Corie Brown, "The Years Without Ross," *Premiere*, January 1996, 78.
11. Nancy Haas, "Marvel Superheros Take Aim at Hollywood," *New York Times*, July 28, 1996, n.p.
12. Thomas Schatz, "The Return of the Hollywood Studio System," *Conglomerates and the Media*, Erik Barnouw, et al., eds. (New York: The New Press, 1997), 94.
13. *Newsweek*, July 28, 1996, 42.

14. Thomas Schatz, " The Return of the Hollywood Studio System," *Conglomerates and the Media*, 95.
15. Kathleen Kernin, "Hi-ho, Hi-ho, A-Marketing We Go .... And Go," *Business Week*, June 25, 1990, 54.
16. *Variety*, 14-20 October 1996, 1.
17. Thomas Schatz, "The Return of the Hollywood Studio System," *Conglomerates and the Media*, 97-98.
18. *Variety*, "Wall Street bell rings for Disney: Shares boost as analysts predict turnaround in new year," (3-5 January 2003): 10.
19. Prince, Stephen, *A New Pot of Gold: Hollywood Under the Electronic Rainbow, 1980-1989* (Berkeley: University of California Press, 2000), 89.
20. Ibid.
21. *Variety*, September 30-October 6, 1995, 1.
22. Stephen Prince, *A New Pot of Gold: Hollywood Under the Electronic Rainbow, 1980-1989* (University of California Press: Berkeley, 2000), xi.
23. David Bordwell, *On the History of Film Style* (Cambridge, Massachusetts: Harvard University Press, 1997), 71-72. Of course, both pre- and post-Bazin we have enjoyed various other hermeneutic and critical ways to approach film. Bazin's idea of what cinema is comprises but one of many critical opinions—many more complex than Bazin's, others less so. For the sake of example, however, Bazin was chosen for his more easily approachable study of film and was embraced by many in the New Wave (and thus, by many "auteurs" during the period being studied).
24. Stephen Prince, *A New Pot of Gold: Hollywood Under the Electronic Rainbow*, 1980-1989, xii.
25. Jon Lewis, "The Corporate Era," *The New American Cinema*, 97.
26. Ibid., 98.
27. Ibid., 99.
28. When Seagrams purchased MCA/Universal, the producers, directors, and stars under contract were not happy. To express their collective thoughts on the merger, the producers, directors, and stars of the newly purchased company made a film that recently surfaced on youtube.com that lampoons and parodies the sale titled, "Universal Corporate Film #304," "Your Studio & You." In this short film, Steven Spielburg, Angela Landsbury, Demi Moore, John Singleton, Michael J. Fox, Bruce Willis, Brian Grazer, Ron Howard, Sylvester Stallone, Kevin Misher, Sean Cassidy, James Cameron, among others, all share their "thoughts" on working for Universal City Studios, or UCS, collectively agreeing at the end of the film that, "It's UCS for me!" which clearly sounds more like

"It Sucks For Me!" rather than what was written on paper. This hidden gem of a film can currently (retrieved August, 20, 2014) be viewed on youtube.com in two parts as: Your Studio & You Pt 1 (https://www.youtube.com/watch?v=-gRS9NnWP2w)Your Studio & You Pt2 (https://www.youtube.com/watch?v=4SdVKTPDWLA)
29. Jon Lewis, "The Corporate Era," *The New American Cinema*, 97-99.
30. Prince, Stephen, *A New Pot of Gold: Hollywood Under the Electronic Rainbow, 1980-1989*, xiv.
31. Ibid., 45.
32. Wolfgang J. Koschnick, "I Can Think of More Important Things Than Being Loved by Everybody," *Forbes* (27 November 1989): 102.
33. *Time*, "Fast Forward," 5 December 1983, 74. *Raiders of the Lost Ark* with 420,000 units sold quickly became the number one home video sell through champion. *Flash Dance* initially sold over 200,000 units. See also Justin Wyatt, *High Concept*, 82.
34. Quoted in Joseph McBride, ed., *Filmmakers on Filmmaking* (Los Angeles: Tarcher, 1983), 174.
35. Stephen Prince, *A New Pot of Gold: Hollywood Under the Electronic Rainbow, 1980-1989*, 162.
36. Michael Pye and Lynda Myles, *The Movie Brats: How the Film Generation Took Over Hollywood*, 9.
37. *USA Today*, 19 October 1984.
38. *The Economist*, "The Batmogul and the Abyss" (26 August 1989), 73.
39. "US Movie Marketing Summary 1995-2010," *The Numbers*, retrieved August, 5, 2011. Available from *http://www.the-numbers.com/market*
40. William J. Palmer, *The Films of the Eighties* (Carbondale: Southern Illinois University Press, 1993), 308.
41. Ibid.
42. Ibid., 309.
43. For an in-depth look at Coppola's life and work, see Jon Lewis', *Whom the Gods Wish to Destroy*.
44. Greg Hernandez, "Franchise features often mean big bucks so they keep coming," *LA Daily News & Greensheet*, July 20, 2002, 1, 4. *Daily News*, Greg
45. *Cinema Editor*, 52, no. 4, (Fall 2002): 26-39
46. *Daily News*, Greg Hernandez, "$9 Billion boxOffice, Industries purse building in record year," 1, 11, 30 December 2002, 1.
47. *American Cinematographer* 63, no. 8, "Computer Research and Development at Lucasfilm," (August 1982): 773-75.

48. William J. Palmer. *The Films of the Eighties*, 15.
49. Paper presented at University of Austin, Texas, *American Popular Culture Convention*, in February 2002 by Michael Blake on "Ford, the Searchers and a Code of Honor."
50. Stephen Prince, *A New Pot of Gold: Hollywood Under the Electronic Rainbow, 1980-1989*, 342.
51. Barry Norman, *The Story of Hollywood* (New York: NAL Penguin, 1987), 336.
52. Andrew Button, "Blissing Out: The Politics of Reaganite Entertainment," *Movie* 31/32, 23.
53. David Bordwell, *On the History of Film Style* (Cambridge, MA: Harvard University Press, 1997), 263.
54. Robin Wood, *Hollywood: From Vietnam to Reagan* (New York: Columbia University Press, 1986), 163-164.
55. Robin Wood, *Hollywood: From Vietnam to Reagan* (New York: Columbia University Press, 1986), 174.
56. Stephen Prince, *A New Pot of Gold: Hollywood Under the Electronic Rainbow, 1980-1989*, 204.
57. ILM Timeline (for the most part) outlined in: Randal Lane, "The Magician," *Forbes*, 11 March 1996, 123. see Appendix I
58. Ron Magid. "George Lucas: Past, Present, and Future," *American Cinematographer* 78, no. 2 (February 1997): 49, 52.
59. From a telephone interview with Allan Daviau, A. C. E. January 1, 2003.
60. Prince, Stephen. *A New Pot of Gold: Hollywood Under the Electronic Rainbow, 1980-1989*, 208.
61. Janet Wasko, *Hollywood in the Information Age: Beyond the Silver Screen* (Austin: University of Texas Press, 1994), 241-242.
62. Thomas Elsaesser, "The Blockbuster: Everything Connects, But Not Everything Goes," *The End of Cinema As We Know It*, Jon Lewis, ed. (New York: New York University Press, 2001), 17.
63. Ibid., 13, 15.
64. Thomas Schatz, "The Return of the Hollywood Studio System," *Conglom-erates and the Media*, Erik Barnouw et al., eds. (New York: The New Press, 1997), 98.
65. Cited in Janet Wasko, *Hollywood in the Information Age: Beyond the Silver Screen*, 248.
66. Michael Conant, "The Paramount Decrees Reconsidered," *The American Film Industry*, 539. See also, Gomery, *The Hollywood Studio System*, 297-300.

67. Greg Hernandez. "Film Exodus Grows," *Los Angeles Times*, July 10 2002. See also David Finnigan, "Woe Canada: Guilds cite $10 Billion in Lost Prod'n," *The Hollywood Reporter* (June 25-27, 1999): 1, 8.
68. Ibid.
69. Joel Kotkin, "Runaway Productions Pose Challenges for Hollywood," *Los Angeles Times*, Business, March 27, 2002, M1, 6. Also see *Variety*, "Down Year in LA as Jobs Fade Out," March 27, 2002.
70. Ibid.
71. Ibid.
72. Thomas Elsaesser, "The Blockbuster: Everything Connects, But Not Everything Goes," *The End of Cinema As We Know It*, Jon Lewis, ed., 18.
73. *Variety* (December 27, 1993), 62.
74. Cited in Thomas Schatz, "The Return of the Hollywood Studio System," *Conglomerates and the Media*, Erik Barnouw et al., eds., 99.
75. Ibid., 102.
76. Ibid.
77. As cited in Pat Mellencamp, "The Zen of Masculinity: Rituals of Heroism in The Matrix," *The End of Cinema As We Know It* (New York: New York University Press, 2001), 83.
78. Ibid., 84-85, 93.
79. Jon Lewis, ed. "The End of Cinema As We Know It and I Feel . . . ," *The End of Cinema As We Know It* (New York: New York University Press, 2001), 8.
80. Wheeler Winston Dixon. "Twenty-Five Reasons Why It's All Over," *The End of Cinema As We Know It* (New York: New York University Press, 2001), 360.
81. Ibid.
82. Thomas Schatz, "The Return of the Hollywood Studio System," *Conglomerates and the Media*, 97-98.
83. Justin Wyatt, "The Formation of the 'Major Independent': Miramax, New Line and the New Hollywood," *Contemporary Hollywood Cinema* (New York: Routledge, 1998), 87.
84. Dana Polan, "The Confusions of Warren Beatty," *The End of Cinema As We Know It*, 142.
85. Pat Mellencamp, "The Zen of Masculinity: Rituals of Heroism in the Matrix," *The End of Cinema As We Know It*, 93.

Chapter 5

Digital Beginnings

> What's exciting for me is that we're going into an area that nobody's tried before, that seems totally impossible—in terms of new technology and production techniques—and everybody is going, "Oh, my God, what's going to happen?"
>
> George Lucas, "The Force Never Left Him," 1997

> I've never focused on making the money. I've always focused on not losing the money.
>
> George Lucas

Digital Beginnings: Special Editions, A Series of Historical Film Firsts

By the end of the 1990s, Lucas had been recognized for his achievements by the Academy with the Thalberg Award. Skywalker Ranch had grown to an immense empire, with sales of $300 million a year, pretax profit of $120 million, making Lucas's holdings valued at roughly $5 billion. His personal assets likewise approximated $5 billion. Since *Star Wars,* Lucas has transformed corporate synergy into an art form, a method carefully copied by the studio conglomerates who have all watched and learned.

To date, the licensing of *Star Wars* merchandise tops $3 billion, and all but one of the twenty-one *Star Wars* (and more since this writing) related novels have made the New York Times bestseller list and the animated *The Clone Wars* (2006-present) television series thrives, having won a day-time Emmy in 2013.[1] Total merchandizing in 2011 topped over $22 billion. In a popular culture awash now with brand names, *Star Wars* is more than just a popular logo. For under forty-aged moviegoers, it is probably the most informative experience of a generation.

After twenty years of "wishing he could make it better," George Lucas, in 1997 got his wish, and forged new ground. He released a "Directors Cut" of the *Star Wars* trilogy---the version he always wanted film-goers to see—and they showed up in droves. The new "Special Edition" trilogy, released over a two-month period (February and March) in the winter-spring of 1997, made an astounding $35.9 million its opening weekend on 2,104 screens, the highest ever for a film reissue and the eighth largest opening weekend of all time—a strong marketing assessment based on a lack of any competing blockbuster fare. In contrast, the original *Star Wars* opened twenty years before on forty-three screens and made $1.6 million in its opening weekend. By the end of its run the reissued *Star Wars* made over $100 million, taking *Star Wars* alone to a total box office of $461 million domestic by the end of 1997.[2]

Lucas's reasons given for reissue of a twentieth anniversary *Star Wars* Special Edition are threefold: (a) to make improvements to the films that had been bothering him since the film was first made on a $10 million budget, (b) give something back to *Star Wars* fans the world over, and (c) provide a large screen venue for his four-year-old son, Jett, to see the movie as originally intended and conceived.[3] Lucas states,

> The most obvious thing that's happened is we've gone back to the original negative, cleaned it up considerably, redone a lot of the optical effects, the wipes, the dissolves and improved the quality of the film, because it was deteriorating. One of the things I wanted to do was preserve the film so that it could still be a

Digital Beginnings 213

> viable piece of entertainment in the twenty-first century. Films do deteriorate, and they disappear. This one had deteriorated a lot more than anybody expected in twenty years. So that was the primary concern. The audience will get a brand new print that's very clean and actually better than the original release in terms of technical quality. It's less grainy, it's less dirty, and it's just a better print.[4]

Since the original negatives had deteriorated to the extent they needed to be completely restored, Lucas made the decision to restore the original and then re-release the films once more—a brilliant restoration and marketing decision. New digital technology, which Lucas had pioneered and developed, enhanced the special effects and sound. Three years and $15 million later, the Special Edition trilogy was ready for the theatres, and the theatres were as anxious as Lucas to screen them. Lucas said,

> We were hoping to get 200 theatres, maybe 400. We had no idea. But then theatre owners began to get really excited during the summer after we ran some trailers and it started getting standing ovations. We began to say, "This is going to be more than just a limited event for fans. This is going to be a big thing for everybody." I realized that maybe there were more people like me that wanted to see it with their kids on the big screen.[5]

Once again, Lucas presented the film industry with a new "first." He was the first to ever re-issue and screen " *Star Wars: Special Editions*," of his films--making something old, entirely new. But the "firsts" don't end there. The *Star Wars: Special Editions* releases mark another "first"— the first time a film was re-released with significant changes made to the original work. The marketing blitz highlighted these new, *Star Wars: Special Editions* technical, digitally-enhanced changes, including the addition of new and updated scenes. *Star Wars: Special Editions* releases of *Star Wars: A New Hope* had 69 differences from the original, the *Empire Strikes Back* had fifty-five, while *Jedi* contained thirty-eight. Most agreed that the most significant changes to the trilogy came in the expansion of Mos Eisley to make it look like a bustling metropolis, a scene with Han

Solo and a re-animated Jabba the Hutt where ILM artists were able to replace a real actor with an animated counterpart (something that was not possible twenty years ago), a reinstated Biggs scene, an establishing shot of Obi Wan Kenobi's home on Tatoonie, dozens of TIE fighters placed strategically in the final Battle of Yavin, enhancements to the Wampa ice creature and dew back, the redecoration of Cloud City, the addition of Jabba's 'Jedi Rocks' band, and the extended Endor celebrations.[6] Other changes were made as well to character and story (e.g., Han Solo no longer takes the first shot at the bounty hunter in the Mos Eisley bar). "You try to make the movie that you wanted to script, and along the way, you have to make a lot of compromises," Lucas said.

> There's never enough time, never enough money; some things just aren't possible. So you have to rewrite, change and you have to cut things out that you planned to have in the movie. Sometimes you cut things out because they don't belong in the movie—because the idea didn't work and the film looks better if you cut it out...special effects don't make the movie. Story makes the movie. All the special effects do is allow you to tell a particular story.[7]

And so, the historical significance of Lucas's Special Editions continues. Not only was George Lucas the first to clean up and theatrically re-release his *Star Wars* films as *Star Wars: Special Editions*, as well as to be the very first filmmaker to have the technology available to do so (because the had invented and developed it), but also the very first filmmaker to make significant changes to his original work (because he outright owned the film himself). No filmmaker has EVER accomplished anything similar in the recent history of film. EVER.

Not surprisingly, in 1998, distributors followed Lucas's lead and re-issued both *Gone With The Wind* and *Wizard of Oz*, making a tidy profit. In the past, these type of blockbuster films might have toured the globe (ie. D.W. Griffith's, *Birth of a Nation*), but the original creative work always remained intact. The idea of re-cutting or adding scenes to a classic film might have been considered, but never done. Suddenly, the digital technology of George Lucas made that a reality.

DIGITAL FILMMAKING: REALITY ENDS HERE

If the changes to the *Star Wars: Special Editions* were purely technological our discussion would end here, but the addition of scenes and actual change to original character and narrative begs further examination. These changes, specifically to character and narrative, which sparked discussions among fans and more casual viewers, was tied to how people experience shared cultural artifacts. Shared cultural artifacts are called "shared" for a reason. The release of the *Star Wars: Special Editions* reinforced the idea that a film (and most creative works) are not merely stand alone cultural artifacts, like a piece of bone or a pottery shard dug up at a archeology site. Instead, there exists a shared space between the audience and the creative work that becomes charged and invested with emotional and psychological reactions which are filed away into memory and, thus, become part of the viewers personal history and identity. While the creator (George Lucas, in this case) owns the work (film) the space experienced between the creator (film) and the audience is shared by both. It stands to reason that when changes are made to existing stories and a shared experiential space is challenged, especially one with the cultural impact of *Star Wars*, some audience members will react favorably, others, less so. At stake, for some, is nothing less than their childhood memories and sense of personal identity.

We are storytelling creatures. It is through the telling, retelling, and discussion of stories (every day, mythic, religious, etc.) that we experience the world and come to understand our place in it. Our lives and relationships are a series of shared, intermingled stories (that we tell ourselves and others) that form our memories, our identities, and our sense of "self." These stories become our reality. They embody our personal truth. It is in this shared storytelling space that exists between ourselves and others where our history lives and meaning dwells. To change a story is to change our fundamental understanding of the truth. Even the most subtle changes to our favorite stories about the world and ourselves creates havoc with the world as we perceive it. So it follows, changes, especially those to the story, character and narrative in the *Star Wars* epic, became a topic for discussion.

Star Wars: Special Editions became a cause for detailed comparisons that involved countless hours of scrutiny, mostly conducted as a solitary process involving much construction of personal theories and interpretations, a very different experience than watching the film as a group in front of the TV or in the theatre. One example is the change made to Han's character during the cantina scene. In the original *Star Wars*, Han took out his gun from his holster, keeping it under the table, while cornered by Greedo, a bounty hunter trying to collect for Jabba. Han shoots Greedo under the table and leaves. In the *Star Wars: A New Hope Special Edition*, Greedo fires first but misses, justifying Han's retaliation. Some viewers responded negatively to this change and felt Lucas had gone too far by making Han the "nice guy"—it is antithetical to his nature and later motives and downplays his arc from hardened mercenary to a rebel with a cause. What is significant here is that the audience refused to accept Lucas's changes to the reworked *Star Wars* universe over their own understanding of it—especially when the changes directly flew in the face of what they had determined characters would or would not do. Will Brooker, in his book, *Using the Force: Creativity, Community and Star Wars Fans,* points out *Star Wars*, "characters and stories have escaped the original text and grown up with the fans, who have developed their own very firm ideas of what *Star Wars* is and is not about."[8]

While Lucas champions artists' rights to fix their own projects, he does not agree with completely altering a film. Colorization, and "panning and scanning" video, are things that lead to viewing films in a way not intended by the creator. On these issues Lucas comments:

> They're adding scenes, re-cutting things, changing the political content of the movie, the aesthetic content of the movie. A movie is

Digital Beginnings

a very fragile thing. All you need to do is take out a John Williams score and put in Madonna, and you have a very different kind of movie ... The idea of a film as a dynamic, forever changing medium should put film in the same category as all other art forms. Artists are continually changing their work ... the artist can come back and doodle on it. It's a curse of the process, which is that you always see things that you wanted to fix. And yeah, I've been accused of being a perfectionist. I don't believe that in my mind; it's who I am. But to make it right and the way it should be, we had the opportunity to fix it, so we're fixing it.[9]

In Lucas's words, "I'm very aware as a creative person that those who control the means of production control the creative vision. It is not a matter of going down and saying, 'You're going to let me have the final cut.' Because no matter what you do in a contract, they will go around it. Whereas if you own the cameras and you own the film, there's nothing they can do to stop you."[10]

Since the release of the *Star Wars: Special Editions*, other filmmakers have opted to go back in and "fix" a film which was produced under tight deadlines, tighter budgets and running-time pressures. Francis Ford Coppola, for one, did, and changed the title of *Apocalypse Now* to *Apocalypse Now Redux*, clearly signaling to the audience that they were going to be seeing something new. Steven Spielberg also made some changes to the 20th Anniversary release of *E. T.* (2002), but the changes were subtle, claims the director and Kathleen Kennedy, Spielberg's long time producer. Kennedy states, "George went in and he redid whole scenes and sequences. In contrast, *E. T.* is receiving a wide variety of subtle changes."[11] These "subtle" changes include: tweaking of E. T.'s performance through CGI (computer graphic imagery), a new scene with Elliott and E. T. in the bathtub, the elimination of all guns from the film, (e.g., the cops carry walkie-talkies instead of guns while chasing E. T. and Elliott), the removal of Elliot's mothers' line "No, you're not going as a terrorist" in response to Elliot's preference in Halloween costumes, and a few others. Kennedy says, "We were running the movie and looking at the finished shots and we heard the line, and both Steven and I had completely forgotten that it was even in there, and we just felt hearing it that it was probably, in light of what has happened [on September 11th], it's an inappropriate line, and we elected to take it out." Spielberg, later would come to regret all the changes, saying, "I realized that what I had done was robbed the people who loved E.T. of their memories of E.T.." As recompense, Spielberg demanded that Universal include both the 1982 version of *E.T.* as well as the digitally enhanced 2002 version in the 20th Anniversary DVD release. In 2012, both the original version and the digitally enhanced version were digitally re-mastered and included in the 30th Anniversary release of the film. George Lucas followed suit and on May 12, 2004 released the original unaltered *Star Wars* films (1977, 1980, 1983) on DVD in a two-disc set along with a re-mastered version. Kennedy said, "It would be a big controversy if the studio was going to make a bunch of changes to movies and then release DVDs, because they felt the movie was better or something. But if a director is releasing a movie and wants to go in and make adjustments, that's entirely up to the vision of the director."[12]

One can only imagine what would happen if one of the studios went back and decided to change *The Wizard of Oz* or *Casablanca*. These films, these shared cultural artifacts, are as much about our culture as they are about the people who watch them. Movies are products of their times and a part of our cultural history. Countless, pre-civil rights films —many that are considered American classics—feature offensive and embarrassing portrayals of African American characters while many (especially early) James Bond films were unabashedly sexist and James Bond, on par with Han Solo in the original *Star Wars: A New Hope*, when confronted, shot first. Like some activists, we might make strong political arguments that these images should be erased like the guns the cops carry in *E. T.* But would we be better served as a nation if the blatant racism of D. W. Griffith's *The Birth of a Nation* or tacit racism of Fleming's *Gone with the Wind* were struck from all current and future screenings? In this regard, the ability to manipulate images and the

Digital Beginnings 219

narrative of shared cultural artifacts with CGI and the digital imaging not only effects the film business, but also our collective historical past, present, and future, as well.

It seems more and more every day our collective memory is jarred and fragmented as history is reworked, revised, and changed on television, in print, and online. As history, one realizes, becomes more fabricated and suspect, it becomes just one more form of entertainment (as evidenced in television "news" broadcasts). Case in point, in response to Colin Powell's address to the United Nations Council on February 5, 2003, regarding issues of Iraq's noncompliance, the Iraq ambassador said, "It is all fabrications . . . a typical American show, complete with special effects and stunts." In this day and age of "Wag the Dog," the potential for a fabricated reality does cause momentary pause and concern. There are still some people who do not believe that the United States astronauts actually went to the moon, but instead were filmed on a movie set in a secret sound stage. "Maybe they could have made it all up" is not an uncommon knee-jerk reaction—because the potential is there. The reissue of *Star Wars* and *E.T.* and other films, helped in a small way, to highlight the digital possibility of historical fabrication. Ever since the birth of photography and film, which promised viewers a manipulated reality, people have questioned what is "real." As the death of history, as posited by the postmodernists, becomes complete, truth and fiction begin to intertwine. The genie has been let out of the proverbial bottle on a multitude of levels. CGI and the digital revolution effects not only the film business, but also our culture and world view.

The digital revolution allowed filmmakers (and distributors via colorization) to make changes to their work, but also opened the door to consumers who can now digitally alter the Hollywood hits on par with the studios. New software available to the public now makes it possible to "insert product placement in movies or . . . make a New York skyline resemble Tokyo."[13] Some consumers, unhappy with the onslaught of PG-13 or R rated films, have begun to edit mainstream films specifically for family viewing (e.g., skip violent or sexual content, tone down the language, clothe Kate Winslett during her nude scene in *Titanic*, etc.). Demonstrating this editing technique with a demo tape to an audience of film directors, *MovieMask* software developer Breck Rice, upset all those in attendance. Swords in *The Princess Bride* were replaced with light sabers, voice-overs, such as "you funny people" were added over offensive language and Jack Nicholson's lips in *A Few Good Men* were altered as well. "It was heated. The directors did feel threatened," said Warren Adler, the associate national director of the DGA. "The terrifying implication of what you're saying is that any small interested parties are entitled to change anything to suit their own particular will. Where does that leave you? That leaves you in anarchy and chaos," director Michael Apted said, continuing, "It's fascism to me." Michael Mann also had something to say on the subject, "The idea that someone else. . . can arbitrarily take our works apart and destroy them in any manner they want and represent it as still being that film . . . is a breach," Mann says resentfully. "There's no polite word for it—it's stealing. It's stealing from the consumers . . . from the copyright holders [the studios] and it's certainly stealing from us. That's not the film that I made." "It's the tip of a very dangerous iceberg of digitizing," adds Apted. "This would appear to be a benign issue—making a family version—which could easily go a thousand other ways: making pornographic versions of films, political versions of films, any way you wanted to." The directors' outrage is lost on Richard Ray, a chiropractor and father of seven who, on the day a reporter visited the Mesa CleanFlicks, was returning an edited copy of *We Were Soldiers*. "They may talk about artistry and all that other stuff, but when it comes down to it, they made the movie and then some editor came and cut it, and the reason they cut it was to make it a marketable movie," Ray says. "They cut out scenes they thought may have been great, and then it goes to the airlines. They OK that. It goes to TV, they edit that. And they're making money all along the way and nobody hears anything about their artistry being cut down."[14]

The directors respond that such editing is permitted only because it is licensed by the studios. But this is a technicality that does not engage most Mesa CleanFlicks customers. One by one, the customers tick off the movies that had made them uncomfortable—for themselves or their children—and drove them inside this store: the bedroom moments in *Bridget Jones's Diary,* the sex scene in *Dances With Wolves,* the language in *My Cousin Vinny* and *Good Will Hunting*. The store's manager, Karen Huggans, a mother of six children who invested in the business as a way to raise the family's income, still remembers the cursing in *White Men Can't Jump,* a comedy she had looked forward to seeing. "The next day I was speaking to a youth group of kids about doing good things, and I could still hear those words ringing in my head."[15] Rice argues, "In the privacy of your own home, consumers have whatever liberties they want to take with property they own or have paid for the rights to use. No studio or director should be allowed to tell parents how to protect their kids."[16]

Experts sometimes offer conflicting impressions. Michael Marsden, a professor at Eastern Kentucky University who edits a journal on film and television, decries edited videos as "almost vigilantism." Jeremy Hunsinger, who directs a center for "digital discourse" at Virginia Polytechnic Institute, describes it as merely the latest example of the way digitizing dilutes reality—an extension, for example, of the way TV superimposes ads on stadium fences or the yellow first-down line on football fields. Ernest Miller, a fellow of the Information Society Project at Yale Law School, says directors have overreached by trying to outlaw home software that masks content of a DVD: "The issue is whether Hollywood can dictate how a viewer experiences a movie in the privacy of his or her own home." "Look," says director Jon Turteltaub, "You can't treat the work we spend years on as though it were a cookie-cutter project. We put our emotions and anxiety into our films. People like Marva Sonntag are fooling themselves if they think they're watching a Tom Cruise movie. They're simply watching *clips* from a Tom Cruise movie." "Look," says Mann, "You're crossing a line. If we were manufacturing a game we'd call it a game. But this isn't a game, it's a motion picture, and it has a narrative." The parts of a film "bear complex relationships that, in architecture, without that kind of engineering, the building falls down ... The experience is degraded."[17]

You can hear a dialogue in the two sides' exhortations, but it promises no compromise. Studios and the guild have filed suits alleging violation of trademark law while CleanFlicks video store claims protection of editing practices under federal copyright law. Unless the two sides reach a settlement, the court will have to decide whether the editing companies are illegally making "derivative" works, or whether the changes are so minor that they comply with a "fair use" exemption.

Another key question is whether software that allows a viewer to block content on an unedited DVD violates a director's "artistic rights," as the DGA claims, or is as harmless as hitting the fast-forward button on your remote. Directors say they realize their absolutism may be a hard sell in a culture where, as Turteltaub says, "People have the right to have things the way they want it .... I don't think it's surprising we do not have a lot of money for art in our schools when we have a society that feels when a piece of art is done, it's OK to cross things out that you personally don't like or edit it yourself or maybe put a black line through something that looks offensive to your group."[18] It appears that most of the alarm on both sides of the isle centers on what happens when a narrative that supports or constitutes a collective historical, cultural, or personal identity and memory is changed. Our current understanding of history is undergoing this same examination and questions of how a historical narrative is told, recorded, or remembered, or acted out in ritual are being noted. With every change made to a film, we might reflect and consider how our cultural history might have changed, in some small way, as well.

Moving Into the Millennium: The Prequels

> The scripts to the last three films I'm finishing now are a lot darker than the second three, because they are about a fall from grace.... *Star Wars* is ultimately about redemption.
>
> George Lucas, *The New Yorker*, January 6, 1997

For years, Lucas had talked about making the first three "prequels" to the *Star Wars* trilogy, shutting down the *Star Wars* movie-making machinery in 1983 after the opening of *Return of the Jedi*. Lucas had mapped out *Episodes I, II,* and *III* at the same time he had written *Episodes IV, V,* and *VI,* which detailed the early life of Obi Wan Kenobi and Darth Vader, then called Anakin Skywalker (Starkiller). From the beginning, Lucas is quick to say, the *Star Wars* saga has been the story of Anakin Skywalker, not that of his son Luke.

> The first three films are about his fall [Anakin], while the second three are about his redemption ... we will watch *The Phantom Menace* with the dark knowledge that sweet little Anakin Skywalker ... is headed for a particularly pronounced fall from grace.[19]

Probably no other film has received as much hype as Lucas's latest *Star Wars* film installments, and American audiences embraced the hype with open arms. *Star Wars* for many had almost become a secular religion. In *Star Wars* moral judgments such as good and bad, or right and wrong meant something. For many, the moral element of *Star Wars* rates high on the scale as a reason to go see the film. Brandon Eckert, a *Star Wars* fan states,

> We didn't grow up on King Arthur, we grew up with *Star Wars*. Lucas calls it a legend for our generation ... This film also speaks of the good and evil in everyone, that you must choose to be good.[20]

While the mythic dimension gives the story size and a grandeur, the "moral message hidden in the details" makes the stories last for viewers like Eckert.

The *Star Wars* canon certainly has had the ability to bring in an audience long before the actual film was ever screened. In New York City, where three theatres were granted the privilege of sneak previews of the *Phantom Menace*, it has become common knowledge that grown men took the day off from work—some traveling over an hour and a half by commuter trains from Connecticut—and paid $9 for a matinee screening of *Meet Joe Black*, just to see the teaser. Once they had seen *The Phantom Menace* trailer (2 minutes and 10 seconds of it), it was further reported that these same men quietly got up from their seats and left the theatre, only to return home and tell other folks via fan chat rooms what they had seen.[21] According to Tom Sherak, head of Fox distribution, business at theaters showing the trailer was up 140 percent the first night it was shown.[22] Not bad for two minutes worth of film and a good indicator of box office revenues to come. "I think everyone feels very strongly that this is going to be a huge-grossing film," said Chan Wood, executive vice president and head film buyer at Pacific Theatres in Los Angeles. "In my estimation, it probably is the only film that has any chance at all of unseating [all time box office king] *Titanic*."[23]

Because of *Titanic's* phenomenal success late in the preceding year, it was hard not to compare the two films. There were many similarities, but just as many differences. *Titanic*, unlike *Star Wars: Phantom Menace*, is a blockbuster, not a franchise. The year it came out, *Titanic*, shattered all box office records and surpassed the combined domestic box office total of *Star Wars* (*Star Wars*, 1977 & *Star Wars*, 1997) in the third month of its release, and knocked *Jaws* off its tenth place pedestal in little over a month's time (of course, these ratings would be different if box office totals were adjusted for inflation). Nominated for fourteen Academy Awards, including Best Picture, winning eleven, and walking away with the Golden Globe, *Titanic* exceeded all expectations of the studio and its producer-writer-director-editor, James Cameron. *Titanic* was not just a blockbuster, it was a box office phenomenon.[24]

Playing wide on over 3,110 screens (in THX theatres), *Titanic* grossed a steady $20 million a weekend. Even after four months, it did not slow down. It was at this time that Lucas made the comment that he would not be surprised if *Titanic* knocked *Star Wars* out of first position (a position *Star Wars* held after displacing *Jaws* for highest grossing film). Lucas even jokingly took out a full-page congratulatory ad in the trades depicting the cast of *Star Wars* sinking into the Atlantic (as of May 1, 1998 the top three highest grossing domestic box office films were: *Titanic* = $551 million, *Star Wars* = $461 million, *Jaws* = $399 million).[25]

A lot of the success of *Titanic*, like *Star Wars* and *Jaws* can be credited to smart advertising, packaging and marketing. Unlike, the corporate structure of the 1970s, where Lucas had to invent the merchandising wheel, the synergistic media conglomerate of the 1990s (based on the Lucas model) was fully mobilized to serve the needs of *Titanic*. Along with ad-blitzes on TV and radio, pop songs by well-known artists helped to sell the sound track which, besides being nominated for an Academy Award, also set new sales records. Licensee Harper-Collins meanwhile pushed forward on the publishing front with a "behind-the-scenes making of" book that topped the bestseller list at No. 1. Unlike *Star Wars*, *Titanic* is a blockbuster, or what some call a "closed" franchise. There certainly cannot be any sequels, no toys, or novel serializations, so it is forced to make its money from licensing (i.e., Pepsi, etc.), record sales, and rely on repeat audience business driven by those who are overwhelmed by the spectacle and special effects, and/or are attracted to the characters (Leo Di Caprio, in particular). Closer to *Jaws* in merchandising strategies, *Titanic* allows movie-goers multiple viewing, along with consumption of home videos, but does not really have the potential to exploit "take home" commodities like *Star Wars*. All things considered, the media conglomerates were happy with the situation and, even if *Titanic* failed, it would be felt as a long series of "hiccups" along the synergy chain

—nothing near the earth shattering noise it could have made in the 1970s. Fox and Paramount, snuggled within the safe diversity of the conglomerates, could afford to take some risk.

During his long directing hiatus, Lucas wisely bided his time and waited until the technology was there for him to tell the *Star Wars* story his way. After *Jurassic Park* had made its debut (and T-Rex's lived and breathed convincingly), Lucas knew it was time to move forward with his plans for *Episode I.*

The Phantom Menace was budgeted early on for $120 million, only half as much as the $200 million budget of *Titanic* a few years before. In comparison, a $120 million budget looked spare. The only difference was that Cameron's *Titanic* was financed by Fox and Paramount, and *The Phantom Menace* would be totally financed by Lucas who was "betting the Ranch" again. But there was freedom in such a gamble. Since Lucas was funding the prequels, he never had to answer to any one but himself.

Of course early marketing, tie-ins, etc., all helped to finance the film as well. The advertising, merchandising and promotional blitz were amazing. Billions came into play. Hasbro invested heavily in its licensing deal with Lucasfilm to the tune of nearly $600 million for royalties, etc., over nine years for toy sales tied to the three *Star Wars* prequels. "Lucas also received warrants to purchase 15.8 million shares of Hasbro, or about 7.4 percent of the company."[26] The price was steep, but kept Mattel at bay. Many analysts estimated that *Star Wars* toys would account for $1 billion in sales in 1999 alone and they were right. "Even if the movie isn't good, I think toy sales will be huge," said Chris Byrne, editor of the *Toy Report Newsletter*. On May 12th, nine days after toys hit the market, Taco Bell, Pizza Hut, and KFC restaurants join in the marketing hoopla. Tricon Global Restaurants, who own the three fast-food eateries, transformed them into three "planets," KFC–Naboo, Pizza Hut–Coruscant, and Taco Bell–Tatooine; each of these planets had twenty-eight collectible toys to choose from. When the *Star Wars: Special Edition* came out a few years

Digital Beginnings

before, Taco Bell reported a 4 percent increase in business attributable to the promotional tie-ins in stores that had been open for more than a year.[27]

In late May 1999, *Star Wars* merchandise was everywhere. Sunday paper inserts advertised *Star Wars: Phantom Menace* on every page. Pepsi cans, Lay's potato chips, party ware, soundtracks, Nintendo games, Playstation games, candy, trading cards, computer software, action figures, toys, bedding, towels, clothes, rollerblades, underwear, and all this merchandise was for sale on just three pages of a Target insert mailer ("Capture the Goods"). JC Penny claimed, "The Force is with us!," while Sears bragged that "A new saga for the hottest stuff: Blast into Sears" had arrived, and Macy's shouted from the page "In a Macy's Galaxy Near You."

Merchandising got an even bigger push when LucasArts Entertainment announced the addition of two new video game titles that were tied to the film (a *Phantom Menace* adventure game for the Sony PlayStation and a *Phantom Menace* adventure game for the Nintendo 64)—marking another brilliant "first" for Lucas. The practice of releasing video games simultaneously with the release of the movie on which they were based first occurred at this time. "*Star Wars: Phantom Menace*," new media author Don Tapscott said, "will be the first film that will make money even if nobody buys a ticket," regarding the latest video offering of *Star Wars* games.[28] The blitz was on.

It was not long before everybody got into the act and helped make *Star Wars: Episode I—The Phantom Menace* a success. Opening on midnight, May 18, 1999, the latest installment of the *Star Wars* trilogy brought in $121.1 million gross its five-day opening weekend, also racking up a record $28.5 million opening day, surpassing Universal's *The Lost World: Jurassic Park* which had a $26 million single-day gross in 1997.[29] *The Phantom Menace* became the first film to top $200 million domestically in less than two weeks, beating the previous record for the shortest time to hit the $200 million milestone by an astounding eight days.

Star Wars: Episode I—The Phantom Menace blasted past the milestone set by *Independence Day* in 1996.[30] By July 26, 1999, the film crossed the

$400 million dollar mark, becoming only the second film in history to do so in its initial release. *Titanic* was the first. *Phantom Menace* "crested that rarefied box office strata in sixty-seven days, one day longer that it took *Titanic* to reach that level"[31] Brian Fuson, a reporter with the *Hollywood Reporter* continues, "The summer box office season is blazing a trail where no box office season has gone before as the first eight weeks of the session have racked up a record $155 million—a convincing 20 percent better than last year's comparable period . . . the box office pace of the top films far outstripped that of their counterparts last summer, as the aggregate box office for the five most popular films this year was a remarkable 57 percent higher. Led by the stellar performance of Twentieth Century Fox's *Star Wars: Episode I—the Phantom Menace*, this year's top 5 films grossed an impressive $847 million, while the comparable films a year ago pulled in $538.0 million . . . with a little more than half the season gone by, five films have grossed more than $100 million." [32]

In July 1999, the *Phantom Menace* was also breaking records across the Atlantic and set a four-day opening record in the United Kingdom with $14.4 million, knocking *Men in Black*, with $11.8 million, off the top rung in the British four-day opening box office championship.[33] By the beginning of 2000, "The Force continued to be with . . . *Phantom Menace* as the prequel claims(ed) the second-highest worldwide theatrical box office gross of all time with receipts of $922.5 million to date . . . *Phantom* vaulted ahead of *Jurassic Park* (1993), which falls to No.3 with a world wide gross of $920 million. *Titanic* . . . leads with $1.8 billion worldwide—almost equal to the combined worldwide grosses of *Phantom* and *Jurassic Park*."

The biggest part of *Phantom's* worldwide box office came from foreign markets. The domestic total for the sci-fi mega hit is $431.1 million, compared with an international cumulative of $491.4 million. *Phantom* can claim the unique distinction of being the only film other than *Titanic* to gross more than $400 million in North America on its initial release.[34]

Digital Beginnings

For any of you reading who might have missed it, in a nutshell, *Phantom Menace* endeavors to tell the story of what takes place a generation before the original *Star Wars* occurs. The peaceful Galactic Republic is struggling to retain its rule as turmoil engulfs the galaxy. While rescuing Queen Amidala of Naboo from an attack by the Trade Federation, the Republic's Jedi Knight Qui-Gon Jinn and his apprentice Obi Wan Kenobi encounter nine-year-old slave, Anakin Skywalker—who is "strong with the Force." Freed from slavery by the Jedis, taken on by Qui-Gon Jinn as a potential apprentice (Obi Wan "ends up with him" after Qui-Gon is killed by the Sith), the future Darth Vader begins a fateful journey that will change his destiny.

To put the entire *Star Wars* narrative into perspective this outline can be offered:

Episode I. Anakin Skywalker, a child slave on Tatooine, gained his freedom with the help of the Jedi Qui-Gon Jinn, who recognizes "Force" potential in the young boy. Forced to leave his enslaved mother, Shmi, behind, Anakin helped the Jedi and Queen Amidala liberate her home world in the Battle of Naboo. When Qui-Gon Jinn was slain by a Dark Lord of the Sith, his apprentice, Obi wan Kenobi, begrudgingly took on the responsibility to raise the boy as a Jedi. Although Anakin was older than most recruits, the Jedi Council eventually allowed him to enter the order (against the advice of Yoda).

Episode II. Anakin, grown to a young man and "strong in the Force," meets up with Padme Amidala, former Queen of the Naboo again (Queens on Naboo only serve four year terms). Although such a romantic relationship is forbidden to the Jedi (since they are celibate), Anakin falls in love with Padme. As both are caught up in the chaotic events of the time (read: *The Clone Wars*), Anakin seems drawn to the dark side of the Force (for one, he slaughters the Sand People who have kidnapped and killed his mother). Anakin and Amidala are secretly married.

Episode III. Anakin's children, Luke Skywalker and Princess Leia Organa, are born and are hidden from their father for their own protection.

Anakin eventually comes under the sway of Emperor Palpatine—who finally reveals himself as a Dark Lord of the Sith. Anakin betrays the Jedi, causing their partial destruction. He sustains injuries at the hands of his former master, Obi-Wan, that require extensive cybernetic replacements. He is reborn as Darth Vader, a Dark Lord of the Sith, a being seemingly bereft of any humanity.

Episodes IV-VI. Luke and Leia grow to adulthood and join the Rebel Alliance. Darth Vader kills his former master, Obi-Wan. Throughout, Luke learns the way of the Jedi (first from Obi-Wan, then Yoda). During a duel, Vader reveals himself as Luke's father. Luke, captured, is brought before the Emperor aboard the second Death Star. Unable to see his son killed, Vader slays the Emperor. Darth/Anakin dies a short while later —finally redeemed for his transgressions.[35]

About the film critics remarked, *Phantom Menace* delivers on spectacle; the pod race was terrific . . . easily this film's biggest thrill . . . it is in this kind of visual creation of other worlds that *Phantom Menace* lives up to expectations and reveals its strengths; the many visuals were stunning and imaginative. For the first time fully digital characters seamlessly interacted with live actors on the screen while fantastic landscapes and environments tantalized the eye—another Lucas and film history "first." We learned about and lived pod races and were introduced to a whole new world of odd and interesting characters. A true digital fete.[36] Lucas explains, "On *Phantom Menace* we started to develop digital characters. At the time, we had dinosaurs that could look good running through a real environment. But we never had anything that could actually act and look good and be believable with real actors."[37]

ANAKIN & LUKE: TWO DIFFERENT TYPES OF HEROES

In *Phantom*, as in *Episode IV*, Lucas used the hero quest myth as the foundation of his story. Considering the Prequels were written at the same time as the original *Star Wars* trilogy, this approach was not a surprise. As outlined earlier, according to Joseph Campbell, the film follows the journey of the archetypal hero quite well: Anakin is born of a virgin (the origin of Luke's mother is likewise obscure), he harkens to the call to adventure and leaves his familiar world, is "chosen" and aided by protective forces in the guise of the "Wise Old Man/Good Father" archetype (Obi Wan), goes through initiation via a series of trials where he meets and rescues the princess, battles his "shadow" (or his capacity for evil), survives supreme ordeals, and gains his final reward.

Anakin, our hero, doesn't refuse the call to adventure as part of his journey, but *he is refused himself* by the Jedi Council. Here is the striking difference between the two heroes: where Luke is immediately accepted by those who can teach and guide him, Anakin is not. This change to the "normal" hero myth structure is significant. Anakin, rather than following a 'Hero's Journey," decidedly takes, what appears to be the less familiar, "Heroine's Journey." Rather than believing in and aiding the young hero in his quest, the supernatural guides act as Harsh Mentors or Threshold Guardians and thwart his every move. The only individual who stands up for Anakin, Qui Gon Jinn (the Wise Old Man/Good Father), must prove over and over again to his Jedi "brothers" the child's worth. But no one in the Jedi council deems the young hero worthy—or worth their time to guide and instruct (perhaps reflective of our current society where absent fathers proliferate). In fact, they accuse the child of being too powerful, too prone to losing control. The Jedi committee of supposedly Wise Old Men/Good Fathers (more like rival brothers really—on parallel to Robert Bly's notion of the sibling society) [38] in this scenario want to "get rid" of the child instead of help him, and do not want to help him hone his extraordinary qualities (Anakin gets punished for his unique abilities instead!). Hence, the "good" Jedi who should be helping the child to learn how to strike a balance between right and wrong and learn self-control, instead, through short-sightedness or own fear that the child might eclipse their own power, become Anakin's Bad Fathers (and consequently, the true "Bad Fathers," the Sith of the Dark Side, accept and cherish Anakin, and, in a perverse twist, become his Good Fathers).

This archetypal reversal sets the stage, then, for our hero to steer away from the "positive" side of his nature and embrace the negative, or "dark."

Extremes in anything create an imbalance, which on a mythic level, has the capacity to destroy not only an individual, but the entire universe. The Jedi, in their hubris, try to repress the negative aspects of Anakin's nature, instead of helping him learn how to control and balance it. This is their downfall. A "shadow" repressed or denied is a shadow that will return with a vengeance—and does in the guise of Darth Vader. Eventually, Anakin, shunned by his Jedi "brothers/potential Wise Old Men/Good Fathers," is eventually duped by the bad (Sith). He does not belong anywhere. He is a liminal character, not of this earth. Demi-god, he is betwixt and between the worlds and does not fit in—so he begins to sulk and rebel. And it is no wonder he is angst-ridden. He is the ugly duckling, a little child lost, unloved and unappreciated—and very, very angry (Oddly, Anakin had it better as a slave on Tatooine. He was praised for his pod racing abilities, although "used" is more like it. He at least belonged on Tatoonie, was loved by his mother, and was cherished for his talents and abilities).

Luke, on the other hand, is aided, loved and cherished throughout his entire life by all his "Good Fathers" (Uncle Owen, Obi Wan Kenobi, Yoda); he fights his "Bad" father (Anakin/Darth Vader), who eventually turns into his "Good" father via a deathbed reconciliation, and in doing so, Luke overcomes the capacity for evil—and learns to control and balance the two parts of his human nature. Luke finally recognizes himself in his father and forgives him (and, in doing so, forgives himself his own dark potential and shortcomings). Both father and son find redemption in each other. Anakin growing up does not have it so easy. Hell is murky, so Lady Mac Beth is fond of saying, and Anakin's story is a bit of a modern day *Paradise Lost.*

In the second installment, *Attack of the Clones,* Anakin becomes more lost and more angry. His heroism is never acknowledged, merely discussed by committee. Anakin's mother dies alone because he was

Digital Beginnings

not there to help her--his out-of-touch father archetype interferes once again and denies him any interaction with his mother. Throughout his Jedi training, Anakin is denied access to his emotions, or his feminine side (the Jedi are celibate priests) as personified in the women in the film, most notably his mother and the Princess Amadala. But to be a fully integrated, balanced individual, he must reconcile his emotional/feminine side with the masculine/intellectual side of his human nature, a balance of yin-yang, anima/animus, and light/dark is required to become a fully individuated human being. The important journey for Anakin is an interior one. Joseph Campbell has said that "all journey's lead inward," none so much as Anakin's. To do this, Anakin must make a very hard choice: either remain a child and blindly obey those in authority, or make his own decision and grow up. Tales of transgressive redemption, which the *Prequels* clearly are, requires the hero to listen to their own hearts, and make their own choices, and take responsibility for those choices. In order to grow up, and find balance and harmony, a hero needs to be able to make their own decisions, not live by someone else's. [39] And Anakin does make his own choice, but because he still must learn self-control and learn how to strike a balance between what is good for a society vs what is good for the individual, as well as weigh the consequences between immediate gratification and long term success, he stumbles. No one is there to teach him how to strike this balance—both the Jedi who are clearly associated with the "good" and the Sith who are positioned as "bad" do not have the capacity to help him integrate "both sides." The worlds these opposites live in are a place of "either/or"—but Anakin, in order to become a fully integrated individual, needs to live in "both." As a liminal character Anakin must negotiate between the two worlds (good/bad, right/wrong, masculine/feminine, yin/yang) and balance them both within himself. The archetypal image of the man with the angel on one shoulder and a devil on the other isn't far off the mark. Only after listening to both sides can he truly make his own decision.

So, Anakin decides and defies the rules of the celibate Jedi and marries Amidala (integrates his feminine/emotional and intuitive side). At every turn, Anakin's better judgment, common sense, and intuition (his feminine anima) is being tested by out of touch "superiors." Again, this resistance is part of Anakin's quest, his Grail. As long as he marches to the beat of someone else's drum he is doomed. He is continually cut off from his own feelings, his own better judgment. Emotions, denied or repressed in this way return with a vengeance. In psychological terms, to be a Jedi means to guard against being possessed by power, greed, lust and other primal impulses and to work for individual human transformation, not just in society, but within one's personal life as well. A balance is required. But if the pendulum swings too far in either direction and emotions are denied and an individual is cut off from their true feelings (and the Jedi and Anakin are at opposite ends of the bell curve: one feels too little, the other too much), then the dark side (shadow) will 'cut through' the denials and gain power. Of course, since the prequel and trilogy are about the redemption of Anakin Skywalker, it follows that the narrative is about redemption from identification "with archetypal energies," especially destructive ones like anger and hate or fear, which can cause us to do things we might otherwise regret, triggering a loss of our humanity. These negative actions feed the monsters we must acknowledge, overcome, and control in ourselves.

These archetypal energies are expressed in our myths, both old and new. To fail to recognize them for what they are and to ignore or deny them is to lose one's soul. When this happens, as this story demonstrates, we need the help of others–as well as a conscious understanding of the nature of the transformation of archetypal energy so that lost aspects of the human personality can be restored... Luke's final vision [of Anakin Skywalker, Yoda, and Obi Wan Kenobi together in spirit] suggests that he has succeeded in healing a wound that has been carried forward from the past, in particular, Ben and Yoda's loss of Anakin to the dark practitioners of the Force. At the end of *Episode VI*, "Leia steps forward to invite Luke back to the celebration and to what may lie ahead for all of them. The film ends with the theme that initially awakened the young hero: a beckoning of the feminine principle to enter a new age, an

Digital Beginnings 235

invitation to go forward in life in conjunction with the transformation of problems held over from the past. This brother-sister, yin-yang pair, and their companions become new symbols for the future." [40]

While some may argue that the Force is God, it is never set up as such. Instead, the Force is an elusive and mysterious supernatural "thing" that exists. The good guys use it for good, and the bad guys use it for evil. Accordingly, the Force is like any natural force of nature, like fire, which can be used for good or ill. It has no inherent moral nature, it simply is. Perhaps it is how the individual decides to use the Force which ultimately defines it. Certainly, it is our decisions in life that define who and what we are.

FANS REACT

Fan reactions, like those for the *Star Wars: Special Editions*, were divided. Many fans loved the new *Star Wars* films, others didn't. As a shared cultural artifact, these films were not "just a movie," they had become a part of their lives. Some fans tried to "make it better" through repeat viewings that were an attempt to see the saga in a new light. Others would go as far as to actually reedit the film or make their own version of the new *Star Wars* epic. The irony being that these were the same people who had criticized Lucas for making edits to the original trilogy in the *Star Wars: Special Editions* years before. Still others would turn to writing fan fiction to enhance and accommodate their own reading of the films, while others would go to the internet and post threads on discussion boards and debate other fans who had enjoyed them.

Any "let down" feeling, Booker contends in his book, *Using the Force: Creativity, Community and Star Wars Fans*, was due to how much of an impact the film had made in some of the fans' lives.[41] *Star Wars* had figured in many fans' development as a child, they had played "it" and acted "it" out at home and at school; kept "it" alive while viewing it in groups or studied "it" while watching alone. They had used their own sweat equity to emotionally invest and identify with the *Star Wars* characters, who after so many years, had become fully integrated into their lives, and hence, an integral part of their identity. The films acted as a social touchstone and icebreaker and had helped these people build a sense of community and belonging throughout their lives. *Star Wars* was a "secret password" that enabled fans to make instant connections, and in doing so, share an immediate sense of communal culture. Viewed within this context, it is no wonder, then, that the fans would take the prequels personally. One fan remarked:

> I care about the characters in the SW universe. In a way, I share a sense of fellowship with them. I know the difference between fantasy and reality, and though the characters in SW will never be as precious to me as my "real" friends, I still wish the best for them. Through the years, I have become invested in their lives. From that first moment I felt a bond form with that lonely farm boy on a planet in a galaxy far, far away, I have followed the exploits of the SW family, in their triumphs and sharing their tragedies.[42]

For many, *Star Wars* was more than a movie, the people in them more than movie characters. These characters had, in many ways, become part of an extended "family," a very important part of the fans' real and imagined lives. How many films can really boast this kind of deep identification with the characters? Not many outside the *Star Wars* oeuvre. This phenomenon in itself is a true tribute to the storytelling power of George Lucas.

The most likely reason for the divided fan reaction was due to an aging fan base. Perhaps, as the fans of the original *Star Wars* trilogy grew older they wanted to recapture the same feelings they had watching *Star Wars* for the first time when they were seven or seventeen—but could not. To recapture the wonder, awe, and magic they originally experienced at a younger age is impossible. This is the lure of nostalgia. How can anything compare to a first love, a childhood Christmas morning, or the "best 8th birthday ever"?

> I have been a *Star Wars* fan for over twenty years. I'm old enough to have seen the original trilogy in the cinema. I remember the phenomenon that was *Star Wars*. My first reaction to the film that I had been looking forward to for so many years was... It was nothing like the original trilogy.[43]

This issue centered around age seems to bear out, since many of the younger crowd who saw *The Phantom Menace* before being exposed to the original trilogy appear to respond to it extremely favorably and enjoy the high-end, sophisticated effects and martial arts fight scenes. Many of these kids have been weaned on *Star Wars* Nintendo and Game Boy video games that parallel many of the scenes in *The Phantom Menace* and *Attack of the Clones*. Polls on *Star Wars Kids* (a junior version of the *StarWars.com* site) asked visitors for their favorite characters and *Menace's* or *Clones's* Obi Wan Kenobi won out over Han Solo while Amidala and Leia, as well as the young Obi Wan Kenobi and Luke Skywalker all enjoy equal status.

Despite the debate, the fans still love *Star Wars* and base it on their own personal involvement with the saga. In many ways, *Star Wars* no longer belongs solely to Lucas anymore, not in the literal sense. *Star Wars* characters and stories have escaped the boundaries of the original text and have grown up with the fans that have developed their own sense of what *Star Wars* is and is not. So, when Lucas revisited the *Star Wars* universe in 1999, he found resistance on the part of the fans who had created via play, discussion, and identification, their own version of the *Star Wars* epic. Both the fans, who appropriated *Star Wars*, and Lucas, the writer, director, and owner of copyright, can be considered "creators" and co-owners of this shared cultural space.

THE LUCAS EFFECT: EXPANDING THE DEFINITION OF FILM: A NEW FILM APPROACH

Clearly, the circulation of *Star Wars* in our culture, by fans or others, goes beyond the simple definition of a film either as a noun or a verb.

As a noun, film has traditionally been described as a thick strip of plastic or other material coated with light-sensitive emulsion for exposure in a camera used to produce photographs or motion pictures, as a story or event recorded by a camera, or as cinema--pertaining to art or an industry. As a verb, film is something that captures images, or is a thin membrane that covers things. Film has grown beyond these limited restrictions. Film, "post-Lucas," has evolved as a noun from celluloid to digital capture, from a story or event recorded by a camera into theme park rides and pillowcases, and as a verb shifted from the mere filming or viewing of images, into the active manufacture, consumption, appropriation, and circulation of images in our culture. As mentioned earlier in the book, a film is no longer just a film.

Most critical approaches today still use the piece of celluloid or projected image on the screen as their primary focus of study. The actual projected film is a good starting point for examination, but it is only the starting point. It follows then, that what defines a film needs reworking, and in turn, new critical approaches based on these new definitions need to be developed. A more synergistic model is needed. Synergy, the cooperation or interaction of two or more organizations, subsidiaries, or agents to produce a combined effect, more closely resembles how film functions today. From the original idea of the creator to screen, and then to market and theme park, the original film, as well as its narrative, goes through a series of important transformations. There are points along this transformational chain (or production line) where the film is used, by one entity or another, for different purposes. From being a piece of celluloid or digital image, the film changes into a product, place, or idea. We need to capture these points of transformation, as well as examine the people, agents, organizations, or subsidiaries who are involved as collaborators in this transformational process, along the way. Not only is a film watched, but is being *used* and experienced differently. Old measures of study and evaluation that theorized film only using a piece of celluloid as reference point will no longer suffice in a system of active praxis. We need a more holistic system of evaluation and measurement. To capture the true measure and impact of a film (in all its various forms) and assign value, we need to develop a synergistic, and/or transmedia model that will take into consideration and can capture all the transformations of the original film throughout its lifetime. We need to consider not only how a film: 1) is historically significant, but, 2) the various ways it is used and experienced in our culture as a shared cultural artifact (how the film is circulated, appropriated, and disseminated), 3) how it has impacted film industry practices and business strategies (marketing, distribution, licensing, franchise strategies used to accommodate film synergy among corporate affiliates, etc.), and 4) its impact on various economies (local, national, and global; examine fiscal impact, box office, ties to GNP, etc.). Only then, after careful consideration, can we get a true understanding of what a film is and has become, including its true value. Use and synergy must be examined across platforms of expression to extrapolate meaning when film has become more than just a film. When considered within this model, Lucas's contribution to film and film history is unprecedented.

Domestic Box Office Hits $9 Billion—Highest Ever

The *Star Wars* audience when asked whether they would be lining up for the next *Star Wars* installment, answered with a resounding "yes" and made *Clones* (and *Spider Man)* their film of choice at the box office, making the four-day 2002 Memorial Day weekend the biggest in box office history, combined gross receipt totals reaching $200 million. *Star Wars: Episode II - Attack of the Clones* was the top film with an estimated $61.2 million for the four-day holiday frame and *Spider Man* came in second in its third week of release at $36.5 million (with a cumulative of $334.3 million). For the week ending May 23rd, the national box office was up an amazing 68 percent from the comparable seven-day period in 2001 ($242.4 million vs. $144.4 million). The year-to-date total for 2002 vaulted to a stunning 23 percent improvement the year before ($3.31 billion versus $2.70 billion). In just twelve days, *Clones* went on to make $202.5 million, the second fastest to that mark after Sony's *Spider Man* which took nine days to reach that goal (*Phantom Menace* took thirteen days to hit that level). In twenty-two days, *Spider Man* hit an estimated gross of $334.3 million, making it the sixth highest-grossing domestic film of all time, passing *Forrest Gump* ($329.7 million) and coming close to Universal's *Jurassic Park* ($357 million).[44] By the end of the summer, one would have thought *Clones* would have been the one to beat at $300 million, but *Spider Man* ended up out-grossing *Clones* by more than $100 million ($431.1 domestic).[45]

Although lagging behind *Spider Man*, *Clones* consistently brought in 70 percent of the domestic gross of its predecessor, *The Phantom Menace* ($431.1 million domestic), an amazing feat for any sequel (which at best brings in around 60 percent of the original in the series). Internationally, *Clones* brought in another $324.3 million bringing the total box office to $624.3 million worldwide (within the same time frame *Spider Man* hit the $800 million dollar mark).[46] Another film to challenge *Clones* was *Lord of the Rings: Two Towers*, which opened its first weekend with $61.5 million, more than *Clones* received its first week out, taking only eight days to reach the $100 million mark.[47] This combined total for the week made LOTR the biggest December opening by any movie in film industry history, doing an unheard of 33 percent more than the previous year's first installment in the trilogy, *The Fellowship of the Ring*. The film also was the twenty-second in 2002 to gross more than $100 million, tying 2000's record total.[48] Touted by many as "this generation's *Star Wars*," *The Lord of the Rings* trilogy brilliantly set up a situation in which people were excited to go to see the next in the series, and grosses clearly reflected that sentiment.[49]

By the end of 2002, Hollywood had a lot to celebrate. The year ended up recording the biggest gains in more than a decade in both number of admissions and total box office dollars. Sony's *Spider Man* led the pack with *Attack of the Clones* ranking a close second.

Digital Beginnings 241

Theatrical box office in the United States surpassed the $9 billion mark for the first time and admissions posted their highest tally since 1957. *The Hollywood Reporter* states:

> The total for the national box office in 2002 for a normalized fifty-two week year was a record shattering $9.46 billion - an extraordinary increase of more than $1 billion from the previous year's $8.41 billion - a marked improvement of nearly 13 percent, according to projections ... the year-to-year percentage increase at the box office is the largest since 1989, when revenue increased nearly 13 percent from the previous year. Even more significantly, more people went to the movies in 2002 - a great deal more— as admissions climbed a stunning 150 million from 2001 .... admissions for 2002 were 1.642 billion, up 10 percent from the previous year's 1.487 billion and the highest in the past forty-five years. In year-to-year increases, 2002 represents the biggest gain in ticket units since 1982, when admissions jumped 10 percent from the year before.
>
> Since 1998, theatrical film admissions in the United States have hovered in the 1.4 billion area but never quite reached the heights of 1959, when 1.488 billion admissions were recorded. Until last year, 1959 had been the admissions benchmark against which the past few years were measured. But after last year, 1957—when 1.73 billion admissions were recorded—is the new standard against which the past year can be compared.[50]

As mentioned in Chapter 1, theatrical admissions hit their highest point in 1946 in the United States when 4.1 billion tickets were reported sold. But when TV hit the airwaves, admissions went into steady decline (homes with TVs in 1947 was at 2 percent and climbed to 90 percent by 1961). The decline continued until it bottomed out in 1971 with a record low of 820 million admissions. After 1971, though ticket sales began a steady upturn culminating in the stunning showing of 2002. What can account for these increases? There is a strong correlation between increase in admissions with increase in box office, suggesting that the increase in attendance can be attributed to a steady increase in ticket price. Releases also helped account for the rise, up from 130 in 2001 to 139 in 2002 while screen count remained stable. But a larger number of film releases does not guarantee higher admissions.

In 2000, there were 135 releases and admissions were tame (1.42 billion), and in 1996, there were 139 wide releases but admissions remained modest (1.34 billion)—almost 300 million fewer than 2002. What seems to be the biggest contributing factor was the quality of films.

> Last year witnessed a record number of films that reached $100 million. By year's end, there were twenty films that grossed more than $100 million, which bests the previous record set in 2002, when nineteen films reached that level by the end of the year. A record seven films hit the $200 million mark last year: *Spider Man, Attack of the Clones, Harry Potter and the Chamber of Secrets, Signs, My Big Fat Greek Wedding, The Lord of the Rings: The Two Towers* and Austin Powers in *Goldmember.* The old record was six in 2001.
>
> Additionally, the winning pictures were spread among more studios. For the first time, three North American distributors racked up more than $1 billion each in domestic box office. Sony was the box office champ by a wide margin, with the company joining the $1 billion club for the second time and logging around $1.56 billion—the biggest gross ever tallied by a distributor in a single year. The studio had five films that grossed more than $100 million each—*Spider Man* ($405.7 million), *Men in Black II* ($194.2 million), *XXX* ($141.2 million), *Mr. Deeds* ($126.2 million) and the 2001 release *Black Hawk Down* ($108.6 million).[51]

More than any other film, *Spider Man*, starring Tobey Maguire and directed by Sam Raimi, contributed to Sony's outstanding year and shocked the industry as it broke every industry record on the books to date.[52]

The most popular rating by far among the top twenty-five films was PG-13 and fourteen films, or 56 percent, carried that particular rating. Films rated with PG were the next most popular with six followed by R-rated films (4) and one rated G. But among the top twelve of the year, PG-13 and PG tied—each tallying six each. As a rule, family friendly films were abundant in the top tier in 2002, with the majority in the top twelve. Concept also contributed to a films' success in 2002, eclipsing the popularity of movie stars. Statistically, stars were not a significant factor in the top twenty-five films of the year.[53]

Christmas week (Friday through Thursday) also logged the very first $300 million week ever recorded with $308 million. The following New Year's week even exceeded that amount with $346.5 million. It was not very long ago that Hollywood positioned its most expensive "froth"—popcorn flicks—for summer releases, while using the holiday period to screen more "adult," or Oscar-oriented fare. Not so anymore. Now we see more and more sequels, remakes, spin-offs and other low-risk, mass market fare pushed by a desire and need for fast money at the box office. With the movement of the Academy Awards from the month of April (or late March) to late February in 2004, this practice may change to showcase possible Oscar contenders. The film's December release coupled with a short/early Oscar voting period has been blamed for its poor award showing.

The holiday season is now viewed as the best twelve to fourteen days of the year and the big conglomerates need the dollars funneled off ($9 billion in 2003) from the studios they own to help keep the beleaguered media giants afloat. To do this, studios need to keep hedging their bet as the cost of making a movie continues to escalate. The average cost to make a movie rose from $9.4 million in 1980 to $52.8 million in 2000 (according to the Motion Picture Association of America). The cost of selling and distributing such a picture has also risen. The movie in 1980, which cost $9.4 million to make, took $4.3 million to market; the same movie in 2000, which took $52.8 million to make cost $31 million to market. That is for an "average" picture. Add all the special effects and larger budget for a popcorn flick and you are looking at more like $40-$70 million to market. *Titanic's* successful release can be pointed to as the major reason in the blockbuster move from summer to the midwinter season. *Titanic* was originally scheduled to be released during the summer, but delays due to post-production problems pushed it until the holiday season.

Titanic eventually brought home $1.8 billion worldwide. Now, all of a sudden, the holiday season looked really good to distributors who had a popcorn flick or two that could use a little less summer competition. As a result the holiday season which spanned roughly fourteen days, now reaches into November (e.g., *The Santa Claus 2* which opened in November 2003 grossed over $100 million).[54]

Let's Go Digital: Technical, Commercial and Artistic Implications: Another First

Lucas's second installment of the prequels, *Star Wars: Attack of the Clones* (2002) was *a technical benchmark in filmmaking*. It had the distinction of being *the first feature film to be shot entirely on high-definition digital video* (it was shot with a 24p digital video-cam especially developed by Sony, with newly developed Panavision lenses)—changing both the look of film and the standards of filmmaking. The shift from Lucas using complicated matte visual effect composites (opticals) for specific shots in *Star Wars* in 1977 (developed by ILM) to the use of time saving digital technologies to replace these complex celluloid opticals (and use of miniatures, puppetry, etc.), along with the inclusion of more extensive green screen elements (*Jurassic Park*, 1993; *Star Wars: Special Editions*, 1997); naturally evolved into the wall-to-wall use of digital technology to replace all celluloid in the production of the entire film—especially if the screenplay called for the creation of new worlds, alien people, and never-before-seen creatures (*Star Wars: Attack of the Clones*, 2002). The technical breakthroughs on *Clones* are evident in every frame. Never before had so many previously impossible shots and visions appeared in one film, nor on such a large scale. "With digital, you have to learn how to do things differently than you've done in the past," says Lucas, "The core part of making a film, which is directing the actors and writing the

Digital Beginnings 245

script, stayed the same. But telling the story and having digital characters and sets took a little figuring out to actually pull it off."[55]

While much of *Phantom's* live-action footage was recorded on "old-fashioned" celluloid, *Clones* was not—almost every environment visited by the film's characters is either totally or mostly computer-generated (even though the film was produced on four continents). "There are approximately 2,000 visual-effects shots in the movie," notes visual-effects supervisor John Knoll, "That's about three or four times what we would normally think of as a big visual-effects production."[56]

The statistics for *Episode II* are: seventy minutes of animation compared to *Episode I's* sixty minutes worth; approximately sixty-five different alien species and double the number of hard-surface models (i.e., vehicles, weapon systems and the like) as in the previous movie; 95 percent of the shots in the final cut are reported to have some kind of computer generated element or another. Countless man hours went into making them all look and move right. The art, design and tech team heads met with Lucas every Tuesday and Thursday for eighteen months, watched their latest footage on high-definition television and then worked out any kinks in the visuals back and forth over computer linkups. Of the thousands of elements *Clones* required, Lucas was most concerned with the movements of Yoda. Probably thirty people at ILM were involved with making that character. It was five years of research and development.[57] But while Yoda was being developed in the computer, real actors had to work with invisible Yoda's on the set—which took some doing. "We actually had the puppet, so when we had to do a reference shot, they would just put him in there and I'd know where to look," said Samuel Jackson. It was not so easy for Hayden Christensen the actor who played Anakin. "It was tricky sometimes, in terms of trying to keep your head straight as to where you are supposed to be looking and deliver a line at the same time . . . . It definitely was challenging." The final battle in which Anakin is battling droids and clones while on the back of a hippo-like creature called a Reek was all captured while the actor was on top of a bucking mechanical bull on an empty Australian soundstage.[58] Early versions of Yoda still did not come across as "real," nor did Gollum in first installments of the *Lord of the Rings* trilogy. No matter how many man-hours went into it, Gollum in *Fellowship of the Ring* never seemed "real"—he appeared not to have bones, was too rubbery, and unnatural. Michael Blake, veteran actor, friend, and long-time film makeup artist, in an email dated May 10, 2001 considered the "reality" of CGI characters:

> Recently, I was at a video store and was watching a film done in CGI. There was a big parade scene and all the people in the scene were cheering and waving. I was watching it from a distance and was struck at how "unreal" the extras looked. The sets, background players, etc. Compare, if you will, the big parade number in *Hello, Dolly!* The sets were real and so were the extras. They have a substance that CGI lacks. Of course, as time gets better, I am sure CGI will improve on these problems . . . . then again, maybe not. Anyway, I was struck by this and I felt kinda sad. Yes, I know scenes like that parade for *Hello, Dolly!* would be way too expen$ive nowadays, just like the big ball sequences in "Marie Antoinette" would have a UPM reaching for a gun to shoot themselves. But it hit home that those wonderful days of filmmaking when we had BIG scenes like that are gone and CGI has yet (if ever) to reproduce that "human" and "realistic" feel for such sequences on film. Anyway, just the rambling thoughts of an old makeup artist who pines for the good old days of the studio system. [59]

To give an example of how complex and involved the CGI process and directing in post at ILM was, consider this, then multiply it by 2,000:

> Under George Lucas' direction, ILM used its computers to manipulate live action plates to an unprecedented degree. 'We've literally taken parts of four different shots to make one shot,' says Lucasfilm's Martin Smith, one of the movie's editors. 'We've even changed people's eyeballs to establish eye contact. It's very much like directing in post.' One such scene depicts a conversation between the character Padme (Natalie Portman) and the young Anakin Skywalker (Jake Loyde). Since Lucas preferred each actor's performance in different takes, the shot became a split-screen,

Digital Beginnings 247

composed of elements from two separate takes, says ILM Editor David Tanaka. ILM Compositing Supervisor Greg Maloney created the split by getting the two plates to lock together using proprietary Repo (Repositioning software). "This scene hadn't been shot with pin-registered cameras, so there was movement in the plates.... The procedure I used involved making one shot the 'hero side'—in this case, the Anakin plate—and stabilizing that." After locking that down, Maloney used the information to stabilize the other side. Making the actors appear to interact convincingly, however, took some finessing. "Padme is first supposed to look at Anakin, then at the floor.... But the only footage that was actually photographed was of Padme looking down at the floor first, then looking up at Anakin. So Padme's action was run backwards." However, the footage of Padme showed steam rising in the background. Once her action was reversed, the steam appeared to be going in the wrong direction. Artists had to perform intricate rotoscoping around Padme so that her performance could be thrown in reverse motion while the steam continued to rise. Padme's hand also passes in front of Anakin, so a rotoscoped holdout matte was needed in order to allow her hand to pass beyond the split onto Anakin's action from the other take. To accomplish this, Greg Maloney used Avid's Matador for the mattes and ILM's proprietary software Comptime for compositing. "The historical notion of film editing is that once material has been shot, on the whole, that will dictate the cut ... basically that's out the window. From now on, don't ever believe anything you watch. Anybody who says 'the camera never lies' is a liar!"[60]

Calling into question our understanding of filmed reality.

"Just by the nature of what *Star Wars* is, there are a lot of big environments that were not really practical to build as sets, either economically or just because of how big it is," said John Kroll. [61]

Lucas's digital breakthroughs at ILM led to more and more directors embracing digital filmmaking. An early digital trailblazer, Robert Zemeckis made *The Polar Express* entirely with digital cameras in front of a blank screen with sets that were filled in later by computers. "The actors will be covered in motion-capture sensors so that each move of the arm, each flicker of the eyelid and each wrinkle of a lip will be stored on a computer and used as guide for the digital animators who will create the actual movie footage."[62]

The film, for those who may not have seen it, is about a boy who refuses to give up his belief in Santa Claus and is whisked to the North Pole in a train called *The Polar Express*— opened wide at theatres in 2004, and starred Tom Hanks (or should we say, a digital character that actually looked like Tom Hanks). The technical crew took over a year in experimenting with ways to map out Tom Hanks' facial and muscle structure in order to capture it convincingly on the "screen" (screen is a relative term here). "The whole film rests on whether this illusion works or not," said Zemeckis, "All you can hope for is for technology to save us."[63] For his sake, it did. According to boxofficemojo.com, *The Polar Express* opened on 3,650 screens on November 10, 2004, and was #2 at the box office. Since, 2004 the film has grossed over $300 million worldwide. Audiences flocked to see the Zemeckis film. It wasn't long before other directors and producers began to follow suit and join in the digital revolution.

And it is a revolution...the shift to digital represents tremendous change in the filmmaking industry. Consider the dilemma in which the Academy of Motion Pictures and Sciences board of governors finds itself. Can *Attack of the Clones* be nominated for a film award if it is not technically a "film"? Changes in the medium were enough to prompt the board to send summons out to the film elite (e.g., Tom Hanks, the late Conrad Hall, Michael Mann, etc.) to help refine the technical definition of "digital" cinema. Such questions included: "What does it mean to be digital? Can an all-digital production be considered a film? What if the movie never touches celluloid, as in *Star Wars Episode III*? The discussion, though engrossing, was brief. Raising his voice, Academy President Frank Pierson simply asked, "Who's going to call George Lucas and tell him his movie can't be nominated for an Oscar?"[64] No one wanted to make that

Digital Beginnings 249

call. The vote by the Academy committee was unanimously—*"film" is no longer required to make a movie*, marking another George Lucas first.

The discussions around what constitutes a film are raised every time a new technological shift occurs. Sound wreaked havoc in the film industry when it was introduced, inter-title artists and live music, hence musicians in the theatres, and actors who could not "speak," all became obsolete. The introduction of color likewise caused changes in everything from wardrobe design to lighting techniques and color composition. In every case listed thus far, the whole of Hollywood was affected in a myriad of subtle, and, not so subtle ways.

The most glaring change with a shift toward digital comes in the form of contracts - the deal memos - that unions and workers sign with producers when they are hired for specific jobs. It was not so long ago that guilds may have forgotten the costly mistakes they made when they shrugged off (missed the boat) the power of new technologies such as cable TV. Sad to say, writers gave up incredibly lucrative residual payments for programs written for cable channels like HBO - the loss of these potential residuals still hurt today. The wounds have not yet healed in many cases. The fur flew when actors began to question who had jurisdiction over their pay scales on digital TV productions--did it fall under the guidelines of SAG or AFTRA? Both argued they had rights, but in the end agreed to divvy up the shows on a case-by-case basis. In any event, both sides agreed that their contracts did not address new technologies in a significant way (e.g., digital cameras which currently rely on videotape for storage, and I say currently because new chips and storage technologies have been developed that no longer require videotape - impact actors' pay because they are often paid less for work done on videotape vs. film).

Then there is the problem with more and more movement toward motion capture, or real time animation. A live actor (who usually is the voice for the CG character) wears a helmet device and a set of motion sensors anchored to various parts of the body with straps. The sensors send information back to the computer where the actor's movements are recorded and translated into a computerized image on the screen. With a little postproduction tweaking here and there, the effect can look surprisingly realistic. Andy Serkis, who has turned motion capture acting into an art form, first starring as Gollum in the *Lord of the Rings* trilogy and most recently as Caesar the ape in *Rise of the Planet of Apes* (2011), is a testament to how realistic an animated character can become. Motion capture can be used when creating cyborg characters or, as in the case of a place called Virtual Celebrity in Los Angeles, it can be used to wed what the live actor is doing with scanned features of a dead celebrity to star in a movie or sell the latest car. [65] No longer are ad companies or film companies tied to what a celebrity did in old footage, with the help of motion capture, these dead celebrities, like Groucho Marx, Marilyn Monroe, Audry Hepburn, or W. C. Fields, can be literally resurrected on the screen.

Even the DGA (Directors Guild of America) has had problems on high-tech shoots, including: variations in pay for film and digital television crews, and replacement of certain workers when film cameras are exchanged for electronic gear, which has required the DGA to create an internal committee to work with producers specifically on this matter. As the use of different media by filmmakers in one production becomes increasingly commonplace, pay rates, at least, need to remain stable but even that becomes complicated by changing job titles protected by the guilds. For example, stage managers and assistant directors often perform many of the same duties. The only difference is that stage managers only work on productions shot on videotape (or with digital cameras), while assistant directors work on productions shot on film and digital cameras. At the end of the day, assistant directors make a lot more than their stage-managing counterparts. To keep everyone happy and employed, the guilds struck a common ground and leveled out the pay scales so that workers could move from format to format without getting hit in the wallet.

Digital Beginnings

But job titles are not the only issues on the table; take for instance, shifting job responsibilities. The computer tools used in postproduction and production are similar and it is easy for a worker to be hired for one job and then be required to handle an entirely different job when production begins. New contracts are required for new duties, but this rarely happens and the craftsman's pay can be a lot less than what the union job calls for. Producers agree that these job duty ambiguities are cropping up more and more, especially in the areas of art, art direction, and set design where the technological tools available to the artisans frequently allow them to take on expanded roles and duties which, in some cases, may require more work for less pay.

And then there is the downscaling of talent, crew, craftspeople and vendors on a "digital set." Everything is impacted, from A-list actors to prop rental houses. A $150 million dollar budget is spent quite differently for a "traditional" film vis a vis a fully "digitalized" film. On a digital set, for example, many human actors might be replaced with computer generated characters, live extras exchanged for CGI, locations might be created in the computer instead of constructed and built on a studio lot. When you consider how creative people using a computer can replace 1000's of people employed on a traditional film production, the implications are staggering. While the lengthy credit sequence of *The Hobbit: An Unexpected Journey* (2012) suggests that there are many jobs available for talented people in Hollywood, the landscape and skillsets of those jobs are changing.

So, not only are job duties changing, but there is an increased need for new skillsets in the traditional jobs and more training on new equipment. Cinematographers, for example, will need to learn a new language of luminance and chrominance, pixel density, bit rates, RGB values, and lux levels. They will have electronic shutters replacing the old which will be able to capture hundreds or even thousands of images per second. Blurred backgrounds that normally occur in a whip pan will not happen unless the director, or cinematographer, wants them. Editors likewise can expect new training for the digital tools now available, since, for example, they will be able to drop frames, freeze frames, and morph between frames whenever they want to. Implications of technology, but also style are undergoing change. Even more than before, editors will be able to dilate and compress time, split screens and combine images—all this perhaps leading to a new on-screen imagery vocabulary. It is true that we are not "watching movies being made. Rather we're watching history being made."[66] "Definitions are changing on everything, even what the word digital means," said John Manulis, chief executive of the digital movie production firm, Visionbox Media Group.

> There are so many technologies that are encompassed in that one word [digital] . . . The one thing everyone agrees on is that "digital" equals change. This is an industry that operates largely out of fear, and not unreasonably so because change is threatening.[67]

According to Manulis, digital does not always mean "quality" to buyers. Many in the "smaller film" arena play down the fact they have shot on digital. "Digital camera makers have been running around town telling everyone, 'This is cheap, cheap! . . . cheap is a bad, bad word for us because buyers will refuse to pay a lot of money for something they hear is cheap. . . . It doesn't take a marketing genius to figure that out,'" added *Tortilla Soup* associated producer Meyer Gottlieb. When Samuel Goldwyn began to shop *Tortilla Soup* around, they decided it would be in the best interest of future deals to record the digital movie onto a 35mm print and play it on a traditional projector. After foreign and domestic deals were signed, it became known that the film had digital roots and organizers for digital film festivals came knocking—but Goldwyn was not budging. Goldwyn refused the requests taking the position that no amount of free publicity was worth the risk of undermining future deals. "For us," Gottlieb said, "there is no value in embracing the word 'digital'" . . . it equates to something filmed off the cuff . . . . something that looks terrible.[68] Perhaps that sentiment was true in 2002, but times and attitudes toward digital have rapidly been changing, and many producers, cinematographers, and even film schools, in the past decade have embraced the technology.

Notes

1. Stephen Sansweet, *Star Wars: From Concept to Screen to Collectible*, 56-57.
2. Claudia Puig, "Star Wars Appeal is a Surprise Even to Creator Lucas," *Los Angeles Times* February 4, 1997, pp. F1, F4.
3. Ibid., F1
4. Interview with George Lucas, starwars.com (January 15, 1997).
5. Ibid., F4.
6. Will Brooker, *Using the Force: Creativity, Community and Star Wars Fans* (New York: Continuum, 2002), 63, 65.
7. Constantine Nasr, "George Lucas: Recaptures the Force," *Daily Trojan*, January 29 1997: 10.
8. Ibid., 77.
9. Cited in Constantine Nasr, "George Lucas: Recaptures the Force," *Daily Trojan*, 29 January 1997, 10.
10. Randall Lane, "The Magician," *Forbes* (March 11, 1996): 125. Perhaps all the recent edits made by Lucas on his *Star Wars* films in some way makes up for the other "final cuts" he was denied by the studios on *THX 1138* and *American Graffiti*.
11. Mark Caro, "Spielberg Alters Scenes in 'E. T.' for Twentieth Anniversary Release," *Los Angeles Times*, 5 November 2001, p. F9.
12. Ibid.
13. Goy Gentile, "Video Sanitizing Business Angers Movie Directors," *Los Angeles Times*, 3 February 2003, p. 1.
14. Ibid.
15. Bob Baker, "Are these videos rated C for clean or compromised?," *Los Angeles Times*, 14 October 2002.
16. Goy Gentile, "Video Sanitizing Business Angers Movie Directors," *Los Angeles Times*, 3 February 2003, p. 1.
17. Bob Baker, "Are These Videos Rated C for Clean or Compromised?," *Los Angeles Times*, 14 October 2002.
18. Goy Gentile, "Video Sanitizing Business Angers Movie Directors," *Los Angeles Times*, February 3, 2003, p. 1.
19. Stewart Silverstein, Greg Hernandez and Diane Seo. "Star Wars Glows at Center of Marketing Constellation," *Los Angeles Times*, 1 May 1999, pp. C1, C2.

20. M. S. Mason. "Fans Love This Saga of Good and Evil," *Christian Science Monitor* 91, no. 118 (May 14, 1999): 17. Others in the article state, " It's good fun adventure about the triumph of good over evil."
21. Annie Leibovitz, "Star Wars: The Force is Back at Last," *Vanity Fair*, no. 462 (February 1999), 118-129. For more information regarding the preppies, see also Bob Strauss, "The Force," *Daily News*, May 19, 2002, pp. U4-5, 8.
22. Steve Daly. "A Monster Movie," *Entertainment Weekly*, no. 478 (March 26, 1999): 32.
23. Annie Leibovitz, "The Force is Back at Last," *Vanity Fair*, no. 462 (February 1999), 118-129.
24. Many had predicted before its December 19, 1997 release that Cameron's $200 million plus production would sink in a sea of red ink, along with the job of at least a few executives at Fox if it proved to be a box office loser. Anticipating escalating costs even before the production began shooting (due to the nature of the film, through no fault of Cameron), Fox asked Paramount for $65 million against a 60/40 split of profits. (This partnership between studios signaled a trend in sharing both profits and losses during this decade which continues today.) Paramount, ever hungry for software and secure with the "brand name" of Cameron at the helm, agreed. Not only did everyone's job remain secure, but shares in Rupert Murdock's News Corp—Fox's parent media conglomerate holding company—surged more than 17 percent, based primarily on the "software" success of *Titanic*.
25. Jack Mathews, "Saber Rattler," *Los Angeles Times, Calendar*, 17 January 1999, pp. 4-5, 51.
26. Robert W. Welkos, "In a Theatre, Near, Near You . . . ," *Los Angeles Times, Calendar*, 17 January 1999, p. 2. See also Louise Kramer and Wayne Friedman. "Star Wars Tie-In Deals Fail to Rise Above Clutter," *Advertising Age*, 21 June 1999, 70, no. 26, 1; Ben Pappas. "Star Bucks," *Forbes*, 17 May 1999, 163, no. 10, 53; Philip Kerr. "Starbucks and Filthy Lucas," *New Statesman*, 29 April 2002, 131, no. 4585, 36; David Kaplan and Adam Rogers. "The Selling of *Star Wars*," *Newsweek*, 17 May 1999, 133, no. 20, 60. Kaplan and Rogers showed that in 1997 Pepsi signed tie-ins with Lucasfilm for $2.5 billion (Frito-Lay, Taco Bell, KFC and Pizza Hut) that would run through 2005, Hasbro guaranteed Lucasfilm $500 million, Ballantine paid $1 million for book rights, and Lego paid $50 million for the rights to *Phantom*, in its first licensing deal ever.
27. "Highest Grossing Movie," *Entertainment Weekly* 429, 1 May 1998, 21.

28. Scott Hettrick. "Phantom new master of video game spinoffs: E3 gets a sneak preview from Lucas Arts," *The Hollywood Reporter* (May 14-16, 1999): 1, 35.
29. *Hollywood Reporter*, 19 May 1999, 1.
30. "Hollywood in Action," 1 July 1999, *Celebrity News Magazine*, 1.
31. Brian Fuson, "'Haunting' Fills House in DreamWorks' Best Bow," *Hollywood Reporter*, CCCLVII, 41 (July 26, 1999): 1, 35.
32. Brian Fuson, *Hollywood Reporter*, "Summer of Love at Box Office: Grosses Are Running 20 percent Ahead of Last Year's Record Results," July 26, 1999, 35, 39. The May 21st release of *Phantom Menace* included an update to many exhibitors' sound systems, *which included the new Dolby Digital Surround EX system* (along with the Vision2 Premiere film stock from Kodak). Audiences were to be fully surrounded by sound due to a discreet rear channel, fed separately from the other speakers, which creates a much stronger sense of sonic spatiality. "When watching a spaceship battle or light saber duel, for instance, audiences will see and hear ships and aliens move past the camera, travel to the side and then to the back." Brian Fuson, *Hollywood Reporter*, "Deep Impact," 26 February 1999, C-32.
33. Hy Hollinger, "Britain Falls to Phantom in Record Opening," *Hollywood Reporter*, 19 July 1999, 1.
34. Brian Fuson, "Int'l Fans Make Phantom No. 2 on All-Time B. O. List," *Hollywood Reporter*, 9 February 2000, 6, 23.
35. "Your Guide to Episode II: Star Wars: Attack of the Clones," *Daily News*, 16 May 2002, 14-15.
36. While countless hours went into creating the digital environments in post-production prior to release, the actual digital exhibition in theatres of the film in 1999 was uneven. While personally watching *Phantom Menace* projected in digital at the Winnetka Theatres in May 1999, banding and pixelation was evident in a few scenes. Most notably, large bands appeared in the lower right hand corner of an early scene with Qui-Gon Jinn and Obi Wan Kenobi (when they were attacked while trying to keep peace during trade negotiations). Some digital characters in scenes appeared much sharper in focus while their non-digital counterparts (actors, etc.) seemed less so. This "splitting" of the frame into sharp and soft focus areas was somewhat distracting in places (most notably when Jar Jar Binks appeared on screen . . . maybe subconsciously this on-screen focus issue caused some people to react negatively toward the character?).

37. Bob Strauss, "The Art of Wars," *Los Angeles Daily News*, 16 May 2002, p. U13.
38. Robert Bly. *The Sibling Society* (New York: Vintage Press, 1997).
39. Patti McCarthy, "Walking the Labyrinth: The Heroine's Journey: Reclaiming the Feminine," paper presented at the *University Film & Video Association Conference*, Chapman University, Orange, CA, 2 August 2013. The Heroine's Journey is similar to the Hero's Journey, but decidedly different. While the Hero's Journey is outward and focused on external adventures (the princess, the castle, the sword...the girl, the house, the car), the Heroine's is focused on internal discoveries and revelations. The Heroine begins her journey when she discovers that she's been living a lie and been duped in some way. She makes a decision to leave her present situation to rescue or save loved ones, she picks up or is given a feminine, bladeless "magic" talisman (only to find out later, none of them work because she needs to believe in herself, not external things), encounters a Harsh Mentor who reveals her flaws and forces her to make her own decisions. She faces a series of trials and symbolic deaths, but must ultimately learn how to say "no" and make her own path—no one can do it for her. She learns true sacrifice and shares her "win" with others and, in doing so, passes her knowledge on to future generations.
40. Steven A. Galipeau. *The Journey of Luke Skywalker: An Analysis of Modern Myth and Symbol*, 252.
41. Will Brooker, *Using the Force: Creativity, Community and Star Wars Fans*, 82.
42. Ibid., 86.
43. Ibid., 87.
44. Brian Fuson, "Record H'wood Heatwave," *The Hollywood Reporter*, 28 May 28-3 June 2002: 1, 54.
45. Gregg Kilday, "Summer Tentpoles Stake B. O. Records," *The Hollywood Reporter*, 3-9 September: 1, 65.
46. Brian Fuson, "Clones a $300 mil B. O. Force," *The Hollywood Reporter*, 28 August 2002, 1, 23.
47. Brian Fuson, "A Tower-ing B. O. Weekend," *The Hollywood Reporter*, 23 December 2002, 1, 23.
48. Greg Hernandez, "'Towers' Breaks December Box Office Records," *Los Angeles Daily News*, 23 December 2002, pp. 1, 6.
49. Ibid.
50. Ibid., 22-23.

51. Ibid., 23-4.
52. Ibid., 24.
53. Ibid., 24. "*Spider Man* was the first film in history to shatter the $100 million mark on its opening weekend as the adventure rocked an amazing $114.8 million on its debut frame. It also was the fastest film to hit the $100 million mark, doing so in three days; its opening Friday and Saturday logged the biggest single days in box office history with $39.4 million and $43.6 million, respectively; and it was the first film to surpass the $40 million mark in a single day."
54. Rick Holson and Laura M. Holson, "Christmas Film Face-Off," *Los Angeles Daily News*, 24 November 2002, pp. 1, 23.
55. Bob Strauss, "The Art of Wars," *Los Angeles Daily News*, 16 May 2002, p. U12.
56. Ibid.
57. Ibid. For very technical and involved descriptions of what occurred digitally during filming, also see: Debra Kaufman, "HD Breaks BG," *Hollywood Reporter*, May 30-June 2, 2002, 44-45. *Advanced Graphics & Animation*, "Who's the Boss? How Industrial Light & Magic Created a Virtual Actor for *The Phantom Menace*," 5, no. 8 (August 1999): 24-32; Steve Siberman, "G-Force: George Lucas Fires Up the Next Generation of Star Warriors," *Wired* 7, no. 05, May 1999, pp. 133-134, 182.; Ellen Wolff, Inside the ILM pipeline," *Millimeter Magazine, Star Wars*: June 1999, 27, no. 26, pp. 30-42; Audrey Doyle, Virtual Sets: How to Make Them," *Millimeter Magazine*, 27, no. 26 (June 1999), pp. 55-60; See also George Lucas, "The Future Starts Here," *Premiere 1*, no. 6 (1999, February): 58; *Cinema Editor*, "The Art of Editing & The Disappearance of Film," 51, no. 3 (Winter 2002): 22-28, 44-46, 54.
58. Ibid., U13.
59. Michael Blake in email to the author dated May 10, 2001.
60. Ellen Wolff, "Star Wars: Inside the ILM Pipeline," *Millimeter Magazine* 27, no. 26 (June 1999): 32.
61. Ibid., 32.
62. P. J. Huffstutter, "Rewriting the Script," *Los Angeles Times*, December 2, 2002, p. C1.
63. Huffstutter, P. J. "Oscar Enters the Picture in Film vs. Digital Debate," *Los Angeles Times*, 3 December 2002, Business, C 1.
64. Ibid., C7.
65. Bill Machrone, "Film's Dead. Are Actors Next?" *PC Magazine* 18, no. 15 (September 1999): 85.

66. Cited in P. J. Huffstutter, "Oscar Enters the Picture in Film vs. Digital Debate," *Los Angeles Times*, 3 December 2002, p. C 7.
67. Ibid.
68. Ibid.

Chapter 6

The New Age of Film

It's the end of cinema. No, I believe that the cinema will last forever.
Godard, *Le* mepris (1963)

Recently, the film industry as a whole has been hit hard by a number of difficult challenges. These challenges include a loss of jobs to run away productions, de facto union strikes that for all intents and purposes shut down the industry in 2001/2002, the fear of terrorist attacks targeted at studios after the September 11th tragedy (jobless rates reached an eight-year high according to the Valley Industry and Commerce Association [VICA]—the entertainment industry alone lost 8,800 jobs as a direct result of the attacks), and changes made in digital technology. All have had an impact on industry jobs.

In the Los Angeles area, the information industry which includes publishing and film companies is currently No. 1 in terms of local payroll. The sector, according to VICA, "accounts for $4.7 billion or 17 percent of the San Fernando Valley's $27.8 billion payroll. Employment in the entertainment industry decreased by 8.3 percent for 2001."[1] Although the year 2002 brought about the biggest domestic box office ever ($9 billion),

Hollywood continues to feel the pinch and impact of current events. "It is a dangerous time to be a media mogul," states Daniel Gross of *Slate*,

> Vivendi [Universal] just sent CEO Jean-Marie Messier to the guillotine, and Bertelsmann deposed CEO Thomas Middelhoff. At AOL Time Warner, once the biggest and baddest of all the sprawling media conglomerates, Jerry Levin and Bob Pittman have been cashiered. Most of the media bosses who survive—Rupert Murdoch at News Corp., Sumner Redstone at Viacom, and Charles Dolan at Cablevision—can't be fired because they essentially own the companies. And then there is Disney's Michael Eisner who survives against all odds, all explanation, and all common sense. The company he has run since 1984 is sputtering on all cylinders. Theme-park attendance and bookings are down. The movie business is the typical hodgepodge of hits—*Signs* and *Lilo & Stitch*—and expensive misses—*Bad Company* [*Treasure Planet*]. Television is similarly mixed. ESPN prospers, but the third ranked ABC network is broken . . . Standard & Poor's has put Disney's long term credit rating—historically one of its strengths—on watch for possible downgrade. On Monday, Disney's stock slipped to levels not seen since 1994. In the past two years, and in the past five years, Disney has performed worse than all but three of the Dow stocks [AT&T and Hewlett-Packard]. Yet Eisner remains, bestriding the media world like a wooly mammoth.[2]

Left and right media conglomerates during 2002 reported staggering fourth-quarter losses: AOL Time Warner, $44.9 billion; Vivendi Universal, $8.61 billion, while ABC Disney posted losses of over 42 percent for the year. Other conglomerates posted similar losses. The reasons are many and varied, ranging from a soft economy and the bear market, to lack of proper synergy tactics, poor management, or too much investment riding on a beleaguered Internet market.[3] At least the media conglomerates were not involved in other recent corporate strategies such as defrauding investors, cooking the books or trying to hoodwink the IRS or employees as did Enron et al. But such losses and the aggressive "mega-mergers" of conglomerates which continue at an alarming rate to combine the largest firms already highly concentrated in certain industries, have raised the

The New Age of Film

eyebrows of Federal regulators regarding antitrust concerns—concerns that haven't been raised since 1948.

Although the Federal Trade Commission and the Justice Department are not challenging a significantly larger percentage of mergers, they are taking a much closer look at what have been termed so-called strategic mergers that result in greater market concentrations. "If everyone wants to be No. 1 or No. 2, then you are going to see a lot of markets where there are only going to be one or two competitors," said William Baer, who heads the FTC's Bureau of Competition.[4]

The total number of merger transactions announced in 1997 between U. S. companies totaled 9,992 worth $845 billion. That is double the 4,950 deals completed in 1992. Since the 1990s, merger regulation was, for the most part, ignored in order to help big U. S. conglomerates become bigger to help them compete with foreign rivals. These same big companies are now rushing to buy the capabilities they need to create new markets, such as putting video over telephone lines or putting the Internet over cable systems, which no single company has the ability to do.

Sectors like defense are also seeing major firms attempt to vertically integrate, giving them the capability of building all the constituent parts of their products. This process is at the heart of many of the media giant conglomerates. These types of firms can lock out competing parts makers and also control the market. The key question when viewing these new mergers comes down to "are prices likely to rise as a result of eliminating competition?" This basic question seems to be the touchstone of all current antitrust analysis. While many do not want to waste their time in an unlikely merger and many predicted that tighter scrutiny by the Feds would help slow down many of the mega-mergers, the heightened antitrust enforcement doesn't really seem to have had much effect and business is being carried out "as usual."[5]

Father of Digital Filmmaking

If George Lucas can be "blamed" or given sole credit for anything, it is not only for bringing back the blockbuster per se, but the move toward digital filmmaking. On June 24, 2005 it was announced by Lucas Ltd. Pressroom that,

> Opening the door to the future of digital arts, filmmaker George Lucas and nearly 2,000 guests today celebrated the unveiling of the Letterman Digital Arts Center, a 23-acre, 860,000-square-foot production campus in the heart of city's historic Presidio. The Letterman Digital Arts Center is devoted to the production of digital cinema and videogames and the creative exploration and innovation of new digital tools that allow artists to bring anything they can imagine to life. "The digital revolution began in San Francisco, and digital arts and entertainment have only begun to show their potential," Lucas said during the opening gala. [6]

Lucas has hopes that San Francisco can rival Hollywood as a producer of entertainment. "San Francisco's always had a quality of filmmaking that most people have not been able to recognize. We always get shoved under the title 'Hollywood,'" Lucas has been quoted as saying. "I think this will begin to put a stake in the ground for San Francisco as a filmmaking community, as a creator of world cinema."[7]

Since 1999, Lucas has been working toward this end where a transmedia convergence of entertainment and technology industries will become centered in San Francisco. As a result, more and more film production, creative and technical talent and profits, may, in theory, move North away from Los Angeles. As digital effects become more widely used, the need (again in theory) to shoot real-life characters on real-life sound stages and locations may be reduced, which could ultimately lead to more blue-collar job losses in Hollywood than runaway production. As long as USC and UCLA continue to invest in their film programs, Los Angeles will still continue to be the place where most students will go to learn how to become filmmakers. The Bay Area may be the place

The New Age of Film

where all the digital components come together and eventually become the digital center of the film industry. Probably the most consequential effect of the "Lucas empire's move into the heart of San Francisco will boost the Bay Area's ambition to be the global capital of the twenty-first century... While it [the Bay Area] is currently home to many important information-technology and biotechnical companies, including two of the world's most influential universities—UC Berkeley and Stanford—and [it] dominates the world's most important new communication medium —the internet—it [the Bay Area] has no center.[8]

In 1999, Lucasfilm and Letterman Digital Arts Ltd., housed over 2,000 workers ("guests") and consisted of a 860,000 square foot production campus. Plans allowed for a clear view to fantastic landmarks like the Golden Gate Bridge and the Palace of Fine Arts and consists of four buildings that frame a park within a park with a lovely pond at its center. The current campus houses five Lucas companies at the former Letterman Army Hospital owned by Lucas including: ILM, LucasArts Entertainment Company (a leader in interactive software), THX, Lucas Learning Ltd. (an educational software developer), and Lucas OnLine (focuses on e-commerce and the Internet). The complex also houses the George Lucas Educational Foundation and a visual effects archive (opened to researchers and the public). Lucasfilm and Skywalker Sound will remain at the Ranch in San Rafael.[9]

Lucas has always been at the forefront of the digital revolution that is changing the ways films are made, distributed, experienced and used, creating new possibilities for a convergence of media and technologies. As discussed earlier, new high-definition video cameras and digital editing equipment challenge the long-time supremacy of film. These tools may be more flexible and cost less, but are frightening to artisans accustomed to using film. The final cut of a digital motion picture will eventually be sent directly, via satellite or fiber optic cable (ala Netflix, et al), from a computer screen to hard drives at theatres around the world. This system, were it realized would reduce a major source of the big studios' leverage over independent filmmakers (like Lucas) and control of distribution would be reduced.

At a screening at Skywalker Ranch in 2002, Lucas assembled a group of friends and A-list directors—Steven Spielberg, Oliver Stone, Francis Ford Coppola, and Robert Zemeckis—to let them know that celluloid film was dead and digital filmmaking was the way of the future. He warned them all to take note or be left behind. "Film is what we do. It's what we use," Stone is reported to have told Lucas. "You'll be known as the man who killed cinema." Lucas, it is likewise reported, merely rolled his eyes as Stone went on about the poetry of celluloid and the coldness of pixels —this to a man who had recorded his latest film in a series of 1's and 0's with high-definition digital cameras, edited with digital equipment and, in a few specially equipped theatres, distributed and projected digitally. "Just watch," said Lucas. Raising a hand, he cued his demonstration and told the group about what they would see: a series of identical clips that had been stored on different formats from *Monsters, Inc.*. The first clip was completely electronic. It was put together in a computer, stored on digital tape and projected digitally. The footage looked like you were experiencing a real world through an open window. It was crisp, clear and rich in tone. The next clip was on film—film that had spent four weeks in a mall theatre. The clip was clearly faded and degraded by the heat from the projector and dust that had filled the air. Out of focus, the film reel image jiggled and popped on the screen. The difference was radical. No one spoke for a long time after the lights came back up. [10]

True to his word, Lucas shot the final installment of his prequels epic, *Star Wars: Episode III: Revenge of the Sith (2005)*, digitally, doing away with film entirely. Since 1889, film stock has not changed that much; chemicals that are layered on the surface of the film react when they are exposed to light and changed into hues that match the light's wavelength. While the process remains the same, film has gone through a series of developments to keep pace with the competition or fulfill the needs of the industry. Most recently Eastman Kodak Co. has come up with a new film stock, Vision2, that approximates digital technology in order to protect its $1 billion entertainment business. The new Vision2 line is a high-speed camera negative film that is particularly good for use during night shoots and was designed to address cinematographer complaints regarding the digital's flexibility. Kodak's sales worldwide took a 4 percent drop over the first nine months of 2002 compared with the same period the year before. The drop in sales continued and Kodak was forced to file for bankruptcy in 2011. Changing technology, the stalled economy, bad product marketing and choices, along with the constant threat of Hollywood union strikes have all been blamed for the drop in sales. The rise of reality television, and use of digital technologies to produce such fare, may be another factor.

The acceleration of digital use by the networks and the explosion of reality television shows is no coincidence. The lower costs and ease of using digital technologies perfectly coincides with the shoe string budget and cinema verite approach to reality television. Out of thirty-seven television programs produced by major networks, nearly 30 percent of the prime time line-up was shot with high-definition digital cameras because digital costs less. Successful reality television productions, such as *Survivor*, are shooting at about 99% digital, due to ease of shooting and cutting, or editing, "on the fly." Normal 35mm stock runs approximately 50 cents a foot or $58 per minute of shooting, while digital transfers to the cheaper videotape, or even cheaper yet, is stored via internal hard drive in camera or on memory cards, then downloaded directly to an editing system on the computer. A blockbuster can easily go through 300,000 feet of film during production at an expense of $175,000 or more, not including developing, processing and costs of dailies, etc. In stark comparison, digital cameras use inexpensive videotape which costs roughly $27 for forty minutes[11] (or store data on hard drives or memory cards).

Cost is an issue for production, but the cinematographers having to make the choice between traditional film stock and shooting digitally are not completely convinced. "I don't know one cinematographer who would choose digital over film, "said the late cinematographer Conrad W. Hall, "Producers choose digital over film." Hoping to impress cinematographers and put the pressure on producers, Kodak regularly polls the artisans and asks them to test new stocks. Vision2 had been tested quietly for almost a year to insure satisfaction before going public with the new film stock.[12] Even Rick McCallum, Lucas' producer had something good to say about the new Vision2 stock which was used to strike prints for *Phantom Menace*: "It makes the images seem almost electric. The blacks are really rich and real deep, very saturated. All the colors are much more vivid. We count on the ability to take advantage of blacks and shadows, and before that's always been a debilitating process."[13]

The stock worked very nicely with the film's innumerable special effects. With more than 2,000 effects shots, *Phantom Menace* is a very digital movie and much more of the color correction in the effects shots was actually done on computer. "McCallum cites the ability of the Vision Premiere stock to reproduce the color timing as key, bringing the final print right back to the colors cameramen actually shot. And you can count on having total uniformity across all the release prints."[14]

Digital cameras, rather than using celluloid, use computer chips that convert light into electronic pulses, which are then translated into data and stored on videotape or, much more frequently, converted to memory cards or an internal hard drive in the camera. It won't be too long until this more streamlined digital transfer of image to memory card or internal drive replaces videotape altogether. Sony Corp. and Panasonic (and others) over the years have developed better and better cameras that could deliver far more detail and a wider range of color. In the summer of 2003, Thomson Grass Valley brought out a "new line of cameras that captures almost five times as much detail and twice the range of color as previous high-definition models," said Jeff Rosica, Vice President of Marketing.[15]

Advocates of digital insist that the technology cuts costs, partly by eliminating key parts of the movie-making process. The push toward greater and greater frugality is pushing studios and filmmakers to consider

The New Age of Film 269

digital tools. This need to cut production costs led the team behind the Twentieth Century Fox Television series *The Education of Max Bickford* to "go digital." The tactic worked. Producers saved over $35,000 an episode in post and filming costs, but without good writing and poor direction, the series failed. Tools are only tools and while contributing to the creative process, certainly do not define it.[16]

Rich McCallum, Lucas' producer also boasted a savings of $3 million in production costs on *Episode II* by replacing film in the cameras with videotape and speeding the work flow. Three million dollars is a lot of money, but a drop in the overall $150 million budget, when all is said and done.[17] Of course, with the recent failings of the conglomerates (e.g. AOL Turner, etc.), coupled with a declining local and national economy, the aftereffects of September 11th, a chronic war in Afghanistan and Iraq, ex-facto strikes, runaways to Canada, and pressures of a stalling economy, it is not surprising that corporate managers, driven toward higher profit margins, will try to hasten the move toward digital.

"With film, you get 60 percent of what you want," says director Robert Rodriguez. "In film, cinematography is the art of guessing." Certainly each mistake and each re-shoot eats up a production's time and money, but, even though you can view digital images instantly and thereby make corrections early, the problems inherent on a digital set are daunting. The inevitable "bugs" of a new technology can eat up just as much time and money as film and all the savings that the digital process promises producers. A particularly good example of how these "bugs" have and will run up a budget occurred on an independent shoot in the Mojave Desert helmed by one of Coppola's nephew's, Chris Coppola. "This was supposed to be a $600,000 independent film," said Coppola. "Now, [because we used the high-definition gear] we're way, way over budget."[18] The camera's computer chips which are sensitive to distance require a lot more set up time than traditional cameras and then, a strange "single blue pixel" randomly appeared in random spots in much of the footage—for no reason. Even Sony had not a clue as to how to solve the problem. All the footage had to be re-shot.

For this reason and others, cinematographers are still skeptical about using this kind of gear, but as time passes and digital becomes more standardized, less so. Mistakes mean money and money means lost jobs and bad reputations. Many cinematographers are facing a nasty dilemma: What happens if you are not equipped to continue telling stories in an industry where the narrative tools have fundamentally changed? Certainly the latest shift toward DSLR and the 3-D revival craze in filmmaking and exhibition practices falls within this category. Many see these changes as "just another way of telling the story," perhaps not a better way, but a different way, while others may be left behind who do not possess the same skills or initiative. The push toward digital is certainly on, but no one knows right now if and when a full shift will occur. As Roger Deakins, ASC has said so eloquently, "Film is rather like the magic lantern. There is a sense of mystery, because you don't know what's going into the black box camera until you send the film to the lab... With digital it's all very businesslike. We're not businessmen. We're artists and magicians."[19] Lucas, it can be said with some certainty, is both.

We stand at the edge of a new age in filmmaking. We can embrace or refuse the call to such an adventure. New technologies have quickly gone beyond the mere erasing of "flying" wires or of making dinosaurs walk, and will have uses that will

continue to revolutionize filmmaking far into the new millennium. Perhaps the new "digital studio" will be the closest thing to bridging the gap between imagination and what can be convincingly shown on a movie screen. No longer will the director or producer be constrained by real people or actual locations. This is George Lucas' legacy. The sky is the limit.

So, is cinema dead, as some have warned, with the advance of technology? No. Not hardly. Technologies may change, styles may come and go, but cinema, in one form or another, whether experienced on the screen, ridden in a theme park or circulated within a fan culture, will live on. As we move into the new century, digital production and distribution will transform the film viewing landscape. "...far from dying," Wheeler Winston suggests, "the movies are reinventing themselves for the patrons of a new era...we'll never see the like of *Casablanca* again, or *Pillow Talk* (1959), or *Psycho* (1960), but then again, the late twentieth century novel is an all together different affair from the days when F. Scott Fitzgerald commanded the public's attention." Perhaps, as Winston suggests, the masterpieces of the past no longer "speak to our present condition," but they do "haunt us and inform our collective consciousness of mid-to-late twentieth culture." [20]

From the very beginning, "film 'as we know it' has always been dying and is always being reborn. "What we are witnessing now is nothing more nor less than the dawn of a new grammar, a new technological delivery and production system, with a new series of plots, tropes, iconic conventions, and stars," suggests Wheeler. "We must be content to speculate, and realize that no matter how the cinematic medium transforms itself in the coming decades, it will always continue to build on, and carry forward, the past." [21]

And one can be sure that George Lucas, more than any other who has come before him, or even after, will continue to carry on the filmmaking tradition, while remaining the industry's greatest visionary and advocate for change.

SUMMARY

George Lucas, more than anyone or anything else during the past thirty-plus years, can be credited as the premiere catalyst of change in the Hollywood film industry. His establishment of the blockbuster franchise acted as the first domino to fall in a series and chain of events that have made Hollywood, and therefore, a good part of our culture, what it is today. George Lucas and the subsequent "Lucas Effect" deserves the recognition and acknowledgement currently granted others for his part in the making of the New Hollywood and our current understanding of what is film.

As one domino fell, others soon followed. Briefly, Lucas reinvented the blockbuster as a blockbuster franchise, which then led to the adoption of high concept, big budget, visceral films that were/are heavy in special effects. These blockbuster films typically have happy endings and can be exploited for ancillary markets both domestic and foreign.

The insatiable studio desire for "big," blockbuster product and even bigger pay-off fostered a need to hire strong producers, executives, and entrepreneurs (instead of relying on directors or auteurs) who watched the budget and stayed on schedule, a play-it-safe practice which rapidly developed a reliance on stars and brand names, or the "sure thing," guaranteeing a profit at the box office. This need for a "sure thing" quickly evolved into "the sequel" which rapidly replaced the production of genre films. Corporations, which were quickly buying up the studios, began to go through a series of mergers and acquisitions. These corporate mergers and acquisitions more easily exploited the film as a product and diversified against the spiraling costs of talent, special effects, and production. At the same time, a strong foreign market opened the door to global players. Soon, the corporations which purchased the Hollywood studios, became absorbed themselves by giant media conglomerates that used the blockbuster franchise as "synergistic" software, fueling their many subsidiaries. These subsidiaries, in turn, exploited the original film for endless profit across synergistic platforms: the book became the film and the film became the t-shirt sold near the theme park ride.

Not only does our discussion of the Lucas Effect and the New Hollywood shed light on business practices in the film industry, but challenges current critical film evaluation practices. Theoretical and critical inquiry and evaluation has been too narrowly defined. Inquiry needs to acknowledge the importance of film synergy and how the Lucas Effect has expanded the definition of a film from something that is merely experienced in a theatre into something used and circulated (whether as meaning, actual real-life experiences, a shared cultural artifact, a place, or a thing) amid a series of intertwined and interrelated industries, economies, communities, and experiential practices. As such, what I have termed, The Lucas Effect, has the potential of fomenting a new synergistic critical and theoretical approach to film which recognizes the impact of transmedia and the value and weight of "connectivity" and transformational (or alchemical) relationships.

Finally, it has been acknowledged, that George Lucas, more than any person or any thing, is responsible for a series of "firsts" in the film industry. Lucas was the *first* to create "the" film franchise which completely changed the way films were made in Hollywood. He was the *first* to take advantage of marketing strategies which set the foundation for synergistic practices in the film industry and in our culture, and was the *first* auteur to make the shift to entrepreneur and successfully own and run ancillary filmmaking businesses (Skywalker Sound, Industrial Light and Magic, LucasArts, etc.). These ancillary businesses were strategic and supported his own work and that of other filmmakers in the industry, while at the same time enhanced the film viewing experience in areas such as sound and special effects, to name a few (THX, ILM). He was the *first* filmmaker in history to own the modes of production and successfully create, produce, finance and retain full ownership of his films. He was also the *first* to use and develop new digital filmmaking technologies to better tell his film stories and that of others which ushered in a new digital age of filmmaking, ultimately changing the look, production, and distribution of film forever. Any one of these many "firsts" are significant by themselves, but taken all together, George Lucas' impact on the film industry, our culture, and the world, is unparalleled and indisputable.

Today, George Lucas is one of the greatest and most successful filmmakers of all time. He has single-handedly transformed the boundaries of traditional image-making and revolutionized the art of motion pictures. His devotion to timeless storytelling and cutting-edge innovation, has given us some of the most beloved films ever created. Each of his films celebrate the boundless potential of the individual to overcome any limitations and the promise that anything is possible if you can imagine it—a simple truth he has lived his entire life. His entertainment companies, notably Industrial Light & Magic, and Skywalker Sound, continue to thrive and forge new paths in entertainment, and have collectively received over one hundred Academy Award nominations. Director, producer, and visual and sound effects pioneer, Lucas has himself earned cinema's highest honors, including the Irving G. Thalberg Award, the AFI Lifetime Achievement Award, and the Lifetime Achievement Award form the Visual Effects Society. Lucas was recently awarded the National Medal of Technology by the President of the United States for 30 years of innovation at ILM and honored with the NAACP Vanguard Award for increasing understanding and awareness of racial and social issues. He has also taken a leadership role in applying his technical and storytelling expertise to the classroom and is chairman of the board of the George Lucas Educational Foundation, and is a member of the USC School of Cinematic Arts Advisory Foundation. He recently accepted a day-time Emmy in June 2013 for production of his animated series *The Clone Wars* and on July 12, 2013 received the National Medal of Arts from President Obama for his "contribution to American cinema." In his Irving Thalberg acceptance speech on March 30, 1992, George made one of his filmmaking priorities clear: "all of us who make motion pictures are teachers; teachers with very loud voices." George Lucas, more than any other, has taught us all, from his earliest days in Modesto to present, that with a little imagination anything is possible.

It is certain that Lucas, or his influence, will continue to lead the way in innovation for many years to come. It will be fascinating and extremely educational in the next decade to watch the full "Force" of the "Lucas Effect" on the film industry, our culture, and the world.

Notes

1. Evan Pondel, "9-11 Hit the Valley Hard: Jobless Claims Reach Eight-Year High," *Los Angeles Daily News*, 11 November 2002, pp. 1, 15.
2. Daniel Gross, "The Louse in Mickey Mouse's House: Why Eisner Should Be Fired," accessed 8 August 2002; available from *http://www.Slate.com*. In January 2004, Roy Disney called for Eisner's resignation after he himself resigned from the company his uncle had founded. In March 2004, the Disney board decided to split Eisner's CEO position in reaction to general dissatisfaction with Eisner.
3. Charles Masters, "Embattled Messier Ousted," *The Hollywood Reporter*, July 2-8, 2002, 1, 52. Also see Charles Masters and Georg Szalai. "Viv Uni reports 1 percent dip as music, film struggle," *The Hollywood Reporter*, 11-17 February 2003: pp. 1, 80; *Los Angeles Times*, "Failing Magic at Disney," 29 September 2002;George Szalai. "Turner to exit AOL TW post," *The Hollywood Reporter*, 30 January, pp. 1, 22.
4. Ralph Vartabedian, Tom Petruno, and Debora Vrana. "Fed's Taking a Harder Look at Mega-Mergers," *Los Angeles Times*, 11 March 1998, pp. D1, D10.
5. Ibid., D10.
6. "Letterman Digital Arts Center," *Pressroom* (24 June 2005). Available from http://lucasfilm.com/press/presidiopreview/index.html?page=1
7. Angela Watercutter, "Lucas Stakes Out Hollywood Rival," *Los Angeles Daily News*, 9 February 2003, News 6.
8. Mike Clough, "Lucas Strikes Back," *Los Angeles Times*, 11 July 1999, pp. M1, M6.
9. Ibid.
10. Cited in P. J. Huffstutter and Jon Healey, "Filming Without Film: High-Definition Digital Cameras, Feared By Some Directors, Could End the Careers of Those Unable to Make the Transition," *Los Angeles Times*, 11 July 2002.
11. Ibid.
12. P. J. Huffstutter, "Kodak Banking on Celluloid Having a Lot More Moments," *Los Angeles Times*, 20 November 2002.
13. Brian Fuson, "Deep Impact," *Hollywood Reporter*," 26 February 1999, p. C32.
14. Ibid.

15. Cited in P. J. Huffstutter and Jon Healey, "Filming Without Film: High-Definition Digital Cameras, Feared By Some Directors, Could End The Careers of Those Unable to Make the Transition," *Los Angeles Times*, 11 July 2002.
16. Personal conversation with Loren Dreyfuss, writer on *Max Bickford*, brother of Richard Dreyfuss, CSUN University Club, September 2002.
17. Ibid.
18. Cited in P. J. Huffstutter and Jon Healey, "Filming Without Film: High-Definition Digital Cameras, Feared By Some Directors, Could End The Careers of Those Unable to Make the Transition," *Los Angeles Times*, 11 July, 2002.
19. Ibid.
20. Wheeler Winston Dixon. "Twenty Five Reasons Why It's All Over," *The End of Cinema As We Know It: American Film in the Nineties*, Jon Lewis, ed. (New York University Press, 2001), 365.
21. Ibid., 366.

Epilogue

"The Force is strong in that one."
                Darth Vader, Star Wars: A New Hope, Episode IV

On Oct 30, 2012, George Lucas sold Lucasfilm, Skywalker Sound, video game company LucasArts, and special effects house Industrial Arts and Magic (ILM), to Disney for $4 billion dollars, including all rights to the *Star Wars* characters and franchise. As part of the deal, Lucas received half, or roughly $2 billion in cash, the rest paid in the form of 40 million Disney shares, making Lucas the second-largest non-institutional shareholder of Disney, only eclipsed by share-ownership of the trust of the late Steve Jobs of Apple, Inc..

"For the past 35 years, one of my greatest pleasures has been to see *Star Wars* passed from one generation to the next," said Lucas, "It's now time for me to pass *Star Wars* on to a new generation of filmmakers." Said Disney CEO Roger Iger of the acquisition: "This is one of the great entertainment properties of all time, one of the best branded and one of the best valuable, and it's just fantastic for us to have the opportunity to both buy it, run it, and grow it." [1] Since the buyout of Capital Cities/ABC in 1995 for $19.7 billion, Disney has been driven by corporate acquisitions, including the purchase of Fox Family in 2001 ($5.2 billion), Pixar in 2006 ($7.6 billion), and Marvel Comics in 2009 ($3.96 billion). It doesn't take a wall street genius to understand Disney's corporate strategy and need to control more and more content to feed its ever growing conglomerate presence in the marketplace. Disney, most likely, will be able to quickly recoup the $4 billion paid to Lucas as soon as it taps the full potential of the franchise for more movies (the first installment of a new *Star Wars* trilogy is planned for release in 2015 with *Star Trek* reboot director J. J. Abrams at the helm), theme parks (planned to open in Disney

World, Florida in 2018), and merchandise. Says David Miller, analyst at investment research firm Caris, Lucasfilm Ltd. "is one of the great entertainment franchises of all time." Disney CEO Iger confirmed that Disney was immediately ready to pursue a more aggressive expansion of the *Star Wars* film franchise, including the release on December 18, 2015 of a new *Star Wars: Episode VII* film..

Set thirty years or so after *Return of the Jedi* and after the death of Darth Vader, the story focuses on three young protagonists, along with a cadre of characters from previous *Star Wars* films. [2] Lawrence Kasden, writer-producer of *Star Wars: Episode V (The Empire Strikes Back*, 1980), *Star Wars: Episode VI (Return of the Jedi*, 1983) and the first installment of the Indiana Jones series, *Raiders of the Lost Ark* (1981) has returned to pen the screenplay. J.J. Abrams, who will direct the film, will also act as co-writer. Both replaced Michael Arndt, who wrote the story treatment and was originally attached by LucasFilm to write the screenplay before the company was sold to Disney. Abrams stated, "The key to moving forward with the film would be for it to return to the roots of the first film and be based more on emotion than explanation." [3] *Star Wars: Episode VII* will be produced by Walt Disney Pictures, LucasFilm and Bad Robot Productions and will be the first *Star Wars* film to ever be distributed by Walt Disney Studios Motion Pictures. Twentieth-Century Fox had the past distinction. The film has signed John Boyega, Daisy Ridley, Adam Driver, Oscar Isaac, Andy Serkis, Domhnall Gleeson, Max Von Sydow, Lupita Nyong'o, and Gwendoline Christie to star, with Harrison Ford, Mark Hamill, Carrie Fisher, Anthony Daniels, Peter Mayhew and Kenny Baker reprising their roles from the original trilogy. Fans were especially thrilled to learn several of the original members of cast, specifically Ford, Hamill, and Fisher, will be returning to the screen. Second-unit filming began in April 2014 in Abu Dhabi and Iceland, and principal photography began on May 16, 2014 in Abu Dhabi. Film production will primarily be based at Pinewood Studios in Buckinghamshire, England, near London where most of the original *Star Wars* films were shot. A small portion of the film will also be shot in Los Angeles at the request of J.J. Abram's whose family resides in the southland.

Most interestingly, Abram's has decided, along with cinematographer, Daniel Mindel that the film will be shot in 35mm using Kodak 5219 (and in 65mm IMAX format) and would rely on the use of actual locations and scale models over computer generated imagery to better approximate the aesthetic look and feel of the original *Star Wars* films. [4] Hence, the rush to bury celluloid in the industry may be a bit premature. It's clear that Abram's and Mindel both recognize the need to have celluloid as well as digital technology available to them as filmmaking tools, having used both mediums successfully. Such aesthetic options gives the film artist a wider array of creative choices. A great painter wouldn't be expected to use one kind of brush or color, nor should a great filmmaker be required to do so. This creative decision bodes well for Kodak and other film manufacturers, and may, if the audience responds favorably, prompt other filmmakers (and producers) to consider the use of 35mm stock in tandem with current digital recording practices. The more artistic and creative choices available to the filmmaker—the better.

Whatever the creative filmmaking decisions on *Star Wars: Episode VII*, Disney already has plans for more films, including two new stand-alone films featuring Han Solo and Boba Fett. [5] Disney CFO, Jay Rasulo described these stand-alone films as character "origin" stories. [6] Lucasfilm President Kathleen Kennedy explained that, "These stand-alone films will not cross over into the canon created by the *Star Wars* saga sequel trilogies [created by George Lucas]. Right now *Episode VII* falls within that canon." Additional *Star Wars* novels, comic books, and computer games (written over the years) have expanded the *Star Wars* universe and will, instead, be the focus of the new stand-alone film stories. Kennedy adds, "There is no attempt being made to carry character—from the stand-alone stories—in and out of the saga episodes. " [7] In other words, don't expect to see Luke Skywalker or Princess Leia appear in any of the stand-alone films. On May 22, 2014 it was announced that *Godzilla* director Gareth Edwards would direct the first stand-alone film story scheduled for release on December 16, 2016 and on June 4, 2014 it was announced that *Chronicle* director Josh Trank would direct the second stand-alone installment. [8]

Following the 2015 *Episode VII* release, "our long term plan is to release a new *Star Wars* feature film every two to three years," stated Disney CEO Roger Iger. Case in point, Rian Johnson (*Looper*) has been already tagged to write and direct *Episode VIII*. [9] Iger continued, "We really like *Star Wars*' potential on TV as well, and we think (cable satellite) Disney XD will be a great home for that." [10] Viewers support Iger's point of view. Lucas recently received a daytime Emmy for his animated *Star Wars: The Clone Wars* series, June 16, 2013. Iger has also confirmed expanding the presence of *Star Wars* in the Disney theme parks, as new, stand alone parks in the near future. Doubtlessly, the plans for a *Star Wars* theme park has been underway for some time. As a child who attended the opening weekend of the original *Disneyland* theme park in 1955, and was inspired by the Magic Kingdom so many years ago, having such a park built filled with his characters, for Lucas, would be a dream come true. It stands to reason that if Universal was able to support a park devoted to the *Harry Potter* franchise, a *Star Wars* park would prove to be an even greater draw. Film critic and historian, Leonard Maltin, stated, "Obviously Disney, as they did with Marvel, is investing in a blue chip property that will yield dividends for years to come."

There is also some speculation that Disney's purchase of so many content bearing companies over the recent years indicates that the House of Mouse is out of new ideas and must go out into the marketplace to buy them instead. Fueling this speculation, Disney's Iger was quoted as saying, "We actually determined that we'd be better off as a company releasing a sequel to *Star Wars* than probably most other. I'll call them 'not yet determined' films. So we love the fact that this will take its place in our live-action strategy as an already-branded, already-known quantity." [11] There's no doubt that only new, fresh product will feed its ever growing, insatiable synergistic appetite. David Karger at Fandango, remarked, "Now Disney has Marvel, Pixar, and Lucasfilm Ltd.. Three of the biggest companies that most consistently make mega-blockbusters. It puts Disney in an amazing position to be the leader in tent-pole movies." [12]

While some worry," said Eric Geller, "that Disney is more concerned with capitalizing on Lucas' merchandizing empire than the actual content," others recognize that more than most, Disney would protect Lucas' *Star Wars* history and characters considering the respect paid to characters in the recently acquired Marvel universe.[13] All believe, however, that as long as the company respects Lucas' input, the *Star Wars* brand will continue to be protected and thrive. Since Lucas will become the second-largest non-institutional shareholder of Disney after the deal and remain on as creative consultant, it appears that Lucas' impact on the *Star Wars* universe will continue for a very long time to come. In his current capacity as consultant and shareowner Lucas will also continue to guide and shepherd ancillary companies ILM and Skywalker Sound (LucasArts, the internal game development arm of LucasFilm Ltd., was shut down by Disney in April 2013) and remain instrumental in the shaping of the film industry. Regardless the speculation about the Disney purchase, it was said, by insiders closest to Lucas, that on the day the deal was announced to the world, October 30, 2012, that Lucas was very happy. He was smiling.

Lucas has mentioned throughout his career, that he wanted to try new things, write new stories, and breathe life into new characters and spend more time devoted to education, philanthropic endeavors, and his family. Now, in "retirement," he has that chance. Recent events, such as his June 2013 bid to build a $300 million dollar Lucas Cultural Art Museum on the waterfront dedicated to the art of visual storytelling at the San Francisco Presidio is a big step in that direction. Lucas has promised another $400 million to endow the museum for future upkeep and support. Many have said that the building of the museum is a way for Lucas to "give back" to the city he has called home and loved for many years. The museum will be the world's first cultural institution, Lucas says, "to celebrate creative innovation in the art of telling stories, and a place to inspire the imagination of future generations of visual artists"—just as he was at a young age by artist-illustrators such as Norman Rockwell and Maxfield Parrish. [14] Growing up, Lucas loved to draw and was inspired by the illustrations he saw in adventure books and *The Saturday Evening Post*. An illustrator and artist in his own right, Lucas owns many original prints of both artists. Norman Rockwell's All-American idealism, Lucas has remarked, influenced his film, *American Graffiti*, while the work of Maxfield Parrish directly inspired the feel and look of his *Star Wars* films. "I'm a storyteller at heart and I understand the power of a visual image to tell a story," Lucas wrote in paper submitted to the Presidio Trust in March (2013). "I know how works of art can ignite children's imaginations and change their lives. They changed mine." [15]

Surprisingly, on February 3, 2014, the Presidio Trust rejected Lucas' bid, along with two others, for the 8-acre, waterfront, Presidio "Crissy Field" site. "We simply do not believe any of the projects are right for this location," stated board Chairwoman Nancy Hellman Bechtl, "We didn't think any of them hit the mark." [16] Although Lucas did everything he could to accommodate and adjust his plans to fit Presidio Trust site requirements, concerns over height and museum style won out over strong public, corporate, and political support for his bid, including backing by Gov. Jerry Brown, San Francisco Mayor Ed Lee, U.S. Sen. Diane Feinstein, and House Minority Leader Nancy Pelosi. Although Presidio Trust members hinted during the rejection announcement that other site alternatives for the museum might become available--they came too little, too late.

Quickly acting on San Francisco's failure to secure a site for the museum, both Chiago Mayor Rahm Emanuel and Los Angeles Mayor Eric Garcetti kicked into high gear and began actively wooing Lucas with proposals to move his museum to their cities. A radical change from the frustrating dealings and dithering in San Francisco. On June 24, 2014,

Lucas announced his plans to build his museum in Chicago. "Choosing Chicago is the right decision for the museum, but a difficult decision for me personally because of my strong personal and professional roots in the Bay Area," said Lucas. [17] San Francisco's loss became Chicago's gain. "No other museum exists like this in the world, making it a tremendous educational, cultural and job creation asset for all Chicagoans, as well as an unparalleled draw for international tourists," Chicago Mayor Rahm Emanuel added. "The Lucas project should help provide a strong boost to Chicago's already strong museum scene," said Ford Bell, the President of the American Alliance of Museums, "While the Alliance's database includes more than 22,000 U.S. museums, there are no other narrative art museums," adding, "I think it's unique, which is what you'd expect form George Lucas." [18] Truly, the new Lucas Museum of Narrative Arts will mark another "first" for Lucas, it will be the first museum of its kind. Brooks Peck, curator at the EMP Museum in Seattle, which collects sci-fi, pop culture and music said, "I'm actually super excited about the Lucas museum because there hasn't been anything that looks at quite what they are looking at....it will be highlighting very American art forms, including Norman Rockwell, special effects and sci-fi blockbusters," adding, "These are American inventions." [19]

The Lucas Museum of Narrative Art, formally called the Lucas Cultural Arts Museum, will be built on a choice Chicago lakefront site, home to both the Shedd Aquarium and Field Museum (which houses the exhibits and collections of the World's Fair) and will be, according to the website for the planned museum, "a gathering place to experience narrative art and the evolution of the moving images—from illustration to cinema to the digital mediums of the future. The museum's seed collection—a gift from founder George Lucas—spans a century-and-a-half and features the images and mediums that have profoundly shaped our cultural heritage." [20]

While Chicago Mayor Emanuel is enthusiastic about the plans, there may be some push back from open space advocates on parallel with those

Lucas encountered in San Francisco who might decide to move forward with plans to argue the footprint for the 17-acre site violates Chicago's landmark Lakefront Protection Ordinance. Advocates, however, heavily outweigh adversaries. Supporters don't anticipate any problems with upcoming construction plans. Lucas will submit architectural renderings to the City of Chicago by fall 2014. The museum is planned to open by 2018.

Lucas recently participated in two events that marked important changes in his own life. First, Lucas made an appearance in his hometown on June 7, 2013 during Modesto's "Graffiti Summer" as Grand Marshall of the Classic Car Parade. After accepting several awards from the city and Kiwanis Club, he cruised the Modesto Historic Graffiti Cruise Route (www.modestocruiseroute.com) in a 1946 apricot-colored Mercury convertible first alone, and then with Mellody Hobson, his fiancé, by his side. His first public homecoming in four decades, in the company of his two sisters, Wendy Lucas and Kate Nyegaard, Lucas returned to the place where both he, and *American Graffiti*, were born. [21] Lucas acknowledged the importance of his childhood "home."

Only two weeks later, on June 20, 2013, Lucas unveiled bronze statues of two of his most iconic characters, Yoda and Indiana Jones, in the San Anselmo Imagination Park he donated and then dedicated to the city of San Anselmo. These appearances in both Modesto and San Anselmo support his desire to both "give back" and inspire. [22] His home in San Anselmo, Lucas explained, to the 500, or so, people who attended the dedication ceremony, was located "just up the street" from the new park where both his Indiana Jones and *Star Wars* series were created. [23] Prior to the creation of park, the city of San Anselmo, Lucas stated, did not have a center—a heart—a place where the people could gather as a community. Now it does. Two iconic characters from his films, Yoda and Indiana Jones, will forever stand in the San Anselmo park, a testament in bronze, to his storytelling legacy, and belief that anything is possible if you just imagine it.

A desire to connect emotionally with people is a recurrent theme and a cornerstone of Lucas's filmmaking and life work. These recent homecomings signal new beginnings. Lucas's donations to the public takes his desire to connect on a deep emotional level with others (on film) to a new level. His ability to create communities via film and storytelling is now being used to develop strong "hearts and centers" where others can create their own stories and build new communities in the "real world." These communities can center around a park, a cruise route, or a museum. It doesn't matter. Instead of building worlds in space for the screen, he's giving others the space to create new, and lasting, worlds and identities of their own.

On June 22, 2013 George married his fiancé and long-time girlfriend, Mellody Hobson in a private ceremony at Skywalker Ranch. In a building located in a lush vineyard on the grounds, festooned with white roses, the couple exchanged vows during a ceremony conducted by Bill Moyers. The bride carried a bouquet of blue roses. Family and longtime friends, Steven Spielberg, Francis Ford Coppola, Ron Howard, and John Plummer, among others, were in attendance. Spielberg was said to have good-heartedly joked during a toast to the couple, "The Force finally has a name: Mellody." A large reception was held in the bride's hometown, Chicago, a week later. Lucas states, "Well, now that I'm retired, I have time to be a husband. We're an unlikely match-up. She's a money manager and I'm a '60s guy in San Francisco. But, it works. She lives in Chicago. I live here. We travel. She's the president of a money management company in Chicago as well as Chairman of the Board of DreamWorks Animation SKG," he explains. "When you find somebody who is THE one, it works. She's been raising my son since he was 13-years-old. She adopted him at his request. She is his mother. People say to him, 'I hear your parents are getting married,'" laughs Lucas. [24] According to insiders at the event —George was very happy. He was smiling. The happy couple decided to make Chicago home for half the year. With plans for the new Lucas Museum of Narrative Art to be built there as well, Lucas may be spending even more time in the Windy City.

If George was happy after marrying Mellody in June, then on August 9, 2013, he was even happier still. On that date, George Lucas and Mellody welcomed their first child, a daughter, Everest Hobson Lucas, into the world. The new baby is the first biological child for both George and Mellody. (Lucas has three adopted children: Amanda, 32; Katie, 25; and Jett, 20). It is only fitting that the man who shared his gift of storytelling and "happily-ever-after's" with so many, finally gets the "happily-ever-after" he so richly deserves of his own.

Notes

1. Matt Krantz, Mike Snider, Marco Della Cava, Bryan Alexander, "Disney Buys Lucasfilm for $ 4 Billion," *USA Today* (30 October 2012). Available from http://www.usatoday.com/story/money/business/2012/10/30/disney-star-wars-lucasfilm/1669739/
2. "Star Wars: Episode VII Set To Roll Cameras May 2014." Available from http://www.starwars.com/news/star-wars-episode-vii-set-to-roll-cameras-may-2014
3. Micke Sebastien, "J.J. Abrams Un Livre Et Des Etoiles," *Paris Match* (22 February 2014). Available from http://www.parismatch.com/Culture/Livres/J-J-Abrams-un-livre-et-des-etoiles-549747
4. Chris Taylor, "Star Wars Episode VII to Use Film, Be More Like Original Trilogy." *mashable.com* (22 August 2013). Available from http://mashable.com/2013/08/22/star-wars-episode-vii-film/ . See also Joe Fordham, "Film Renaissance," *Cinefex Blog* (20 April 2014). Available from http://cinefex.com/blog/film-renaissance/
5. Anthony Breznican, "Star Wars' Spin-Offs: A Young Han Solo Movie, and a Boba Fett Film—Exclusive," *Entertainment Weekly* (6 February 2014). Available from http://insidemovies.ew.com/2013/02/06/star-wars-spin-offs-young-han-solo-movie-boba-fett/
6. Marc Grazer, "Star Wars': The 'Sky's the Limit for Disney's Spinoff Opportunities," *Variety* (12 September 2013).
7. Brian Gallager, "Star Wars' Spin-Offs Will Not Crossover with the New Trilogy," *Movieweb.com* (17 January 2014). Available from http://www.movieweb.com/news/star-wars-spin-offs-will-not-crossover-with-the-new-trilogy
8. Borys Kit, "Star Wars' Spinoff Hires 'Godzilla' Director Gareth Edwards (Exclusive)," *The Hollywood Reporter* (22 May 2014). Available from http://www.hollywoodreporter.com/heat-vision/star-wars-spinoff-hires-godzilla-706636. See also "Josh Trank to Direct Stand-Alone Star Wars Film," *StarWars.com* (4 June 2014). Available from http://www.starwars.com/news/josh-trank-to-direct-stand-alone-star-wars-film
9. Justin Kroll, "Star Wars Episode VIII: Rian Johnson to Write, Direct Next Film," *Variety* (20 June 2014). Available from http://variety.com/2014/film/news/rian-johnson-to-write-direct-next-two-films-1201226481/
10. Ibid.

11. Ibid.
12. Brian Truitt, Bryan Alexander, Marco Della Cava, "Reaction: Disney deal for Lucasfilm, 'Star Wars' Empire," *USA Today* (30 October 2012). Available from http://www.usatoday.com/story/life/2012/10/30/disney-star-wars-reaction/1669999/
13. Brian Truitt, Bryan Alexander, Marco Della Cava, "Reaction: Disney deal for Lucasfilm, 'Star Wars' Empire," *USA Today* (30 October 2012). Available from http://www.usatoday.com/story/life/2012/10/30/disney-star-wars-reaction/1669999/
14. Holly Baily, "George Lucas pitches a San Francisco art museum," *Yahoo! News, The Lookout* (14 June 2103). Available from http://news.yahoo.com/blogs/lookout/filmmaker-curator-george-lucas-pitches-san-francisco-art-145650551.html
15. Ibid.
16. John King, "Presidio Trust Shoots Down George Lucas' Plan, 2 Others," SF Gate, (3 February 2014). Available from http://www.sfgate.com/bayarea/place/article/Presidio-Trust-shoots-down-George-Lucas-plan-2-5201301.php
17. Amy Langfield, "The Force Be With You: George Lucas Picks Chicago for Museum," (27 June 2014). Available from http://www.nbcnews.com/business/travel/force-be-you-george-lucas-picks-chicago-museum-n143086
18. Ibid.
19. Ibid.
20. Ibid.
21. In 1997, George Lucas (Modesto's favorite son) was honored by the City of Modesto (and given the keys to the City) for his award-winning work and for immortalizing the city in *American Graffiti* (based on his life in Modesto) with the dedication of the Lucas Plaza at 5 Points (it is called 5 Points because the Plaza sits at a point on the map where 5 different streets come together: McHenry Avenue, 17th, J Street, Needham, McHenry, Downey). In tribute, a bronze statue of a young girl and boy in '50s dress leaning against a '57 Chevy was placed in Lucas Plaza, representing teenage courtship and skillfully recreating the social context for *American Graffiti*--a quintessential coming-of-age story about teenage friendship and romance that will endure forever and will never go out of style.
22. Marijke Rowland, "Celebrated Modesto return for George Lucas," *Merced SunStar* (7 June 2013). Available from http://www.mercedsunstar.

com/2013/06/07/3059622/celebrated-return-to-modesto-for.html. See also Norimitsu Onishi, "Cruising Through Town He Put on the Map," *New York Times*, 7 June 2013. Available from http://www.nytimes.com/2013/06/12/us/george-lucas-visits-modesto-for-american-graffiti-parade.html?_r=0
23. Janis Mara, "George Lucas unveils Yoda, Indiana Jones statues in San Anselmo Thursday," *Mercury News* (21 June 2013). Available from http://www.mercurynews.com/movies-dvd/ci_23510363/george-lucas-unveils-yoda-indiana-jones-statues-san
24. Melece Casey. "George Lucas: Behind the Scenes with Modesto's Movie Mogul," *Stanislaus Magazine* (May/June 2013).

Bibliography

Allen, Robert C., and Douglas Gomery. *Film History: Theory and Practice*, New York: McGraw-Hill, Inc., 1985.

"Animated Features Spur Rising Surge," *Variety*, 18 October 93, 1.

Ansen, David. "Attack of the Groans," *Newsweek* no. 20 (20 May 2002): 64, 139.

Bailey, Holly. "George Lucas pitches a San Francisco art museum," Yahoo! News, The Lookout, 14 June 2013. Available from http://news.yahoo.com/blogs/lookout/filmmaker-curator-george-lucas-pitches-san-francisco-art-145650551.html

Baker, Bob. "Are These Videos Rated C for Clean or Compromised?" *Los Angeles Times*, 14 October 2002. Available from http://www.latimes.com

Balio, Tino. *United Artists: The Company That Changed the Film Industry.*(Madison: University of Wisconsin Press, 1987, 77.

Breznican, Anthony. "Star Wars' Spin-Offs: A Young Han Solo Movie and a Boba Fett Film—Exclusive," *Entertainment Weekly*, 6 February 2014. Available from http://insidemovies.ew.com/2013/02/06/star-wars-spin-offs-young-han-solo-movie-boba-fett/

Barnouw, Eric. *The Golden Web: A History of Broadcasting in the United States, 1933-1953*. New York: Oxford University Press, 1968.

Baxter, John. *Mythmaker: The Life and Work of George Lucas*. New York: Avon Books, 1999.

Alex Billington, "Its Official—New Line Cinema is Dead!" *FirstShowing.Net*, 28 Feb 2008. Available from www.firstshowing.net

Biskind, Peter. "The Young Lions: Raging Days, Boogie Nights," *Vanity Fair*, April 1998, 220-256.

Biskind, Peter. *Easy Riders, Raging Bulls: How the Sex-Drugs--Rock'n'Roll Generation Saved Hollywood.* New York: Touchstone, 1998.

Blake, Michael. Paper presented at the American Pop Culture Conference. University of Austin, Texas in February 2002 by on "Ford, the Searchers and a Code of Honor."

_____. Interview with author 10 December 2001.

_____. Email to author, 10 May 2002.

Bly, Robert. *The Sibling Society.* New York: Vintage Press, 1997.

Bock, Audie. "Kurosawa," *Take One,* March 1979, 34.

Bordwell, David. *On the History of Film Style.* Cambridge, MA: Harvard University Press, 1997.

Bordwell, David, Janet Staiger, and Kristin Thompson. *The Classical Hollywood Cinema: Film Style and Mode of Production to 1960.* New York: Columbia University Press, 1985.

Brooker, Will. *Using the Force: Creativity, Community and Star Wars Fans.* New York: Continuum, 2002.

_____. *Internet fandom and the continuing narratives of Star Wars, Blade Runner and Alien,* in Kuhn, A. ed., Alien Zone II, London: Verso, 1999

Brown, Corie. "The Years Without Ross," *Premiere* 10 (1996 January): 78.

Bruckner, J. "Joseph Campbell: 70 Years of Making Connections," *New York Times Book Reviews* (18 December 1983).

Buck-Morss, Susan. *The Dialectics of Seeing: Walter Benjamin and the Arcades Project.* London: MIT Press, 1991.

Button, Andrew. "Blissing Out: The Politics of Reganite Entertainment," *Movie 31/32,* 23.

Byfield, Ted. "Whether He Knows It or Not: The Creator of Star Wars is Working for the Force," *Newsmagazine 24,* no. 11 (24 February 1997): 33.

Byron, Stuart. "First Annual Grosses Gloss," *Film Comment 12,* no. 2 (1976 March-April): 30.

_____. "*The Searchers*: Cult Movie of the New Hollywood," *New York*, 5 March, 1979, 45.

Campbell, Joseph. *A Hero With a Thousand Faces*. New York: MJF Books, 1949.

_____. *Inner and Outer Reaches of Space: Metaphor as Myth and as Religion*. New York: New World Library, 2002.

_____. *The Power of Myth*. With Bill Moyers, Betty Sue Flowers, ed., New York: Doubleday, 1988.

Caro, Mark. "Spielberg Alters Scenes in 'E. T.' for 20th Anniversary Release," *Los Angeles Times*, 5 November 2001, p. F9.

Casey, Melece. "George Lucas: Behind the Scenes with Modesto's Movie Mogul," *Stanislaus Magazine*, May/June 2013.

Caughie, John, ed., *Theories of Authorship*. London: Routledge and Kegan Paul, 1986.

Clough, Mike. "Lucas Strikes Back," *Los Angeles Times*, 11 July 1999, pp. M1, M6.

"Computer Research and Development at Lucasfilm," *American Cinematographer 63*, no. 8 (August 1982): 773-775.

Conant, Michael. "The Paramount Decrees Reconsidered," *The American Film Industry*, rev. ed., Tino Balio, ed. (Madison, WI: University of Wisconsin Press, 1985), 537-573.

Cook, David. *Lost Illusions: American Cinema in the Shadow of Watergate and Vietnam, 1970-1979*. Berkeley: California University Press, 2000.

_____. "The Film Generation," *American Film History*, Jon Lewis, ed. London: Duke University Press, 1998.

Corliss, Richard. "The Seventies: The New Conservatism," *Film Comment*, no. 16, 35.

Corrigan, Timothy. "Auteurs and the New Hollywood," *The New American Cinema*, Jon Lewis, ed. London: Duke University Press, 1998.

Daily News, "Towers" Break December Box Office Records," December 23, 2002, 1, 6.

Daly, Steve. "A Monster Movie," *Entertainment Weekly*, no. 478 (26 March 1999): 30-41.

Dave Brubeck: In His Own Sweet Way, exec. prod. Clint Eastwood, dir. Bruce Ricker, co-prod. Patti McCarthy (University of the Pacific/Derry Music, 2012).

Daviau, Allan. telephone interview 1 January 2003.

de Certeau, Michel. *The Practice of Everyday Life.* Berkeley: University of California Press, 1984.

Derringer, Darth. "Top Ten Reasons Why TPM Was a Huge Disappointment." Available from *http://www.ezboards.com/officialtpmbasherboard,* accessed 30 June 2000.

Dixon, Wheeler Winston. "Twenty Five Reasons Why It's All Over," *The End of Cinema As We Know It: American Film in the Nineties,* Jon Lewis, ed. New York University Press, 2001.

Doty, Alexander. "Music Sells Movies: (Re) New (ed.) Conservatism in Film Marketing," *Wide Angle 10,* no. 2 (1988): 72.

"Down Year in L. A. as Jobs Fade Out," *Variety (3 March 2002). Variety* (18 October 1993): 1.

Doyle, Audrey. "Virtual Sets: How to Make Them," *Millimeter Magazine* 27, no. 26 (1999 June 1999): 55-60.

Edgerton, Gary. "High Concept, Small Screen," *Journal of Popular Film and Television,* 1991 Fall: 114-127.

Eller, Claudia, "Katzenberg Memo: Rivals' Reactions from Accord to Scorn," *Variety* (31 June 1991): 1.

Ellis Jack C. *A History of Film,* 2nd Edition. New Jersey: Prentice Hall, 1985, 273-274.

Elsaesser, Thomas. "The Blockbuster: Everything Connects, But Not Everything Goes", *The End of Cinema As We Know It,* Jon Lewis, ed. New York: New York University Press, 2001.

"Failing Magic at Disney," *Los Angeles Times,* 29 September 2002, p. M 4.

Farber, Stephen. "Hollywood's New Sensationalism: The Power and the Gory," *The New York Times,* 7 July 1974, sec. E., p.1.

---------. "The Stinky Kid Hits the Big Time," *Film Quarterly*, (1974 Spring): 8-9.

"Fast Forward," *Time* (5 December 1983): 74.

Feurer, Jane. "Reading Dynasty: Television and Reception Theory," *South Atlantic Quarterly*," 88, no. 2, Spring 1989, 446.

Finnigan, David. "Woe Canada: Guilds cite $10 Billion in Lost Prod'n," *The Hollywood Reporter*, CCLXXIII, *21* (25-27 June 1999): 1, 8.

Fordham, Joe. "Film Renanissance," *Cinefex Blog*, 20 April 2014. Available from http://cinefex.com/blog/film-renaissance/

Forkan, James P. "Paramount Exec is A Man of Year," *Advertising Age* (8 January 1979), S2, 1.

Fox, Terry Curtis. "Star Drek," *Film Comment*, July-August 1977, 9.

Friedberg, Anne. *Window Shopping: Cinema and the Postmodern*. Berkeley: University of California Press, 1993.

Fuson, Brian. "Deep Impact," *The Hollywood Reporter*, 26 February 1999, p. C-32.

_____. "Haunting Fills House in DreamWorks' Best Bow," *Hollywood Reporter*, CCCLVII, *41,* 26 July 1999, pp. 1, 35.

_____. "Summer of Love at Box Office: Grosses Are Running 20% Ahead of Last Year's Record Results," *Hollywood Reporter 41, CCLVIII*, 26 July 1999, pp. 35, 39.

_____. "Record H'wood Heatwave," *The Hollywood Reporter, 32, CCLXXIII,* 28 May -3 June, 2002, 1 & 54.

_____. "Clones a $300 mil B.O. Force," *The Hollywood Reporter, CCLXXIV, 48* (28 August 2002): 1, 23.

_____. "A Tower-ing B.O. Weekend," *The Hollywood Reporter*, CCLXXVI, *32* (23 December 2002): 1, 23.

_____. "Big Finish: Box Office Posts Record Gains in a Super Year," *The Hollywood Reporter* (6 January 2003): 22-24.

_____. "Int'l Fans Make Phantom No. 2 on All-Time b.o. List," *Hollywood Reporter CCCLXI*, no. 35 (9 February 2000): 6, 23.

Galipeau, Steven A. *The Journey of Luke Skywalker: An Analysis of Modern Myth and Symbol.* Chicago: Open Court Publishing, 2001.

Gallager, Brian. "Star Wars' Spin-Offs Will Not Crossover with the New Trilogy," *Movieweb.com*, 17 January 2014. Available from http://www.movieweb.com/news/star-wars-spin-offs-will-not-crossover-with-the-new-trilogy

Gentile, Goy. "Video Sanitizing Business Angers Movie Directors," *Los Angeles Times*, 3 February 2003, p. 1.

George Lucas: Creating an Empire: Biography, DVD, produced by A & E Television Networks. (New York: A & E Home Video, 2002).

George Lucas: The Early Years, prod. Patti McCarthy, dir. Andy Crete

(PMC Productions, 2013). https://www.youtube.com/watch?v=c4Edj29BObs

George Lucas: Visionary Filmmaker, prod. Patti McCarthy, dir. Andy Crete

(PMC Productions, 2013). https://www.youtube.com/watch?v=c4Edj29BObs

Goldstein, Patrick, "The Force Never Left Him," *Los Angeles Times Magazine* (2 February 1997): 26.

_____. "Seclusion Has Left Lucas Out of Touch," *Los Angeles Times*, 21 May 2002, p. C1.

_____. "Is Jar Jar Gay?," *Sacramento News & Review* (1 July 1999): 33.

Gomery. Douglas. "Hollywood's Business," *Wilson Quarterly 10* (Summer 1986): 43-57.

_____. "Failed Opportunities: The Integration of the U. S. Motion Picture and Television Industries," *Quarterly Review of Film Studies* (Summer 1984): 219-227.

_____. "The Coming of Television and the Lost Motion Picture Audience," *Journal of Film and Video* (Summer 1985): 298.

Gomery, Douglas. *The Hollywood Studio System.* New York: St. Martin's Press, 1986.

Gottlieb, Carl. *The Jaws Log.* New York: Dell, 1975, 15-19.

Gottschalk, Jr. Earl C., "The Spectaculars," *The Wall Street Journal*, 10 August 1974, p. 1.

Grazer, Marc. "Star Wars': The Sky's the Limit for Disney's Spinoff Opportunities," *Variety*, 12 September 2013.

Gross, Daniel. "The Louse in Mickey Mouse's House: Why Eisner Should Be Fired," *Slate.com*, 8 August 2002.

Gruback, Thomas H., and Dennis J. Dombkowski, "Television and Hollywood: Economic Relations in the 1970's," *Journal of Broadcasting* 20, no. 4 (Fall 1976): 511-527.

Haas, Nancy. "Marvel Superheros Take Aim at Hollywood," *New York Times*, 28 July 1996, n.p.

Harmetz, Aljean. "Burden of Dreams: George Lucas," *George Lucas: Interviews*. Jackson: University Press of Mississippi, 1999, 143.

Hearn, Marcus. *The Cinema of George Lucas*. New York: Harry N. Abrams, Inc., Publishers, 2005.

Hernandez, Greg, "$9 Billion Box Office: Identity's Purse Building a 'Record Year," *Daily News*, 30 December 2002, 1, 11.

_____. "Disney Juggles After Failure," *Daily News*, Business, 4 January 2003, 1, 3.

_____ "Film Exodus Grows,"*Daily News*, 10 July 2002, 1.

_____. "Franchise Features Often Mean Big Bucks So They Keep Coming," *Daily News Greensheet* (20 July 2002): 1, 4.

_____. "Profits Dip at Disney," *Daily News* (31 January 2003): 1, 3.

_____. "Tolkien Characters Become Life Like Sculpture," *Daily News* (20 December 2002): B-1.

_____. "Towers' Breaks December Box Office Record," *Daily News of Los Angeles*, December 23, 2002, p. 1-6.

Hettrick, Scott, "Phantom New Master of Video Game Spinoffs: E3 Gets a Sneak Preview from LucasArts," *The Hollywood Reporter* 14-16 May 1999, pp. 1, 35.

"Highest Grossing Movie," *Entertainment Weekly*, no. 429 (1 May 1998): 21.

Hills, Matt. *Fan Cultures.* New York: Routledge, 2002.

Hilmes, Michelle. *Hollywood and Broadcasting: From Radio to Cable.* Urbana: University of Illinois Press, 1990, 118-119.

Hoberman, J. "1975-1985: Ten Years That Shook the World," *American Film,* Vol. X, no. 8 (1985 June): 34-58.

Holliday, A. *Appropriate Methodology and Social Context.* Cambridge: Cambridge University Press, 1994, p. 204.

Hollinger, Hy. "Britain Falls to Phantom in Record Opening," *Hollywood Reporter, CCCLVIII,* no. 38 (19 July 1999): 1.

"Hollywood in Action," *Celebrity News Magazine* (July 1999): 1.

Hollywood Reporter, 19 May 1999, p. 1.

Hollywood Reporter, January 5, 1995, 1.

Holson, Rick, and Laura M. Holson. "Christmas Film Face-Off," *Angeles Daily News,* 24 November 2002, pp. 1 & 23.

Huffstutter, P. J. "Rewriting the Script," *Los Angeles Times,* 2 December 2002. Available from *http://www.latimes.com*

———. "Kodak Banking on Celluloid Having a Lot More Moments," *Los Angeles Times,* 20 November 2002. Available from *http://www.latimes.com*

———. "Oscar Enters the Picture in Film vs. Digital Debate," *Los Angeles Times* (3 2002 December), C 1.

Huffstutter, P. J., and Jon Healey. "Filming Without Film: High-Definition Digital Cameras, Feared By Some Directors, Could End The Careers of Those Unable to Make the Transition," *Los Angeles Times,* 11 July 2002. Available from *http://www.latimes.com.*

Hurley, Neal. *The Reel Revolution: A Film Primer on Revolution.* Maryknoll, NY: Orbis Books, 1978.

Interview with George Lucas. Available from <*http://www.starwars.com*>, accessed 15 January 1997.

Jameson, Fredric. "Nostalgia for the Present," *South Atlantic Quarterly* 88, no. 3, Autumn 1991, 303-323.

———. "Politics of Theory," *New German Critique* 33, Fall 1984, 54.

———. "Postmodern and Consumer Society," *The Anti-Aesthetic Essays on Postmodern Culture*, ed., Hal Foster, Seattle: Bay Press, 1983.

———. *Postmodernism, or, The Cultural Logic of Late Capitalism*. Durham: Duke University Press, 1991.

Jenkins, Gary. *Empire Building: The Remarkable Real Life Story of Star Wars*. New York: Simon & Schuster, 1997.

John, David, ed. *Star Wars: The Power of Myth*. New York: DK Publishing Limited, 1999.

Jones, Landon Y. *Great Expectations*. Washington, DC: The Brookings Institution, 1982.

"Josh Trank to Direct Stand-Alone Star Wars Film," *Star Wars.com*, 4 June 2014. Available from http://www.starwars.com/news/josh-trank-to-direct-stand-alone-star-wars-film

Kaufman, Debra. "HD Breaks BG," *Hollywood Reporter*, 30 May 30-2 June 2002, pp. 44-45.

Kaplan, David, and Adam Rogers. "The Selling of Star Wars," Newsweek, 133, no. 20 (17 May 1999): 60.

Kernin, Kathleen. "Hi-ho, Hi-ho, A-Marketing We Go . . . . .And Go," *Business Week* (25 June 1990): 54.

Kerr, Philip. "Starbucks and Filthy Lucas," New Statesman, *131, no. 4585* (29 April 2002): 36.

Kilday, Gregg. "Summer Tentpoles Stake b.o. records," *The Hollywood Reporter, CCCLXXV,* no. 1 (3-9 September 2002): 1, 65.

King, John. "Presidio Trust Shoots Down George Lucas' Plan, 2 Others," *SF Gate*, (3 February 2014). Available from http://www.sfgate.com/bayarea/place/article/Presidio-Trust-shoots-down-George-Lucas-plan-2-5201301.php

Kit, Borys. "Star Wars' Spinoff Hires 'Godzilla' Director Gareth Edwards (Exclusive)," *The Hollywood Reporter*, 22 May 2014.

Klemsrud, Judy. "Graffiti is the Story of His Life," *New York Times, 123* (7 October

1973), sec 2, 1.

Kline, Sally, ed. *George Lucas: Interviews.* Jackson: University Press of Mississippi, 1999.

Klinger, Barbara. "Digressions at the Cinema: Reception and Mass Culture," *Cinema Journal 28*, no.4 (1989): 14.

Koschnick, Wolfgang J. "I Can Think of More Important Things Than Being Loved by Everybody," *Forbes* (27 November 1989): 102.

Kotkin, Joel. "Runaway Productions Pose Challenges for Hollywood," *Los Angeles Times* (2002), pp. M 1 & 6.

Kramer, Louise, and Wayne Friedman. "Star Wars Tie-In Deals Fail to Rise Above Clutter," Advertising Age, 70, no. 26 (21 June 1999): 1

Kroll, Justin. "Star Wars Episode VIII: Rian Johnson to Write, Direct Next Film," *Variety* (20 June 2014). Available from http://variety.com/2014/film/news/rian-johnson-to-write-direct-next-two-films-1201226481/

Lane, Randal. "The Magician," *Forbes* (11 March 1996): 123-128.

Langfield, Amy. "The Force Be With You: George Lucas Picks Chicago for Museum," *nbc news.com*, (27 June 2014). Available from http://www.nbcnews.com/business/travel/force-be-you-george-lucas-picks-chicago-museum-n143086

Le Seur, Marc. "Theory Number Five: Anatomy of Nostalgia Films: Heritage and Methods," Journal of Popular Film, 6, no. 2, 1977, 193.

Leibovitz, Annie. "The Force is Back," *Vanity Fair,* no. 462 (1999 February): 128-129.

Leibovitz, Annie. "Star Wars: The Force is Back at Last," *Vanity Fair,* no. 462 (1999 February): 118-129.

"Letterman Digital Arts Center," *Pressroom*, 24 June 2005. Available from http://lucasfilm.com/press/presidiopreview/index.html?page=1

Lewis, Jon, ed. "The End of Cinema As We Know It and I Feel . . . ," *The End of Cinema As We Know It.* New York: New York University Press, 2001.

_____. "The Corporate Era," *The New American Cinema.* Durham, NC: Duke University Press, 1998.

———, ed. *The New American Cinema*. Durham, NC: Duke University Press, 1998.

———. *Whom the Gods Wish to Destroy: Francis Ford Coppola and the New Hollywood*. Durham, NC: Duke University Press, 1995.

———. *Hollywood v. Hard Core: How the Struggle Over Censorship Saved the Modern Film Industry*. New York: New York University Press, 2002.

Litman, Barry R. "The Economics of the Television Market for Theatrical Movies," in Robert Allan, ed., *The American Motion Picture Industry*. Carbondale, IL: Southern Illinois University Press, 1982.

Local Lucas History: Where Were You in '62?, prod. Patti McCarthy, dir. Erik Howell (PMC Productions, 2013). http://www.youtube.com/watch?v=P18CDWvttZA

Londoner, David J. "The Changing Economics of Entertainment," *The American Film Industry*, rev. ed., Tino Balio, ed. Madison: University of Wisconsin Press, 1985, 608.

Los Angeles Times, 17 March 1971, p. 1.

Lucas, George. "The Future Starts Here," *Premiere 1*, no. 6 (1999, February): 58.

Lunk, Tiiu. *Movie Marketing: Opening the Picture and Giving It Legs*. Los Angeles: Silman-James Press, 1997.

Machrone, Bill. "Film's Dead. Are Actors Next?" *PC Magazine*, 18, no. 15 (1999 September): 85.

Mad Men. Prod. Matthew Weiner. American Movie Classics (AMC), New York. 18 Oct. 2007. Television.

Madsen, Axel. *The New Hollywood: American Movies in the '70's*. New York: Thomas Crowell, 1975.

Magid, Ron. "George Lucas: Past, Present, and Future," *American Cinematographer 78*, no. 2 (February 1997).

Mara, Janis. "George Lucas unveils Yoda, Indiana Jones statues in San AnselmoThursday," *Mercury News, 21 June 2013*. Available fromhttp://www.mercurynews.com/movies-dvd/ci_23510363/george-lucas-unveils-yoda-indiana-jones-statues-san

Mason, M. S. "Fans Love This Saga of Good and Evil," *Christian Science Monitor, 91,* 118 (*14* May 1999): 17.

Mast, Gerald. *A Short History of the Movies*, 5th ed., revised by Bruce Kawin. New York: McMillian Publishing Co., 1992, 278.

_____, ed. *The Movies in Our Midst: Documents in the Cultural History of Film in America.* Chicago: University of Chicago Press, 1982.

Masters, Charles. "Embattled Messier Ousted," *The Hollywood Reporter* (2-8 July 2002): 1, 52.

Masters, Charles and Georg Szalai. "Viv Uni reports 1% dip as music, film struggle," *The Hollywood Reporter,* 11-17 February, 2003, p. 1, 80.

Mathews, Jack. "Saber Rattler," *Los Angeles Times, Calendar,* 17 January 1999, pp. 4-5, 51.

Maxford, Howard. *George Lucas Companion: The Complete Guide to Hollywood's Most Influential Film-maker.* London: B. T. Batsford LTD, 1999.

McBride, Joseph. *Steven Spielberg: A Biography.* New York: Simon & Schuster, 1997.

_____, ed., *Filmmakers on Filmmaking,* vol. 1. Los Angeles: Tarcher, 1983.

McCarthy, Patti. "Walking the Labyrinth: The Heroine's Journey: Reclaiming the Feminine," paper presented at the *University Film & Video Association Conference,* Chapman University, Orange, CA, 2 August 2013.

Mellencamp, Pat. "The Zen of Masculinity: Rituals of Heroism in The Matrix," *The End of Cinema As We Know It.* New York: New York University Press, 2001.

Menand, Louis. "Pop Technology—How Star Wars Changed the World," *Slate,* 12 February 1997. Available from *http://www.slate.com*

Monaco, James. *American Film Now.* New York: Oxford University Press, 1979, 169.

Monaco, Paul. *Ribbons in Time: Movies and Society Since 1945.* Bloomington: Indiana University Press, 1987.

Morris, George. "George Lucas' *Star Wars,*" *Take One*, July-August 1977, 9-10.

Murphy, A. D. "1975 Record Film B.O. Nears $1.9-Bil: Variety Key City Grosses Up More Than 90 percent," *Variety* (14 January 1976): 1, 86.

_____. "Universal Pics Make Film History: 1975 World Rentals at All Time High of $289-Mil," *Variety* (21 January 1976): 1.

_____. "Universal's Whale of Pix Biz Share: Jaws Makes U No. 1 with 25 percent of Domestic Gross," *Variety* (11 February 1976): 1.

Murphy, Chris. "George Lucas Grand Marshall 2013 Cruise Parade." *Modesto View*, 20 May 2013.

Nasr, Constantine. "George Lucas: Recaptures the Force," *Daily Trojan* (29 January 1997): 10.

Newsweek, July 28, 1996, 42.

Norman, Barry. *The Story of Hollywood.* New York: NAL Penguin, 1987.

O'Neill, Terry. "When Hollywood Portrays the Moral Universe, It's All Too Often Just Science Fiction," *Newsmagazine* 29, no. 4 (18 February 2002): 2.

Onishi Norimitsu. "Cruising Through Town He Put on the Map," *New York,* 11 June2013. Available from http://www.nytimes.com/2013/06/12/us/george-lucas-visits-modesto-for-american-graffiti-parade.html?_r=0

Palmer, William J. *The Films of the Eighties.* Carbondale: Southern Illinois University Press, 1993.

Pappas, Ben. "Star Bucks," *Forbes* 163, no. 10 (17 May 1999): 53.

Parisi, Paula. "Menace DVD features Lucas' Directors Cut," *Hollywood Reporter,*13 September 2001, p. 19.

Plummer, John. *Interview* for Historic Graffiti Cruise Route, Modesto, 12 September 2012.

Poe, Edgar Allen. *The Portable Poe.* Van Divenster, Philip, ed. New York: Penguin Books, 1997.

Polan, Dana. "The Confusions of Warren Beatty," *The End of Cinema As We Know It.* New York: New York University Press, 2001

Pollock, Dale. *Skywalking: The Life and Films of George Lucas.* New York: De Capo Press, 1999.

Pondel, Evan. "9-11 Hit the Valley Hard: Jobless Claims Reach Eight-Year High," *Los Angeles Daily News* (11 November 2002): 1, 15.

Powers, Stephens, David J. Rothman, Stanley Rothman, *Hollywood's America: Social and Political Themes in Motion Pictures.* Colorado: Westview Press, 1996.

Prindell, David. *The Politics of Glamour* (Madison: University of Wisconsin Press, 1988), 31-32.

Prince, Stephen. *A New Pot of Gold: Hollywood Under the Electronic Rainbow, 1980-1989.* Berkeley: University of California Press, 2000.

Pye, Michael, and Lynda Myles. *The Movie Brats: How The Film Generation Took Over Hollywood.* New York: Holt, Rinehart and Winston, 1979.

Puig, Claudia. "Star Wars Appeal is a Surprise Even to Creator Lucas," *Los Angeles Times,* 4 February 1997, pp. F1, F4.

Rose, Marla Matzer. "NL 'Rings' a New Strategy," *Harvard Register CCCXXVI,* no. 20 (5 December 2002): 1, 37.

Rosten, Leo. *Hollywood: The Movie Colony.* New York: Harcourt, Brace, 1941, 78.

Rowland, Marijke, "Celebrated Modesto return for George Lucas," *Merced SunStar,* 7 June 2013. Available from http://www.mercedsunstar.com/2013/06/07/3059622/celebrated-return-to- modesto-for.html

Rothman, Stanley, and S. Robert Lichter. "Personality, Ideology, and World View: A Comparison of Media and Business Elites," *British Journal of Political Science 15,* no.1 (1984): 29-49.

Russell, Louise B. *The Baby Boom Generation and the Economy.* Washington, DC: The Brookings Institution, 1982.

Sansweet, Stephen. *Star Wars: From Concept to Screen to Collectibles.* Chronicle Books: San Francisco, 1992.

Sarris, Andrew. "Notes on the Auteur Theory in 1962," *Film Culture*, no. 27, Winter 1962/1963.

Sarris, Andrew. "Notes on the Auteur Theory in 1962," *Film Theory and Criticsim*, Gerald Mast, Marshall Cohen and Leo Braudy, eds., 4th ed. New York: Oxford University Press, 1992, 529-540.

Schatz, Thomas. *Boom and Bust: American Cinema in the 1940s, History of the American Cinema, Vol. 6: 1940-1949*. Berkeley: University of California Press, 1999.

_____. *The Genius of the System: Hollywood Filmmaking in the Studio Era*. New York: Pantheon, 1988.

_____. "The New Hollywood," Jim Collins, et al. *Film Theory Goes to the Movies*. New York: Routledge, 1993, 17.

_____. "The Return of the Hollywood Studio System," *Conglomerates and the Media*, Erik Barnouw, eds. New York: The New Press, 1997.

_____. "The Whole Equation of Pictures," *Genius of the System, Film Theory and Criticism*, 4th ed. New York: Oxford University Press, 1988.

Schickel, Richard. "Irreconcilable Differences." *Time* (8 October 1984): 82.

Schiff, Stephen. "The Repeatable Experience," *Film Comment*, 18, no. 2, March-April 1982, 36.

Seabrook, John. "Why is the Force Still With Us?" *The New Yorker* (6 January 1997): 49.

Sebastian, Micke. "J.J. Abrams Un Livre Et Des Etoiles," *Paris Match*, 22 February 2014. Available from https://www.google.com/#q=Micke+Sebastien+J.J.+Abrams+un+livre+et+Des+Etoiles

Siberman, Steve. "G-Force: George Lucas Fires Up the Next Generation of Star Warriors," *Wired* 7, no. 05 (May 1999): 133-134, 182.

Silverstein, Stewart, Greg Hernandez, and Diane Seo. "Star Wars Glows at Center of Marketing Constellation,"*Los Angeles Times*, 1 May 1999, pp. C1, C2.

Sklar, Robert. *Movie-Made America*. New York: Random House, 1976.

Smart, Jessica. "Modesto Historic Graffiti Cruise Route to be Unveiled." City of Modesto Newsroom, 31 May 2012. Available from https://www.modestogov.com/newsroom/releases/prdetail.asp?id=1284

_____. "Modesto Historic Graffiti Cruise Route Walk of Fame to be Unveiled." City of Modesto Newsroom, 27 May 2014. Available from http://www.modestogov.com/newsroom/releases/prdetail.asp?id=1962

"Star Wars: Episode VII Set to Roll Cameras May 2014," *StarWars.com*, 18 March 2014. Available from http://www.starwars.com/news/star-wars-episode-vii-set-to-roll-cameras-may-2014

StarWars.com 15 January 15, 1997.

Sterngold, James. "The Return of the Merchandiser," *The New York Times*, 30 January 1997, sec. C, p. 1.

Strauss, Bob. "The Art of Wars," *Los Angeles Daily News*, 16 May 2002, p. U13.

_____. "The Force," *Daily News*, 19 May 2020, pp. U4, U5, U8.

Stuart, Fredric. "The Effects of Television on the Motion Picture Industry: 1948-1960" in Robert Allan, ed., *The American Motion Picture Industry*. Carbondale, IL: Southern Illinois University Press, 1982.

Sturhahn, Larry. "The Filming of American Graffiti," Filmmakers Newsletter, 7, no.5, March 1974, 22.

Surowiekie, James. "Star Wars Toy Story: A Star Wars Tale for Your Galaxy Enjoyment," *Slate* (25 December 1989). Available from *http://www.slate.com*

Szalai, George. "Turner to Exit AOL TW," *The Hollywood Reporter* CCCLXXVII, no. 4 (30 January 2003): 1, 22.

Taylor, Chris. "Star Wars Episode VII to Use Film, Be More Like Original Trilogy," *mashable.com*, 22 August 2014. Available from http://mashable.com/2013/08/22/star-wars-episode-vii-film/

"The Art of Editing & The Disappearance of Film," *Cinema Editor* 52, no. 3 (Winter 2002): 22-28, 44-46, 54.

"The Batmogul and the Abyss," *The Economist* (26 August 1989): 73.

Bibliography

"The Future Starts Here," *Premiere 1*, no. 6 (1999, February): 58

Thompson, Anne. "George Lucas," *Premiere* 12, no. 9 (1999 May): 68-76.

Ticketmaster.com 20 May 2002

Time, 30 May 1977, 57-58.

Tolkien, J. R. R. *Lord of the Rings: Collector's Edition.* New York: Houghton Mifflin Co., 2nd ed., 1974.

Turan, Kenneth. "The Prequel Has Landed," *Los Angeles Times*, 18 May 1999, pp. F1, F4.

Tusher, Will. "Schwarzenegger as the Tooth Fairy?" *Daily Variety* (29 August 1991): 3.

United States vs. Paramount Pictures Inc., (131: 141-142; 131:146-147; 131:158) 1938.

USA Today, 19 October 1984.

"US Movie Marketing Summary 1995-2010," *The Numbers*, retrieved August, 5, 2011. Available from *http://www.the-numbers.com/market*

Vartabedian, Ralph, Tom Petruno, and Debora Vrana. "Fed's Taking a Harder Look at Mega-Mergers," *Los Angeles Times*, 11 March 1998, pp. D1, D10.

Variety, Oct 14-20, 1996, 1+.

Variety, Sept 30-Oct 6, 1995, n.p.

Variety, 27 Dec 1993, 62.

Variety, 4 Jan 1939, 51.

Vaz, Mark Cotta, and Patricia Rose Duignan. *Industrial Light + Magic: Into the Digital Realm.* New York: Ballantine, 1996.

Von Gunden, Kenneth. *Postmodern Auteurs.* London: McFarland & Company, Inc., 1991.

"Wall Street Bell Rings for Disney: Shares Boost as Analysts Predict Turnaround in New Year," *Variety* (3-5 January 2003): 10.

Wasko, Janet. *Hollywood in the Information Age: Beyond the Silver Screen.* Austin: University of Texas Press, 1994.

Watercutter, Angela. "Lucas Stakes Out Hollywood Rival," *Los Angeles Daily News*, (9 February 2003): 6.

Welkos, Robert W. "In a Theatre, Near, Near You . . . ," *Los Angeles Times, Calendar* (17 January 1999): 2.

White, Dana. *George Lucas*. Minneapolis: Lerner Publications Company, 2000.

"Who's the Boss? How Industrial Light & Magic Created a Virtual Actor for the Phantom Menace" *Advanced Graphics & Animation* 5, no. 8 (August 1999): 24-32.

Wolff, Ellen. "Star Wars: Inside the ILM Pipeline," *Millimeter Magazine*, 27, no. 26 (1999 June): 30-42.

Wood, Michael. *America in the Movies: or Santa Maria: It Had Slipped My Mind*. New York: Basic Books, 1975.

Wood, Robin. *Hollywood: From Vietnam to Reagan*. New York: Columbia University Press, 1986.

Wyatt, Justin. *High Concept: Movies and Marketing in Hollywood*. Austin: University of Texas Press, 1994.

_____. "The Formation of the 'Major Independent': Miramax, New Line and the New Hollywood," *Contemporary Hollywood Cinema*. New York: Routledge, 1998.

Wyatt, Justin, and R. L. Rutsky, "High Concept: Abstracting the Postmodern," *Wide Angle* 10, no.4 (1988): 42.

"Year of the Sequel: More Money Was Spent on Sequels in 2002 Than Ever Before in Movie History: What's the Story Behind Hollywood's Love Affair with Second Acts?," *Cinema Editor* 52, 4 (Fall 2002): 26-39

"Your Guide to Episode II: Star Wars: Attack of the Clones," Daily News, 16 May 2002, pp. 14-15.

Appendix

ILM Timeline

1977, *Star Wars*: The advent of the motion control camera marks the start of the special effects era.

1982, *Star Trek II: The Wrath of Khan* : With the "Genesis sequence," ILM creates the first completely computer-generated scene.

1985, *Young Sherlock Holmes*: ILM develops its first computer-generated character: "the stained glass man."

1989, *The Abyss*: ILM creates the first computer-generated three-dimensional character in The Abyss, using its "Morf" computer program. Introduced the year before in Willow, Morf allows fluid on-screen transformation from one object to another.

1991, *Terminator 2: Judgment Day*: Morphing becomes sophisticated enough to allow the first digitally created major character, the amorphous T-1000 machine.

1992, *The Young Indiana Jones Chronicles*: It proved a ratings flop, but Lucas used his television series for radical experimentation with digital effects and editing. The series' directors digitally created backgrounds and introduced digitally replicated extras.

1993, *Death Become Her*: ILM creates computer-generated skin, one of the key hurdles to digitally created characters.

1993, *Jurassic Park*: Digital technology yields living, breathing creatures, with muscles, skin and texture.

1994, *Forrest Gump*: Numerous Breakthroughs: Digital compositing allow weaving of fictional and historical footage. Gary Sinise's character becomes a double amputee the easy way—his legs are erased. Football crowds, helicopters, Ping-Pong balls, all digitally created. The film wins ILM its fourteenth Academy Award.

1995, *Casper* : Hollywood's first digital lead character. That same year *Jumanji* broke the final barrier preventing digital humans—hair. Monkey fur and a lion's mane were rendered strand by strand.

1997, *Star Wars Special Edition* : The movie's twentieth anniversary edition will demonstrate just how far Lucas has come. Sound and visuals will be enhanced, backgrounds transformed, characters created. And the Harrison Ford of twenty years ago will find himself in an entirely new scene, opposite a digital Jabba the Hut.

1999, *The Phantom Menace*: Technological breakthrough. On June 18th, four theatres began showing *Star Wars: Episode I—The Phantom Menace* using digital projection, marking the first time audiences saw a film-less feature (using digital systems made by CineComm-Hughes/JVC and Texas Instruments). More of the same, but Jar Jar Binks and a large cast of digitized characters are introduced as well—a fully digitized character that replaced the live actor "standing in" for him "lives" side-by-side with "real" actors on the screen.

2002, *Star Wars: Attack of the Clones* was *a technical benchmark in film-making*. It had the distinction of being *the first feature film to be shot entirely on high-definition digital video* (it was shot with a 24p digital video-cam especially developed by Sony, with newly developed Panavision lenses)—changing both the look of film and the standards of film-making.

2013, ILM sold to Disney (October 2013) as part of Lucasfilm, Ltd.

Index

ABC/Capital Cities, 12, 151, 195, 277
ABC/Capital Cities Disney, 12
  See also Walt Disney Pictures
  Abrams, J. J., 69–70, 277–278, 287
  Academy Award, 75, 124, 225, 274, 309
  Academy of Motion Pictures and Sciences, 248
  admission, 240–242
  advertisement, 81, 85, 88–89, 92, 94–98, 104, 127, 130, 145–146, 148, 189, 221, 225–226, 255
  action figures, 122
  Adventure Time, 47
  affiliates, 239
  AFI Lifetime Achievement Award, 274
  AFTRA, 249
  Altman, Robert, 165, 203
  Amblin, 100
American Broadcasting Company (ABC), 12, 86, 147, 151, 166, 195, 262, 277
American Cinematographer, 183, 207–208
American Entertainment Partners, 187
American International Pictures (AIP), 22, 40, 60
American Graffiti, 49, 61, 67–69, 74–77, 79–81, 91–92, 106, 114–115, 123–124, 130, 254, 282, 284, 288

American New Wave, 26–27
American Zoetrope, 31, 44, 59–61, 81, 102, 165
ancillary, 91, 95, 124, 128, 146, 155–157, 159, 163, 170, 180, 195–196, 272, 281
animation, 139–141, 143, 146, 205, 212, 214, 250, 274, 280
Anyone Lived in a Pretty (how) Town, 52
AOL Time Warner (AOL), 166, 193, 262, 269, 275
Apocalypse Now, 61, 81–82, 165, 217
Apocalypse Now Redux, 217
Apted, Michael, 220
archetype, 112, 120, 169, 197, 231–234
aspect ratio, 150
attendance, 8, 14–15, 20, 113, 190, 220, 241, 262, 285
art, 19, 26, 44, 47, 62–63, 77, 79, 84, 87, 101, 104, 108, 110, 121, 126, 135, 139, 150, 161, 201, 203, 211, 217, 222, 238, 245, 250–251, 257–258, 269, 273, 281–283, 285, 288
artifact, 178, 194, 235, 239, 273
Australia, 191–192
authorship, 25–26, 36
auteur, 24–26, 41, 60, 62–64, 71, 90, 101–103, 109, 132–133, 164–165, 202–203, 206, 272
acquisitions, 151, 154, 157–158, 166, 201, 205, 272, 277
Avid, 185, 247

Bad Robot Productions, 278
Baker, Kenny, 254, 278
bankruptcy, 61, 87, 147, 267
Ballard, Carroll, 101
Batman, 142–143
Battle of Naboo, 229
Bay area, 60, 190, 193, 264–265, 283
Baxter, John, 55, 58, 69–70, 73, 79, 105, 129–130, 133–135, 160
Bazin, Andre, 149, 206
BBS Productions, 22–23
Bergman, Igmar, 109
Benchley, Peter, 95
Ben-Hur, 16
BETA, 184
big budget, 2–3, 20, 44–45, 83–84, 191–192, 197, 201, 243, 272
Big Five, 2, 5, 195–196
Berg, Jeff, 114
Berry, Chuck, 48–49
Bestseller, 95, 212, 225
Biskind, Peter, 36, 40, 65, 70, 98, 103, 129, 132–133
Black Stallion, The, 101
Blake, Michael, 111, 133, 208, 246, 258
blind-bidding, 5
Birth of a Nation, The, 218
block-booking, 5, 84
blockbuster, 8, 15, 83–85, 97–98, 103–106, 140, 160, 165–166, 170, 189, 197, 200–201, 243
Blockbuster Entertainment, 151
Body Heat, 77, 164, 180
Bogdanovich, Peter, 31, 101, 165
Bomberger, Dorothy, 65
Bomberger, Paul, 47, 67
Bonnie and Clyde, 21, 63
box-office, 23, 81, 103, 105–106,

box-office (*continued*), 124, 142, 159, 161–162, 167, 200–202, 224, 228, 241
Bram Stoker's Dracula, 165
bricolage, 172
broadcast, 12, 135, 147
Brooker, Will, 216, 254, 257
Buck Rogers, 173
Butch Cassidy and the Sundance Kid, 30
Burstyn v. Wilson, 6
See also censorship
Burton, Tim, 163

C-3PO, 107–108, 122
cable, 12, 34, 147, 149, 152, 155, 157, 187, 249, 280
see also pay-per-view
Cagney, James, 3, 63, 81, 90
Cahiers du Cinema, 25
Cameron, James, 180, 206, 225–226, 255
Campbell, Joseph, 50, 112, 114, 117–118, 120–121, 133–134, 231, 233
Canada, 192
Cannes, 165, 201
Captain Eo, 181
Carpenter, John, 51, 55, 165
celluloid, 149, 238, 244–245, 248, 266, 268, 275, 279
See also film stock, stock
censorship, 6, 9, 19
Center for Entertainment Industry Data and Research, 192
Chewbacca, 134
Chicago, 11, 35, 283–285, 288
Cineaste, 106
cinema verite, 267
Cineplex, 94

circulation of images, 238
Citizen Kane, 42
children's television, 20
Christensen, Hayden, 245
Cimino, Michael, 99, 102–103
Classic Car Parade, 284
clone, 139, 167, 232, 237, 239–240, 242, 244–245, 248, 256–257, 310
"closed" franchise, 225
Coca-Cola Company, 45, 147–148, 153
collectible, 47–48, 106, 113, 283
collectors, 122
colorization, 216, 219
Columbia Pictures, 2, 5, 13, 21, 31, 33, 37, 56, 83, 86, 88, 125, 128, 147–148, 199, 208
Cook, David, 21–24, 29–30, 36, 63–64, 71, 83–84, 94, 97, 129–133, 138, 205
commercial, 71, 88–89, 97, 102, 108–109, 127, 139, 156, 160, 162, 200–201, 244
commercial tie-ins, 97
comic book, 66, 138–139, 147, 279
commodity, 90, 156, 225
communal culture, 236
community, 6, 45, 65–66, 117, 126, 165, 174, 197, 216, 235–236, 254, 257, 264, 284
See also fans
company, 146, 154, 157, 255
competition, 152
compositing, 247, 309
computer graphic imagery, 198, 217, 219, 246, 251
computer-generated, 183, 190, 198, 245, 251, 279, 309
conglomeration, 21, 90–91, 103, 131, 150, 152, 161, 187, 201–202, 225, 255, 277

conservatism, 23, 39, 81, 161–163, 170
consumers, 196
controversial, 178, 218
Conversation, The, 44, 61
Coppola, Francis Ford, 31, 36, 39–40, 42–45, 51, 57–61, 64, 74, 80–81, 83, 90, 94, 101, 111, 116, 132, 164–165, 180–181, 203, 207, 217, 266, 269, 285
Coppola Cinema Seven, 111
copyright, 123, 220, 222, 237
Corman, Roger, 22, 40–41, 43, 60, 135
corporation, 4, 8, 21–22, 60, 73, 81, 90, 103, 126, 128, 144, 148, 150, 159, 161, 187, 193–195, 272
Classical Hollywood, 3, 31, 33, 87, 94, 108–111
   See also old Hollywood, studio system
Cleopatra, 16, 97–98
Close Encounters of the Third Kind, 99, 105
connectivity, 273
Creative Artists Agency (CAA), 104, 158
crash, 50
critical inquiry, 272
cruising, 67–70, 76, 221, 284–285
   the Loop, 49, 68, 70, 76
   the Drag, 68, 76, 79, 92
Crusader Rabbit, 47
culture, 23, 26–27, 119–120, 160–161, 170, 187, 189, 238–239, 271, 273–274
cultural artifact, 194, 235, 239, 273
cultural space, 237

Daniels, Anthony, 278

Dark Crystal, The, 182
Darth Vader, 116, 169, 223, 229–230, 232, 277–278
Daviau, Allen, 183–184, 208
Deakins, Roger, 270
Death Star, 107, 181, 230
Death Wish, 29
Deer Hunter, The, 99, 102
DePalma, Brian, 43, 51, 101
Deregulazation, 152, 187
detective film, 28
Dies Committee, 7
Diller, Barry, 85–86, 93, 193
digital, 84, 134, 153, 168, 178, 181, 183–186, 190, 196, 198, 211, 213, 215, 219, 221, 230, 238, 244–245, 247–252, 256, 258–259, 261, 264–271, 273, 275–276, 279, 283, 309–310
digital capture, 238
digital camera, 184–185, 247, 249–250, 265–270, 275–276
digital character, 168, 181, 218–219, 230, 245, 251, 256, 264, 310
digital effects, 84, 153, 168, 213, 219, 268, 273
digital set, 184, 251, 269
digital technology, 153, 190, 244, 249, 252, 265, 267, 270–271, 273
digital tools, 252, 264, 269
digital video, 221
Dirty Harry, 28, 88, 141
distributor, 21, 84, 164, 242
distribution, 2–3, 12, 15–17, 41, 85, 104, 107, 124, 130, 148–149, 151, 154–155, 159, 180, 186–187, 189, 194, 196, 201, 224, 239, 266, 271, 273
Diversification, 4, 22, 60, 146, 157, 187, 272

Dixon, Wheeler Winston, 199, 209, 271, 276
Dolby Stereo, 29, 84, 124–125, 168, 198, 256
Downey High School, 46, 48, 68
Disney's California Adventure, 147
Disneyland, 48, 149, 181, 280
downscaling, 251
Downtown Disney, 199
DreamWorks, 285
droid, 107, 119, 245
DSLR, 270
DuMont Laboratories, 11
Dykstra, John, 123

Easy Rider, 8, 21–24, 31, 60–63, 83
Eastwood, Clint, 68, 70, 88, 141
economic, 3, 34, 84, 137, 154, 190–192, 239, 262, 267, 269, 273
edit, 25, 46, 59, 219–220, 222
EditDroid, 183
Ecurie AWOL Sports Car Competition Club, 49
Eisner, Michael, 85–86, 93, 138, 140–141, 145, 147, 190, 200–201, 262, 275
Elsaesser, Thomas, 186, 188–189, 194, 208–209
Emperor, The, 52, 57
Emperor Palpatine, 230
Endor, 181, 214
entertainment industry, 192, 261
escapism, 119, 163, 175, 200
E.T.: The Extra-Terrestrial, 126, 179
Evil Empire, 177
exhibition, 2–3, 5, 118, 130, 155, 157, 174, 184, 186–187, 196, 256, 270
    See also theatrical exhibition
evaluation, 238, 272

Index

fans, 107, 112–113, 120, 126, 139, 174, 212, 215–216, 223–224, 235–237, 254, 257, 271, 278
fairytale, 115, 117, 197
fantasy, 93, 112, 115–117, 127, 134, 167–168, 175–176, 196–197, 236
FCC, 152, 196
Federal Trade Commission, 152, 263
Fellowship of the Ring, 113, 240, 246
Fett, Boba, 279, 287
film genre, 3, 20, 22, 24, 29–31, 40, 62–63, 87–88, 92–95, 97, 106–108, 112, 115–116, 166–168, 171–172, 177, 272
film industry, 3, 6, 8–9, 14, 20, 22, 33–36, 52, 58, 83, 87, 97–98, 113, 128, 148, 150, 157, 163, 187–188, 192, 208, 213, 239–240, 249, 261, 265, 271–274, 281
film school, 8, 31–32, 39, 41, 43–44, 51, 57–58, 88, 96, 99, 101, 127, 185, 203
film stock, 4, 22, 24, 36–37, 56–58, 75–77, 79, 129–130, 157, 185, 256, 262, 266–268, 279
Fiat Bianchina, 49
Fields, Verna, 53
film opening, 5, 28–29, 55–56, 79–80, 89, 96, 113, 125, 127, 143, 181, 212, 227–228, 240, 258, 280
filmed entertainment, 141, 148, 150
Fine Line, 161, 201
Finian's Rainbow, 44, 58–59
First Amendment, 6
First Blood, 163, 166
fiscal, 4, 6, 9–10, 41, 239
Fisher, Carrie, 135, 278
Five Easy Pieces, 31

Flashdance, 91–93
Flash Gordon Conquers the Universe, 47, 106, 114, 172
Force, the, 160, 185, 211, 216, 227–229, 234–235, 254–255, 257, 277, 285, 288
Ford, John, 23, 42, 108, 173
Foreign Car Service, 49
Ford, Harrison, 89, 135, 278, 310
Fox Family, 277
franchise, 8, 63, 88, 93–94, 97, 105, 113, 138–144, 146, 191, 193, 196, 205, 207, 224–225, 239, 271–273, 277–278, 280
Frankenstein, George, 46, 51, 66
Freiheit, 52

Galactic Republic, 229
Game Boy, 237
Gandalf the Grey, 112
gangster films, 93, 169
genre, 31, 93, 106–107
See also film genre
global, 147–148, 150–152, 155, 187, 195–197, 272
God, 207
Godard, Jean-Luc, 27, 54, 101–102, 109, 261
Godfather, The, 61, 74, 81–83, 89, 93
Godfather II, The, 81, 89, 93–94
Golden Globes, 75, 81, 224
Good Fathers, 231–232
Gomery, Douglas, 14, 33–35, 208
graphic novel, 147, 151
Griffith, D.W., 214, 218
Grease, 77, 79, 89, 91, 105
Greedo, 216
Gremlins, 164, 179
guilds, 7, 192, 222, 250

See also unions
Gulf & Western Industries, 68, 157
  See also PCI, Inc.

Hamill, Mark, 135, 278
Happy Days, 94
Hard Day's Night, A, 44
Harsh Mentor, 257
Harry Potter, 143–144
Hasbro, 226, 255
Heaven's Gate, 102, 165
"Heirs to the Empire," 139
Hello, Dolly!, 83, 97, 246
Herbie, 52
Hercules, 194
hero, 22, 29–30, 41–42, 48, 107, 112–113, 116–121, 141–142, 171, 178, 197, 203, 230–231, 233–234, 247, 257
Heroine's Journey, 231, 257
Hero's Journey, 112–113, 115–120, 133–134, 231, 233, 257
Hidden Fortress, The, 107, 114
high concept, 8, 64, 73, 82, 86–95, 98, 105, 122, 130–131, 134, 163, 170, 207, 272
Hobbit, The, 113, 138, 251
Hobson, Mellody, 284–285
Hitchcock, Alfred, 25–26, 42, 100, 109
holistic, 238
home viewers, 14, 150, 155, 187, 225, 235
home video, 103, 143, 149–150, 155–156, 163, 201
holy grail, 99, 138, 174
horizontal integration, 194–195
horror film, 29, 43, 63, 84
House Committee on Un-American Activities, 7–11, 18, 21

Huston, John, 25, 181
Huyck, Willard, 40, 51
hybrid, 151, 198, 201
hybridization, 29
hybrid market, 151
hyperspace, 105, 107, 119, 171

ICM (ICM), 96, 104, 158
identity, 142, 175, 215, 234, 236–237, 285
Iger, Roger, 277–278, 280
International Creative Management (ICM), 96, 104, 158
Imperial troops, 108
independent producer, 16
Indiana Jones, 47–48, 138, 166, 168, 179–183, 278, 284, 289, 309
Indiana Jones and the Last Crusade, 166, 179, 181, 183
Indiana Jones and the Temple of Doom, 166, 179, 182
Industrial Light and Magic, 81, 123–124, 134, 153, 182–183, 185–186, 191, 208, 214, 244–247, 258, 265, 273–274, 277, 281, 309–310
Information Society Project, 221
inventory, 66, 145–146
Irving G. Thalburg Award, 179

Jabba the Hutt, 214
Jackson, Peter, 35, 69, 113, 133, 181, 245
Jackson, Samuel, 245
Jameson, Fredric, 42, 65, 77–78, 109, 129, 133
Jaws, 8, 82, 88–89, 94–98, 100, 103–106, 130, 132, 138, 162, 224–225
jedi, 119–120, 229

Jedi Council, 229, 231
Jung, Carl, 112, 114
Jurassic Park, 196, 226–228, 240, 244, 309

Kagemusha, 102, 180
Kasden, Lawrence, 180, 278
Katzenburg, Jeffery, 93, 140–141, 201
Kazanijian, Howard, 51
Kennedy, Kathleen, 74–75, 217–218, 279
Kenner Toys, 122, 124, 127, 135
Kent State Four, 28
Kerkorian, Kirk, 22
Kinney National Services, Inc., 21–22, 57, 60
Kleiser, Randal, 51
Knoll, John, 245
Kurosawa, Akira, 42, 65, 101, 109
Kurtz, Gary, 40, 106–107, 126–127

Ladd, Alan Jr., 114, 123, 127
La Jetee, 54
Laguna Seca Raceway, 50
laissez-faire, 161
Last Picture Show, The, 31
Lego, 138, 255
Lens, 244, 310
Letterman Digital Arts Center, 190, 264, 275
Lewis, Jon, 7–10, 18–19, 25, 33, 35–37, 43, 65, 71, 130, 132, 152, 198–199, 206–209, 276
license, 5, 15, 124–125, 127, 138–139, 142, 144–146, 149, 153, 157, 187, 212, 221, 225–226, 239, 255
liminal character, 232–233
Lippencott, Charles, 126–127

Little Big Man, 30
Little Three, 5
Little Mermaid, The, 140
live-action, 141, 245, 280
Look At Life, 52
Looney Tunes, 144
Lord of the Rings, The, 93, 112–113, 133, 138, 141, 167, 173, 191, 201, 205, 240, 242, 246, 250
low-budget, 2–3, 22–23, 80, 165, 191
Lucas, Everest Hobson, 286
Lucas, George Walton Sr., 45, 65–66
Lucas, Wendy, 46, 65, 67–68, 284
Lucas Cultural Arts Museum, 283
LucasArts Entertainment, 153, 227, 265, 273, 277, 281
Lucasfilm, Ltd., 48, 81, 123, 125, 152–153, 278, 281, 310
Lucas Museum of Narrative Art, 283, 285
Lucas/Spielberg Phenomenon, 31, 40, 43, 51, 99, 101, 103, 126, 153, 160–161, 163, 167–171, 175–178, 180, 183, 185, 199, 202, 218, 266, 285

machines, 66, 167, 201
major-minors, 2
market, 35, 91, 95, 125, 128, 144, 146, 148–155, 157, 159, 163, 170, 180, 186–188, 196, 228, 263, 272
market share, 17, 148
marketing, 24, 90, 93–94, 103, 105, 125, 164, 175, 195
marketing tie-ins, 226
Marvel Comic, 138–139, 151–152, 277
*M*A*S*H*, 21, 23
mass market, 22–23, 115, 243

Mast, Gerald, 13, 19–20, 34–36
materialism, 161–162, 164
Matrix, The, 191, 197–198
matte, 123, 244, 246–247
Matsushita, 153–155
Mayhew, Peter, 278
McCallum, Rick, 268–269
McKenna's Gold, 56–57
media, 33, 35–36, 87, 94–97, 104, 106, 112, 138, 140, 144, 146–148, 150–155, 162, 182, 186–187, 190, 194, 196, 198, 200, 202, 205–206, 208–209, 225, 227, 243, 250, 252, 255, 262–263, 265, 272
media conglomerates, 8, 33, 128, 131, 144, 146, 148, 151, 162, 166, 171, 188, 193–196, 205–206, 209, 211, 225–226, 243, 262–263, 269, 272
mega-mergers, 262–263, 275
Mellencamp, Pat, 197–198, 209
Mengers, Sue, 158
merger, 147, 151, 153–154, 157–158, 166, 201, 205, 262–263, 272, 275
Mesa CleanFlicks, 220–221
metatext, 107
Metro-Goldwyn-Mayer (MGM), 2–3, 11, 22, 63, 127, 144
merchandizing, 64, 90, 123, 125, 138, 142, 144, 194, 212, 227, 278
Midnight Cowboy, 30
Milius, John, 40, 43, 51, 57, 61, 82, 99, 101
Mindel, Daniel, 279
Miramax, 193, 199, 201–202, 209
mise-en-scene, 197
Mishima, 163, 182
Mississippi Burning, 164
modernist, 108–111, 114
Modesto, 45, 47–48, 50, 65–70,

Modesto (*continued*), 74–76, 274, 284, 288–289
Modesto Junior College, 50
Modesto High School, 48, 65
Modesto Historic Graffiti Cruise Route, 67–70, 284
Monaco, James, 36, 107, 133
Monogram Pictures, 2
montage, 150, 172–173
Mos Eisley, 213–214
motion capture, 249–250
Motion Picture Association of America, 7–8, 10–11, 34, 131
MovieMask, 220
movie tie-ins, 88–90, 92, 95–97, 124–125, 131, 138, 142–145, 214, 226–227, 255
Moyers, Bill, 118, 134, 285
MTV, 91, 150, 173, 199
multiple viewing, 92, 110, 116, 125, 174, 225
multiplex, 96
Murch, Walter, 51, 82
Music Corporation of America (MCA), 17–18, 21, 35, 100, 153–154, 206
See also Lew Wasserman
musical film, 29
music video, 92, 131, 147
Myles, Lynda, 37, 81, 97, 115, 130, 132–133, 207
myth, 29–30, 41, 50, 107, 115–119, 121, 171, 173, 234

NAACP Vanguard Award, 274
Napoleon, 102
National Critics Award, 81
National Medal of Arts, 274
National Medal of Technology, 274
National Student Film Festival, 57

National Labor Relations Board (NLRB), 9
negative, 20, 62, 79, 85, 175, 178, 180, 183–185, 190, 212, 232, 234, 267
negative pick-up, 190
New American Cinema, 26, 36–37, 43, 65, 71, 130, 132, 206–207
New Hollywood, 1–2, 6–7, 9–10, 12, 15, 17–18, 22, 27, 30–31, 36, 39, 41, 58, 62, 64, 71, 94, 97, 103–105, 131–132, 138, 141, 144, 152–153, 161, 164–165, 189, 202, 209, 272
  Phase One, 8, 26, 32
  Phase Two, 8, 50
  See also American New Wave, New American Cinema, New Wave-American, post-classical Hollywood
new markets, 152, 188, 263
new media, 190, 227
new skillsets, 251
New Wave, 8, 21, 24–27, 41, 44, 62, 84, 101, 168, 202, 206
News Corp., Ltd., 155
New Line, 93, 135, 152, 201–202, 205, 209, 268
New Zealand
Nintendo, 182, 227, 237
non-theatrical, 149
non-union, 190
novelization, 127
nostalgia film, 76–79, 99, 106, 108, 110, 117, 129
Nyegaard, Kate, 284

Oedipus, 121
Obi Wan-Kenobi, 105, 111, 116, 214, 223, 229–232, 234, 237, 256
old Hollywood, 1, 3, 8, 12–13, 16,

old Hollywood (*continued*), 18, 26–27, 30–31, 41, 58, 87, 91, 97, 123, 141, 152, 176, 189, 195
1:42:08, 52
One From The Heart, 165
opticals, 244
ownership, 4–5, 10–11, 71, 90, 123, 273, 277

Pacific Delta Images, 191
padawaan, 111
Palmer, William, 160, 164, 169, 207–208
Paramount Pictures, 1–2, 5–8, 10–11, 16, 18, 21, 33–36, 61, 84, 86, 93–94, 104, 130–131, 138, 144, 150–151, 153, 156–157, 180, 188, 190–191, 195, 208, 226, 255
Paramount Communications, Inc., 151, 157, 195
parody, 29–30, 42, 108, 110, 170, 176
Parrish, Maxfield, 282
pastiche, 77, 106, 108, 110, 115, 171–172
Patton, 81
pan and scan, 150, 216
Panasonic, 268
Panavision, 244, 310
pay rate, 250
payroll, 261
pay television, 12, 149, 155, 157
PCI, Inc., 157
Pepsi, 156, 225, 227, 255
Phantom Menace, The, 139, 223–224, 226–228, 237, 258, 310
Pinewood Studios, 278
Pixar, 191, 193, 277, 281
Player, The, 165
Plummer, John, 46–47, 49–50, 55, 66–67, 69, 285

Polan, Dana, 202, 209
Polar Express, The, 247–248
Pollack, Dale, 57–58
Pollock, Tom, 55, 70, 127
postmodern, 129
praxis, 238
Presley, Elvis, 48
Prequels, 1–37, 39–71, 73–135, 137–209, 211–259, 261–289, 309–310
Prince, Stephen, 147–150, 154, 158, 170, 179, 186, 206–208
Princess Leia Organa, 107, 134, 169, 229–230, 234, 237, 279
print, 47, 69, 80, 95–96, 114, 132, 184, 213, 219, 252, 268
Presidio Trust, 264, 281–282, 288
products, 6, 16, 19, 65, 90–91, 94–95, 124, 138, 141–142, 144–145, 147, 149, 186, 194, 218, 263
production, 15, 22–23, 25–26, 58, 65, 67, 70, 104, 146, 181, 190–192, 199, 201, 209, 250, 261, 267, 278
Production Code, 18–19
profits, 4, 17–18, 31, 62, 80, 83, 90, 94, 97–98, 104, 124, 128, 194–195, 198, 255, 264
programming, 12, 19–20, 86, 147, 151, 187, 194–195
promotions, 145
publicity, 126–127, 131, 138, 201, 252
Pye, Michael, 37, 81, 97, 115, 130, 132–133, 207

Queen Amidala, 229, 246–247
Qui-Gon Jinn, 229, 231, 256

R&D, 123, 182, 193

R2-D2, 107, 169
racing, 49–50, 68, 76, 230
Raiders of the Lost Ark, 31, 77, 93, 106, 135, 149, 156, 178–180, 207, 278
Rain People, The, 44, 59
Ragtime, 164
Rambo, 163, 166
Ramona Avenue, 45, 48, 66–67
Rastar Productions, 104, 199
rating, 29, 219, 224, 242, 254, 309
Rafelson, Bob, 31
rating system, 18, 20
Rebel Without A Cause, 79
redemption, 103, 165, 180, 223, 232–234
Regan, Ronald, 37
Reagan administration, 163
Reganonmics, 161
re-issue, 213
remake, 167, 243
Repositioning software, 247
resistance, 176, 234, 237
Return of the Secaucus Seven, The, 164
revenge films, 29
revenue, 2, 8, 14–15, 18, 139, 143–144, 146–148, 155–157, 159, 195, 224
rite of passage, 120
RKO, 2, 15
rock n' roll, 22, 24, 77
Rocky, 29, 104, 166
Rockwell, Norman, 45, 282–283
Robinson, Edward G, 3
Roosevelt Jr. High, 46, 48
Ross, Steve, 57, 60
Rosten, Leo, 4, 33
Roth, Joe, 148
rotoscoping, 247

runaway productions, 190, 193, 269

Samuel Warner Scholarship, 57
San Anselmo, 284, 289
San Anselmo Imagination Park, 284
San Francisco, 59–60, 80, 134, 190, 264–265, 281–285, 288
Sansweet, Stephen, 122, 134, 254
Sarris, Andrew, 24, 26, 36
Saturday Night Fever, 77, 89, 91, 105
Sayles, John, 163–164
Savoy, 202
Schatz, Thomas, 1, 3, 33, 63, 70, 95, 97, 131–132, 143, 189, 196, 205–206, 208–209
science fiction film, 115, 117, 167–168
Schrader, Paul, 42–43, 99, 101–102, 163
Schwarzenegger, Arnold, 88–89, 131, 191
Scorsese, Martin, 43, 51, 57, 99, 101, 165
Screen Actors Guild, 7, 191, 249
Screen Director's Guild, 191, 220, 222, 250
Screen Gems, 13
Screen Writer's Guild, 7
Sea Hawk, The, 114
Seagrams, 154
Searchers, The, 88, 99, 108, 132, 169
secularism, 170
self-reflexivity, 109
sell-through, 143, 149, 156–157
serial, 41, 106, 115, 173
Seven Arts, 31, 43–44, 57, 59–60, 104
Seven Samurai, The, 114
Selznick, David, 1, 4
sequel, 77, 97, 139, 166–167, 171,

sequel (*continued*), 225, 243
shared cultural space, 237
see also cultural space
shared cultural artifact, 235, 239, 273
Sheinberg, Sid, 95
Sherak, Tom, 224
shifting job responsibilities, 251
shoppertainment, 145
significant, 89, 150, 214
Sith, 139, 229–233, 266
6-18-67, 57
Shire, the, 112
shoppertainment, 145
Skywalker, Anakin, 223, 229, 234, 246
Skywalker, Luke, 68, 105, 111, 116, 118–119, 121, 137, 229, 237, 257, 279
Skywalker Sound, 81, 123–124, 153, 265, 273–274, 277, 281
slasher films, 163
small budget, 163
small screen, 13, 150, 187
small-town, 164
Soundtrack, 49, 68, 76–77, 92, 97, 147
Solo, Han, 105, 107, 214, 218, 237, 279, 287
Sony Pictures Entertainment, 144, 147–148, 155, 199, 227, 239–240, 242, 244, 268, 270, 310
Sony Playstation, 227
SoundDroid, 183
space fantasy, 116–117, 127
spaghetti western, 191
Special Editions trilogy
See also *Star Wars*
special effects, 45, 84, 95, 106, 108, 113, 118, 123–124, 126, 153, 168, 171–172, 182–183, 197–200,

special effects (*continued*), 213–214, 219, 225, 243, 268, 272–273, 277, 283, 309
    see also digital effects
Spielberg, Steven, 31, 40–41, 43, 51–52, 82, 87, 90, 94, 96, 98–101, 103, 105, 126, 132, 153, 160–161, 163, 165, 167–171, 175–180, 183–185, 196, 199, 201–202, 217–218, 254, 266, 285
Spiderman, 239–240, 242, 258
spin-off, 94, 128
standing-in-line, 3, 41, 56, 89, 94, 126, 138, 141, 167, 174, 192, 197, 239, 263
    See also fans, multiple viewing
star, 2–3, 18, 80–81, 88–90, 124, 131, 135, 141, 159, 188–189, 201, 206, 243, 271–272
Star Tours, 181
Star Trek, 138, 156, 166–167, 182–183, 277, 309
Star Wars, 236
    Star Wars: Episode I: The Phantom Menace, 119, 139, 223–224, 226–230, 237, 240, 256, 258, 268, 310
    Star Wars: Episode II: Attack of the Clones, 139, 167, 232, 237, 239–240, 242, 244–245, 248, 256–257, 310
    Star Wars: Episode III: Revenge of the Sith, 266
    Star Wars: Episode IV: A New Hope, 30, 82
    Star Wars: Episode V: Return of the Jedi, 148, 166–168, 223, 278
    Star Wars: Episode VI: The Empire Strikes Back, 137,

Star Wars
    Star Wars: Episode VI: The Empire Strikes Back (*continued*), 148, 166–167, 213, 278
    Star Wars: Episode VII, 278–279, 287
    Star Wars: Episode VIII, 287
    Star Wars: Special Editions, 213–217, 235, 244
    Star Wars: The Clone Wars, 280
Star Wars Kids, 237
Star Wars trilogy, 166
Stark, Ray, 43, 74–75, 104, 168, 199, 267
stormtroopers, 134
studios, 2–25, 31–32, 39–41, 44, 46, 61–64, 73–74, 80, 83, 86–87, 90, 94, 96, 98, 101, 104, 123–124, 126, 128, 130, 138–140, 145–146, 149–151, 153–159, 166–167, 187–190, 193, 195–196, 199, 201, 203, 206, 218–222, 242–243, 254–255, 261, 266, 268, 272, 278
studio system, 1–5, 8, 11–13, 15–18, 25–27, 30–31, 33, 41, 58, 70, 84, 87, 91, 97, 103, 123, 141, 152–154, 157, 164, 176, 189, 195, 203, 205–206, 208–209, 246
See also Hollywood studio system
Subscribervision, 12
suburbanization, 14
Subscription TV, 12
subversive, 24, 110
subsidiary, 13, 126, 238, 272
Sugarland Express, The, 96
Sylvan Road, 48
symbol, 24, 120, 168, 235, 257
syndication, 144
synergy, 147, 171, 181, 225,

Index

synergy (*continued*), 238–239, 272–273, 281

Taco Bell, 226–227, 255
talent agencies, 15, 17–18, 96, 98, 158
Tanen, Ned, 79–80, 114
Tatoonie, 214, 232
tax incentives, 190
Taxi Driver, 29, 99
technical, 41, 55, 78, 124, 167, 183–184, 213, 244, 248, 258, 264, 274, 310
Technicolor, 16
telecine, 149
television, 12, 14–16, 20–21, 31, 47, 86, 88, 95–96, 104, 106–107, 121, 127–128, 134–135, 139, 146, 149, 152–153, 181, 190–192, 194, 198, 216, 220–221, 225, 241, 249, 280
Ten Commandments, The, 16
tent-pole, 281
Terminator, 89, 167, 169, 191
Thalberg, Irving G., 4, 211, 274
theatrical exhibition, 2–3, 5, 118, 130, 155, 157, 174, 184, 186–187, 196, 256, 270
theatre, 2, 5–6, 13–15, 47, 56, 69, 94–96, 104, 121, 124–125, 127, 137, 139, 149–150, 154, 168–169, 187, 189–190, 195, 198, 213, 224–225, 248–249, 256, 265–266, 310
theory, 26, 36, 80, 129, 131–133, 264
Threshold Guardians, 231
ticket sales, 73, 130, 187, 241
Time, Inc., 152, 155
Titanic, 180, 188, 220, 224–226, 228, 243–244, 255
The Graduate, 91–92

The Robe, 16
The Shadow, 23, 36, 47, 71, 130–132, 205
The Whistler, 47
Theatre attendance, 14
theme-park, 48, 145, 151, 186, 189, 196, 238, 271–272, 280, 285
    See also Disneyland, The Wizarding World of Harry Potter
3-D film, 181, 270
THX, 31, 52–57, 61, 75, 80, 109, 124, 153, 168, 172, 225, 254, 265, 273
THX 1138, 31, 52–53, 55, 57, 61, 109, 254
THX 1138:4EB, 52–53, 55, 57
TIE fighters, 214
tie-ins, 88–90, 95–97, 124–125, 138, 142, 144, 226–227, 255
    See also commercial tie-ins, marketing tie-ins
Tolkien, J. R. R., 112–114, 133, 173–174
Top Gun, 156, 163, 184
Touchstone Pictures, 94
toy, 96–97, 122, 124–125, 127–128, 137–139, 225–227
Toy Story, 140, 145
trailer, 224
Transamerica Corp., 22
transgressive redemption, 233
Treasure Planet, 141, 146–147, 262
Trekkers, 174
Tricon Global Restaurants, 226
Time-Warner, 143–144, 147, 152, 205
transformation, 49, 119, 154, 238, 273
transmedia, 239, 264, 273
Truffaut, Francois, 25–27, 101

Turner Broadcasting, 152, 195, 205
Tusken Raiders, 108
Twentieth Century-Fox, 2–3, 11–12, 21, 89, 108, 114, 122–123, 125, 127–128, 133, 140, 144, 147, 153, 166, 180, 187–188, 191, 193, 206, 224, 226, 228, 255, 269, 277–278
2001: A Space Odyessy, 114, 117, 123
Two Towers, The, 242

UCLA Anderson Forecast, 192
Unions, 6–7, 9, 40, 79–80, 191–192
United Artists, 2, 102, 144, 164
United States Information Agency, 53
United States v. Paramount Pictures, 1–2, 6–7, 10, 16, 84, 130
See also anti-trust decree of 1948, 5
Universal Pictures, 2, 5, 15–16, 21, 35, 39, 63, 74, 79–81, 94–96, 98, 100, 114, 117–121, 127, 130–132, 143–144, 153–154, 193, 206, 218, 227, 240, 262, 280
University of California, Los Angeles, 24, 43–44, 51, 54, 192, 264
University of Southern California, 24, 40, 50–57, 75, 99, 108, 127, 185, 264, 274

Valley Industry and Commerce Association, 261
Variety, 33, 88, 130–132, 141, 145, 205–206, 209, 287
VCR, 187
vertical integration, 3, 15, 195
VHS, 135, 184
Viacom, 151, 166, 193, 195–196, 262

video, 143, 249–250, 267–269
video sales, 138, 187
video rental, 151
Vietnam, 22, 24, 28, 52–53, 74–75, 82, 104, 164, 169, 203
Virtual Celebrity, 250
Vision2, 256, 267–268
Visionbox Media Group, 252
visual effects, 245, 265, 274
See also special effects
Vivendi, 166, 193, 262
See also Universal Pictures

Waldorf Statement, 10
Wall Street, 21, 130, 157, 193, 206, 277
Walt Disney Pictures, 11–12, 21, 47–48, 93–94, 139–141, 143–148, 151, 166, 187, 190–191, 193, 195–196, 199, 201, 205–206, 262, 275, 277–281, 287–288, 310
Wampa, 214
Warner, Jack, 57
Warner Bros., 2–3, 11, 22, 31, 44–45, 57–61, 63, 93, 104, 131, 140–144, 152, 193, 205
Warner Bros.-Seven Arts, 31
Wasserman, Lew, 17–18, 79
Watergate, 23, 28–29, 36, 71, 74–75, 95, 99, 130–132, 171, 205
Waterworld, 146, 198
Wayne, John, 30
Welles, Orson, 25, 42
Wells, Jeffery, 140
Western film, 21, 23, 27, 30, 56, 106–107, 117, 119, 131, 150, 157, 191, 197
Wexler, Haskell, 50, 75
Wild Bunch, The, 63
William Morris Company, 18, 104, 158

Williams, John, 96, 217
Wise Old Man, 231
Wizard of Oz, The, 106–107, 218
Wizarding World of Harry Potter, The, 143
Wood, Michael, 27, 36
Wood, Robin, 37, 175, 178, 200, 208
Woodstock, 23
World War I, 84, 203
World War II, 2–4, 14, 41, 107
Wyatt, Justin, 88–89, 92, 122, 130–131, 134, 201, 207, 209

Yablans, Frank, 104
Yavin, 214
Yoda, 120, 137, 229–230, 232, 234, 245–246, 284, 289
You're a Big Boy Now, 44
youth market, 8, 22–24, 26, 31, 61–62, 74, 79–80, 91, 131
yuppie, 162, 164

Zabriskie Point, 24
Zahn, Timothy, 139
Zanuck, Richard D., 95
Zanuck, Darryl, 4
Zemeckis, Bob, 51

www.ingramcontent.com/pod-product-compliance
Lightning Source LLC
Chambersburg PA
CBHW031250230426
43670CB00005B/117